CHANGING POLITICS OF CANADIAN SOCIAL POLICY

James J. Rice and Michael J. Prince

No one is content with the state of health and social programs in Canada today. The Right thinks that there is too much government involvement and the Left thinks there is not enough. In *Changing Politics of Canadian Social Policy* James Rice and Michael Prince track the history of the welfare state from its establishment in the 1940s, through its expansion in the mid 1970s, to the period of deficit crisis and restraint that followed in the late 1970s and 1980s.

Taking a historical perspective, the authors grapple with the politics of social policy in the 1990s. Globalization and the concomitant corporate mobility affect government's ability to regulate the distribution of wealth, while the increasing diversity of the population puts increasingly complex demands on an already overstressed system.

Yet in the face of these constraints, the system still endures and is far from irrelevant. Some social programs have been dismantled, but others have been reorganized and maintained. Greater democratization of welfare programs and social policy agencies could make the system thrive again. *Changing Politics* provides the much-needed groundwork for students and policy makers while also proposing real solutions for the future.

JAMES J. RICE is Associate Professor at the School of Social Work at McMaster University
MICHAEL J. PRINCE is Lansdowne Professor of Social Policy at the University of Victoria.

JAMES J. RICE AND MICHAEL J. PRINCE

Changing Politics of Canadian Social Policy

UNIVERSITY OF TORONTO PRESS
Toronto Buffalo London

© University of Toronto Press Incorporated 2000
Toronto Buffalo London
Printed in Canada

Reprinted 2000, 2001, 2003

ISBN 0-8020-4232-5 (cloth)
ISBN 0-8020-8074-X (paper)

Printed on acid-free paper

Canadian Cataloguing in Publication Data

Rice, James J.
   Changing politics of Canadian social policy

   Includes bibliographical references and index.
   ISBN 0-8020-4232-5 (bound)   ISBN 0-8020-8074-X (pbk.)

   1. Canada – Social policy.   2. Social security – Canada.
   3. Welfare state – Canada.   I. Prince, Michael John, 1952–
   II. Title.

   HV108.R518 1999   361.6'1'0971   C99-932102-1

This book has been published with the help of a grant from the Humanities
and Social Sciences Federation of Canada, using funds provided by the
Social Sciences and Humanities Research Council of Canada.

University of Toronto Press acknowledges the financial assistance to its
publishing program of the Canada Council for the Arts and the Ontario
Arts Council.

University of Toronto Press acknowledges the financial support for its
publishing activities of the Government of Canada through the Book
Publishing Industry Development Program (BPIDP).

Canadä

Contents

Preface

Changing Politics of Canadian Social Policy examines the current conditions affecting the development of social policies in Canada, and offers a sweeping historical examination and contemporary account of the welfare state and social security. As Canadians enter the twenty-first century, they are grappling with the legacy of the fiscal crisis of the state alongside the tensions between the globalization of the economy and the pluralization of the community. After nearly a generation of neoconservative politics and retrenchment of governments, this book argues for a new balance between the market, the state, and civic society. We maintain that Canada's welfare state and social programs remain relevant and essential precisely because of economic globalism and the growing diversity of community life; and that the role of social policy will increasingly become concerned with the protection of communities and groups against market turmoil, and the recognition of various social and cultural identities within Canadian society.

The scope of the book is limited to an analysis of Canadian social policy, but provides examples from other countries. While it focuses primarily on income security, it examines a range of social programs provided by the federal and provincial governments and the nonprofit sector. The structure of the book leads the reader to understand how the political context is restructuring the fundamental ideas of the welfare state to meet the needs of the global economy.

Our methods include a review of the changing economic and political conditions affecting the development of social policies; an analysis of the changing ideologies influencing the way governments think about social policy issues; and a review of the literature to determine how experts believe social policies will evolve in the future.

We have written this book with three audiences in mind: first, students and teachers in the fields of child and family studies, education, health administration, nursing, political science, public administration, social work, and sociology; second, activists, clients, and workers in community groups and social movements; and third, policy analysts, decision makers, administrators, and practitioners within governments and other public sector organizations – those who wish to understand the evolution of social policy and the welfare state in Canada, including where we are now and where we may well be heading. We have tried to write the book in a way that speaks to each of these groups in a style that is accessible, stimulating, and, at times, personal.

Every book expresses the values of its writer or writers, so first let us be clear as to our beliefs, assumptions, and backgrounds. We believe that to understand Canadian society, social policy, and the welfare state requires a careful consideration of the processes of globalization and pluralization, and the political structures in which these macroprocesses are partially mediated. We believe it is essential to view society from a historical perspective, taking lessons from the past and applying them to the future. We also believe in the importance of finding new ways of building community capacity in order to maintain strong social cohesion, foster environmentally and socially responsible firms and corporations at national and international levels, and democratize the state with a renewed social role. We believe every society must find a balance between the forces that drive production and those that maintain a civil society.

A key underlying assumption in our writing is that context influences policies and practices. For us, context includes the economic, social, and political realms, with special consideration given to the diverse nature of people. Another assumption is that contemporary agencies, programs, and helping professions are influenced by past choices, conflicts, and achievements. History is important. Finally, we assume that social movements, ideas, and programs can and do affect the way people choose to live.

We come to the study and practice of social policy from different disciplinary perspectives and work experience – social work and political science. Together we have been working and writing on aspects of social policy since the early 1980s. The collaboration, we believe, has resulted in a richer and broader approach to social policy theorizing and analysis.

For encouragement, guidance, and feedback thanks are due to Marie Campbell, Bruce Doern, Demi Patsios, Marge Reitsma-Street, Katherine Teghtsoonian, and special thanks to Brian Wharf for his careful review. This book would not have been written and completed without the love, patience, and sacrifice of our families: Robin, Chandra, and Sara; and Karen, Jessica, and Kathleen.

CHANGING POLITICS OF CANADIAN SOCIAL POLICY

Introduction

Three dominant forces are changing the way Canadians think about social welfare: the globalization of the economy, changing needs for social protection, and the desire by diverse groups for community recognition. These three forces are altering the social policy agendas of governments, community groups, interest groups, and social activists. They are creating new debates about the impact of social interventions on economic markets, the relationship between social benefits and labour market involvement, and the implications for social rights for disadvantaged and oppressed groups. The purpose of this book is to explore how and when these three conditions arose and to analyse the implication they pose for the development of new social policies.

The changing politics of social policy are the result of tensions between global economic forces that are constraining governments' ability to provide social protection and diverse groups who are claiming recognition and benefits from social programs. Governments are under pressure from two directions: corporations demand open markets and freedom from the constraints of social policies; and citizens demand protection from the ravages of quickly changing economic conditions. Pressures from both sides are reshaping the old ways of thinking about the welfare state and creating conditions for the development of new social policy interventions.

Most of the contemporary literature on national and comparative social policy, and on the crisis of the welfare state, focuses on globalization. The malaise of the welfare state is explained in relation to economic problems of inflation, low growth, business imperatives, and work disincentives. Major issues examined in this literature include deindustrialization, the changing distribution of work, and the impact of economic globalization on labour markets and the sovereignty of nation states. A trade-off is commonly held to exist between economic growth and international competitiveness on the one hand, and social protection and redistribution on the other.

Typically, the literature on globalization examines the question of what the role of the state should be. Some argue that social programs must be altered, made to be more 'active' and supportive of market forces. This line of analysis argues that the state ought to be downsized and many interventions deregulated or privatized. To be sure, for the past fifteen to twenty years, governments have been adapting and adjusting programs to what have been called 'the new world economy' and 'new fiscal realities.'

A second body of literature focuses on domestic politics and social trends. The welfare state is viewed as either (a) a set of programs and rights offering a social safety net, or (b) a cultural form concerned with the construction of identities and status through the dominant discourse and public policies. This stream of writing treats the welfare state as a political project concerned with nation building, and province building, and, more recently, Aboriginal self-government. Here, social programs and services interact with demographics, identity politics, and intergovernmental relations, and examined issues include population aging, gender relations, new social movements, and the changing racial and ethnic composition of Canadian society. In this line of analysis, many of the challenges facing the modern welfare state derive from the mismatch between existing social programs and the needs and aspirations of a multiplicity of groups. Typical reform ideas call for making institutions, professions, laws, and programs more representative, culturally sensitive, and respectful of differences – in other words, the state needs to be further democratized. For these reformers the politics of social policy relate to the state's struggle to incorporate diverse people into the broader structures of society. This second body of literature thus assumes that the state retains a significant capacity, if not sovereignty, to exercise authority and determine the way people interact.

In this book we connect these two bodies of writing on the state, economy, and society. In looking at economic globalization and social pluralization together, we see that the trade-off is not only between economic expansion and social programs, but also between the quality of life Canadians will have in the new century, the rights and responsibilities people will bear, the nature of their social relations, and their access to resources. The changing politics is about the struggle over who should benefit from the changing economic conditions and how these benefits should flow to groups within the country. It is about what rights and resources corporate interests claim, and the powers they exercise in relation to the state. It is about social status for different groups, and access to health care, education, and housing. It is about how groups in civil society are mobilized, and which succeed or fail in obtaining a voice and recognition. It is about investment, trade agreements, and markets as well as ethnicity, gender, age, and disability. It is about creating new mechanisms for income redistribution that meet the emerging needs of Canadians while improving productivity and economic efficiency. Social policies are the instruments and the welfare state is the institution through which these new politics must be managed if Canada is to develop a more socially inclusive society.

A Framework for Understanding the Magnitude of Recent Changes

To understand what is happening to the relationship between the economy and the community it is useful to look at the principles identified by Karl Polanyi (1957) regarding the transformation from pre-industrial society to a post-industrial social system. His analysis of this transformation provides a powerful parallel for us to use as a way of thinking about how today's society is changing under the pressure of the globalization of the economy and the pluralization of the community. Two crucial ideas emerge from his analysis. The first describes the way community members can be separated from their own economic activities as governments create new economic structures, which lead in turn to social degradation and the inability of community members to care for themselves. The second describes how community members respond to these changes by demanding from their governments greater social protection against the debilitating effects of market liberalization.

In his analysis of pre-industrial society, Polanyi demonstrates how economic activities are deeply embedded in the fabric of social relationships. That is to say, while people labour to earn their living (economic activities) they are involved in their communities and act in ways that ensure community well-being, protect social harmony, and foster social cohesion (social relationships). Community members also maintain social ties through mutual reciprocity and the redistribution of resources. Reciprocal acts bind community members together as they give and receive help in meeting the demands of daily living: in difficult times, for example, community members redistribute food and resources to those in need, and those who contribute the most often receive the highest regard from the community. In this way the community maintains social cohesion.

Polanyi then describes how economic activities were disembedded from the community as pre-industrial societies were transformed into industrial societies. Governments, which were basically the instruments of the new capitalist elites, created markets to allow the owners of capital to produce and sell products. In order to create markets, governments placed constraints on community rights, limited community access to common property, removed traditional barriers to trade and finance, and allowed the owners of capital to treat land, labour, and capital as if they were commodities. Since land, labour, and capital are not natural commodities, the governments had to enforce this fiction through the mechanisms of contracts and laws.

The most damaging part of the fiction is that it undermines the cooperative aspects of civil society. To maintain the separation of the economy from the civil society, business interests and governments sympathetic to them undervalue the cooperation of community members and undermine the importance of reciprocity and redistribution. At the same time, governments enshrine the notion of private property and reinforce the idea that people should care for themselves and become competitive individuals who willingly forsake their communities to find work in the new industrializing societies. Polanyi provides a powerful description of the results when human beings and their communities are treated solely as commodities:

In disposing of a man's labour power the system would, incidentally, dispose of the physical, psychological, and moral entity 'man' attached to that tag. Robbed of the protective covering of cultural institutions, human beings would perish from the effects of social exposure; they would die as the victims of acute social dislocation through vice, perversion, crime, and starvation. Nature would be reduced to its elements, neighbourhoods and landscapes defiled, rivers polluted, military safety jeopardized, the power to produce food and raw materials destroyed. Finally, the market administration of purchasing power would periodically liquidate business enterprise, for shortages and surfeits of money would prove as disastrous to business as floods and droughts in primitive society. Undoubtedly, labour, land, and money markets are essential to a market economy. But no society could stand the effects of such a system of crude fictions even for the shortest stretch of time unless its human and natural substance as well as its business organization was protected against the ravages of the satanic mill. (1957:73)

How does all of this relate to contemporary social policy in Canada? In the changing politics of social policy, we believe that the global economy is being separated from the state in the same way that the economy was disembedded from social relationships in Polanyi's analysis of industrialization. The nation state has less control over economic forces than it did twenty years ago, and the globalization of the economy has lessened the ability of the state to control economic development within its own borders. Governments are creating vehicles for enhancing the power of international corporations such as the World Trade Organization, with legislation such as the North American Free Trade Agreement, and are continuing to seek ways of protecting the rights of investors over the rights of citizens. In the process of creating the global economy, corporations and governments have been prepared to increase the risks community members must bear in meeting the demands of daily living, while reducing their collective abilities to deal with these risks. They have cut back on social benefits, dismantled parts of the welfare system, and removed support for people who are unable to find employment.

Polanyi's history lesson tells us that community members respond to conditions such as these, and that they act to protect themselves and their neighbours from the most damaging effects of economic change. Polanyi claims that community members will band together to demand the creation of policies that safeguard them from the destructive forces of change. He paints a detailed picture of how people developed social movements that were meant to defend them and their environment from the forces of the unregulated market. They called for and introduced factory laws. They organized unions. They created self-help organizations. All of these activities contributed to the foundations of the modern welfare state.

A brief look at this process in Canada helps us to better understand Polanyi's argument. During the development of the Canadian economy in the 1800s and early 1900s, people faced the complex issues inherent in living in an urbanized environment: maintaining social cohesion under stressful conditions; trying to find and maintain steady employment; protecting children in an increasingly dangerous world; and balancing the demands of family, kin, and community. The nature of the problems created by the forces of economic development included unemployment, sickness, disability, industrial accidents, poverty in old age, and the poverty arising so often in large families. For families, it was not just a matter of making small adjustments in the way they lived or how they got along with their neighbours. The problems were deep and systemic.

To protect themselves, people turned to their local communities for help. But charities and municipal governments could only deal with local and immediate issues such as providing emergency shelter or food, so families and local communities increasingly turned to higher levels of government for protection from the destructive forces of self-regulating markets. The provincial and federal governments, sometimes alone and sometimes in collaboration, sought ways to deal with the risks created by the process of industrialization. Over time, structures for administering and providing services changed from those of a local and nonprofessional nature to those that were relatively centralized and professional. New social policy instruments were found to deal with the breadth and complexity of social problems. First social assistance, then social insurance, and finally universal programs were developed to protect citizens. These programs re-created the two fundamental structures found in pre-industrial society: reciprocity and redistribution. They took resources from members of the community who were making money from the industrialization and urbanization process and distributed them to other members to ensure a sense of community and social cohesion.

Throughout the twentieth century, social policies used in the construction of the welfare state created and maintained a new relationship between market forces and the needs of communities. Governments in the industrialized economies organized and delivered a variety of programs designed to provide health care, housing, education, income support, and social services. At the same time, governments intervened in the market to maintain high levels of employment, economic growth, and social stability. The result was the maintenance of a civil society in which a large portion of the population was protected from the turmoil created by economic development. Through political action, community members forced governments to intervene in the operation of markets to ensure a fairer distribution of the fruits of everyone's labour. Governments increasingly taxed individuals, families, and corporations, redistributing the resources to people who were unable to manage successfully in a competitive market environment. Polanyi describes these activities as a 'double movement':

> the action of two organizing principles in society, each of them setting itself specific institutional aims, having the support of definite social forces and using its own distinctive methods. The one is the principle of economic liberalism, aiming at the establishment of a self-regulating market, relying on the support of the trading classes, and using largely *laissez-faire* and free trade as its method; the other is the principle of social protection aiming at the conservation of man and nature as well as productive organizations, relying on the varying support of those most immediately affected by the deleterious action of the market – primarily, but not exclusively, the working and landed classes – and using protective legislation, restrictive associations, and other instruments of intervention as its methods. (1957: 132)

At the dawn of the twenty-first century, governments continue to use social policies to create the social protection described by Polanyi in this double movement. For example, social policies are used to construct the relationship between workers and the labour market. They create the regulations that govern the age at which a person can normally start working and the age at which people can expect to retire. Social policies establish minimum wages, provide workers with the rights to organize and bargain collectively, provide pay equity between the genders for work of equal value, and provide unemployment insurance protection when people are laid off from their jobs. Social policies require employers to create safer working environments, pay better wages, provide job security, and offer employment benefits such as holidays and pension plans. Social policies are used to regulate workers' relationships with their employers by creating labour boards to settle employment disputes and human rights legislation to provide protection from discrimination or sexual harassment. Social policies go beyond the relationships people have with work itself. They provide social security programs based on citizens' rights to old age security, child benefits, health care, social services, and social assistance.

Over the last twenty years the globalization of the economy has put welfare programs under the same strain experienced by the social system during the development of capitalism and the creation of markets. We argue that as threats from the global economy have increased, people have closed ranks and looked for new forms of protection. New social movements represent groups of people who are attempting to articulate their own stories concerning their identity and their history, which in many cases has included oppression and subjugation. Members of these groups are expressing ideas that challenge many of the stereotypes contained within existing social policies. Gays and lesbians, people of colour, people with disabilities, people living in poverty, and community activists, for example, are groups seeking to maintain or reintroduce the old processes of reciprocity and redistribution.

People seeking to re-establish the importance of reciprocity and re-distribution are creating a new language for social policy. They want to demonstrate that social problems 'are part of much wider discourses such that political struggles for welfare occur in many different sites: in the social and cultural relations of sexuality, gender, "race" and ethnicity and age, for example' (Penna and O'Brien 1996:54). These struggles go beyond class and class relations, worker-employer relations, and the relations of the family, while being part of all these relationships. A new struggle for recognition is being developed that respects the differences between people while accepting that there are commonalties in everyone. These new ideas are altering the fundamental idea of what is politically Left or Right by cutting across political boundaries to create new politics based on social identity rather than political orientation.

In addition to economic liberalism (globalization) and social protection (the welfare state) a third movement can be observed, that of cultural recognition (see Table 1.1). Like the others, this movement for cultural recognition provides an organizing principle in society that has specific aims, the support of definite classes and groups; uses distinctive methods; and has preferences for particular forms of social provision, policy, and the welfare state. The cultural recognition movement aims to redress oppressive relations and establish structures for self-determination. It relies on the support and mobilization of marginalized and disadvantaged groups (Drache and Cameron 1985). Economic liberalism, social protection, and cultural recognition provide three distinct orientations to social policy analysis with different aims, supports, methods, and institutional structures. Table 1.1 provides an overview of these policy orientations.

The history of cultural recognition is a long narrative of recurring efforts and battles. In the context of Canada, the most recent period can be said to have emerged in the 1970s. This movement employs affirmative action, employment equity, and human rights petitions, as well as (for Aboriginal peoples) land claims and treaty negotiations. Other

Table 1.1
Three Policy Orientations

Organizing Principle	Economic Liberalism	Social Protection	Cultural Recognition
Aims	Establishing 'self-regulating' markets	Conserving people and the social and natural environments	Redressing wrongs, gaining acceptance of identities, achieving self-determination
Support	Trading classes, business think-tanks, and transnational corporations	Working classes, the young, aged, sick, and unemployed	Various social movements and disadvantaged groups
Methods	Laissez-faire, free trade, contract law, commodification	Redistribution and reciprocity through public intervention, protective laws, mutual aid, trade unions, and self-help associations	Land claims and treaty negotiations, challenging stereotypes, changing every-day discourse, advocacy, and community action
Institutional Sites	Domestic and global economies, World Trade Organization, North American Free Trade Agreement, APEC, etc.	Governments, organized labour, voluntary sector	Aboriginal nations, families, communities of shared interest or identity, voluntary sector
Periods of Ascendancy or Emergence	1800s–1930s 1980s–2000	1940s–1970s	1970s–present
Vision of Social Policy and the Welfare State	Residual social programs and a minimalist welfare state	National system of social security	Diverse range of facilitative/empowering programs and a more democratic state

Source: Adapted in part from Polanyi (1957), and substantially elaborated by the authors.

methods include converting private troubles into public issues by raising awareness, challenging stereotypes, and altering the public's use of language to label peoples and behaviours. The institutional sites of struggles for cultural recognition are wideranging, and include First Nations, community groups, new social movements, and families and kinship networks.

Generally speaking, the vision of social policy and the welfare state advanced by groups seeking cultural recognition is one of an active yet more facilitative state for citizens, one that is enabling rather than overly administrative and controlling of clients. These groups believe that policy development processes should be more inclusive and respectful of differences, while advancing equitable treatment.

The Challenges

A new social policy world is in the making, and as yet it is not entirely clear what this new world will look like. We can make some preliminary observations. First, it looks like many of the old social problems – poverty, unemployment, sexism, and racism – will remain the same, though the context of these problems and the responses to them are changing. For example, in 1980 there were no food banks in Canada, but as we entered the year 2000 nearly three-quarters of a million Canadians used the country's more than 2,100 food banks monthly. Second, the old evils of homelessness and begging have re-emerged and poverty is on the rise. These issues are connected. The rising need for food banks is in part the result of people facing greater difficulty finding work, or, failing that, obtaining employment insurance or receiving social assistance. Third, many new groups are seeking help or protection from the government. Issues such as sexual harassment, abuse, date rape, and neglect of the elderly, which have long remained personal and private, are moving into the public sphere. For example, more people are demanding that they be allowed to die with dignity and to determine when to stop medical intervention. Still others need help in their struggle to live with the ravages of cancer, AIDS, or other life threatening illnesses. Fourth, there are new concerns about individual privacy in a world of instant communications, and a fear that the Internet will continue to be a vehicle for the dissemination of pornography and hate literature. The result of these concerns is that new ideas are entering the welfare debate; new relationships between the public, private, and community realms are being forged; new programs are being developed to deliver welfare services; and new volunteer organizations are being created to help the state manage welfare responsibilities.

The challenge for Canadians is to analyse these ideas, interests, policy instruments, and institutions in order to determine how they will influence the development of social policy. It is clear that the welfare system needs to be redesigned to allow for new relationships between civil society, the market, and the state. New policy designs must be able to tolerate wide differences in family structures, work patterns, learning and training experiences, sexual identities, and ethnic and religious beliefs. The new designs must contribute to the social capital of the country by creating social harmony, safety, and trust while encouraging people to think about the relationship between individual responsibility and social responsibility. The changing politics of social policy must open the process so that the public feels included, and it must seek the advice of those affected by the system. The more people are part of the deliberations, the more ownership of social policy outcomes they will have.

As with all politics, people's views differ about how the system should be changed. Some want to dismantle existing welfare programs and allow markets to solve social problems. Others want to redesign and rebuild the system in hopes that it will work better. Still others want to leave the system more or less as it is. Debates about how to change the welfare system are raging. The greater the difference between people's views, the hotter the debate. In this book we examine how these debates are shaping social policy. We look at the ideas of conservative thinkers who believe the existing system has failed to solve social problems. We compare these with the ideas of people who believe we must find new ways of providing state-sponsored welfare. To this we add the views of those who are seeking a middle way by holding onto the best parts of the existing system while finding new designs that are more inclusive and achieve more integrative goals.

Overview

We have organized the book in a way that traces the building of the Canadian welfare state and examines how welfare programs have been restructured to meet the demands of the global economy, the needs for social protection, and the desire for recognition by diverse populations. The book is based on a fundamental argument: *changes in the economy which threaten people's security lead to renewed community demands for*

social protection and redistribution; and changes in society are creating de-
mands for recognition of diverse identities. We examine the implications of
this argument for the development of Canadian social policy.

Chapter 1 examines in detail the two major forces we feel are effect-
ing the changes to the welfare system: the globalization of the economy
and the pluralization of the community. We argue that the changing
politics surrounding the welfare state are the result of tensions between
global economic forces and the demands being made by community
interest groups for greater protection from the risks created by the
process of globalization. Pressures from both sides have undermined
the support for the existing welfare system and we are entering a new
era of social policy development.

Chapters 2 through 5 deal with the historical background of the
welfare state in Canada and the politics surrounding it. Chapter 2
examines the roots of social policies in Canada and explores the implications these have for the politics of social policy. Beginning with the
pre-colonial era and extending to the years of the Great Depression, we
focus on the movement from local private practices of providing charity to the establishment of a federal-provincial program of social assistance. From a historical discussion of the roots of the welfare state we
describe the four major changes that took place in relation to those who
took responsibility for providing welfare services; the levels of
government(s) involved in social programs; the structures for administering and providing services; and policy instruments and processes.
As we see in later chapters, these four major changes came to play an
important part in the development of the welfare state in Canada.

Chapter 3 continues the exploration of the creation of the modern
welfare state from 1940 until the early 1970s. In this chapter we examine
the changing debate as a new set of ideas came to dominate the social
policy agenda. The Great Depression left no doubt in the minds of
Canadians that social conditions rather than individual behaviours
determined the fate of most families. During the 1930s unemployment
had risen dramatically, leaving hundreds of thousands of people looking for work. Community groups demanded government intervention,
while governments turned to the theories of John Maynard Keynes for
guidance in their efforts to provide social policies that would not hinder
economic development. Keynes claimed that by encouraging consumer
demand through public expenditures, the government could encourage employment, sustain economic growth, and maintain economic
stability. Following the Second World War the Canadian government

had a number of reports prepared which described how it could use Keynes's ideas to protect its citizens against most of the evils witnessed during the depression. The most important of these was the *Report on Social Security for Canada* (Marsh 1943), which urged the government to intervene in the economy by creating programs to help people deal with the problems created by modern industrial society. The chapter examines the effect this and other reports had on the development of a number of essential social programs.

In chapter 4 we examine what we call the crisis politics of the welfare state. By the 1970s critics had begun to complain that the economic system could no longer sustain the costs of the welfare system. There was growing rejection of the Keynesian idea that the welfare system could be used to create economic stability, and new monetarist policy ideas and practices came into vogue. The costs of the welfare system, the Right argued, were destroying the ability of the economy to grow. From this perspective, social programs had to be dismantled and the market had to be allowed to develop in an unfettered way. Writers from both the Left and the Right developed critical reviews of the welfare state. Feminists and other community members soon concurred with this analysis. While many people benefited from the support of the welfare system, it was not without faults. The barrage of critiques in fact destroyed many people's confidence in the welfare system. Chapter 4 then explores the criticisms of each perspective, and adds to it the critical voices of people working within the welfare system as well as those of clients who received benefits through the programs.

Chapter 5 describes three broad policy strategies governments might use to respond to changing conditions: dismantling programs and policy paradigms; remixing the social economy of welfare; or maintaining existing systems of benefits and rights. The Canadian government has used aspects of all three approaches. It has dismantled its universal income security programs, eliminated the Canada Assistance Program, privatized parts of the social service system, and cut back many unemployment insurance and social assistance benefits. At the same time the federal and provincial governments have maintained policy commitments to universal health care and education, workers' compensation, and income support for the elderly. The chapter argues that the cumulative impact of these changes have led to a lowering and fraying of the Canadian social safety net.

The next four chapters speculate about the way the politics of social policy will unfold over the next ten years. They deal, in turn, with the economy, social movements, gender and the family, and the community. In Chapter 6 we argue that globalism must be examined in broad terms. The process includes not only economic factors but cultural and community aspects as well. We examine the case of those who champion the cause of globalization and compare it with the case of those who challenge the benefits it provides. For the most part, Canadian governments have championed economic globalization. They have entered free-trade agreements and opened the Canadian economy to the world, a process that has altered the way Canadians think of themselves. We also analyze the effect globalization is having on a new conception of the welfare state which depicts welfare programs as handmaidens to the economy, programs that do not interfere with the globalization process but rather prepare people to live in a more globalized world.

Chapter 7 examines the changing politics of social policy in light of the evolution of new social movements. While community groups are struggling to have their needs met in the context of the globalization of the economy, they are caught in the tension created between the benefits provided by social policies and the control these policies have over the lives of community members. From the most critical perspective, the state is seen as an extension of patriarchal power whose interests only benefit men. A less critical viewpoint assumes that there are competing power sources, predominantly reflecting patriarchal power but leaving room for the development of wider community involvment in social policy issues. We argue that the new social policy politics entails a shift away from universalism, standardization, and uniformity, and towards particularism, fragmentation, and diversity, which emphasizes subjectivity and difference as opposed to universal and homogeneous experiences.

In Chapter 8, and in parts of chapters 4 and 9, we examine the implications of the changing politics of social policy for women. The needs of women, children, and families have always played a secondary role in the welfare state. Feminist writers point out that policies have supported the dominant role of men in both the workplace and the family. Much of the welfare state was constructed originally to meet the needs of people directly engaged in the paid labour force, its policies based on the assumption that families are the basic building block of the community. The retrenchment of the welfare state has had different consequences for women and men, and the shift back to a more residual welfare system has intensified the tension regarding entitlements and reinforced many inequities and disadvantages facing women. The chapter also explores the changing roles women are playing in relationship to the welfare state.

Chapter 9 examines the implications of the changing politics of social policy for community development. It examines the nature of community and the web of interconnected relationships in which people share resources and care for each other. It compares this with the neo-liberal view which maintains that individuals are independent agents looking out for their own best interests. We argue that the nature of people's connections in the community (whether communitarian or neo-liberal) shapes their ability to help each other. If communities are bound too tightly, members only look towards the community and are not prepared to care for strangers. If communities are made up of independent individuals with little or no connection with one another, no one will share with others for fear of being taken advantage of. When a balance exists, then community resources can be used to help address social problems. The chapter also looks at the way a community's capacity can be used to address social welfare issues. Here, our analysis leads to the conclusion that communities can deal with local problems, particularly those that require one-on-one interactions, but find it much more difficult to deal with systemic problems of poverty or unemployment. The chapter also examines the ways governments have been shifting some responsibility for solving problems back onto the community. This realignment of responsibilities, particularly as it relates to personal caring, has the greatest implications for women, and caution is required in the way communities are expected to provide care.

The final chapter brings the main arguments of the book together. We claim that the changing politics of social policy are the result of tensions arising from the interplay between the globalization of the economy and the pluralization of society. The impact of this interplay can be seen in the restructuring of the welfare system, the changing ideas about the welfare state, the use of new policy instruments, and the changing institutions that have been created to deliver welfare services. We examine the implications of these changes on the fate of the Canadian welfare state and ask what will happen as we move into the next millennium. We argue that a new relationship between market and community must be found, and that a new welfare agenda must be forged.

Throughout this book we focus on the realm between theories and practices, one filled with events, people, and politics that make up the social policy-making process. We are concerned with the questions about how and why the community takes care of its members. The story we tell does not explore, except in passing, the actual programs and services offered by the state, private organizations, or the nonprofit sector. We do not spend much time exploring the regulations or the implementation of particular policies, but concern ourselves primarily with the values that shape social policies and the way these values are translated into interests, instruments, and institutions that determine the course of social policy.

Our analysis is based on the assumption that social change is not part of an evolutionary process leading to greater stability and integration, but rather generates both positive and negative outcomes. Some changes will move the system to instability and disintegration, while other changes will do the opposite. In order to hypothesize about the direction of the changes, policy analysts must be aware of the history of the issues and the context in which the changes are taking place. We seek to demonstrate that the development of social arrangements such as industrialism, capitalism, and the development of the welfare state are interrelated, and that one area cannot be understood without an appreciation of the others.

1

Changing Politics: Social Policy in a Globalizing and Pluralizing Context

This chapter describes and assesses two trends: economic globalization and societal pluralization, worldwide developments which we examine here in reference to the contemporary Canadian context. Economic globalization is, of course, the latest expression of market liberalism and the latest stage in the development of capitalist economics, while societal pluralization refers to the increasing division between people based on gender, ethnicity, sexual orientation, family form, and age or relationship to the labour market. We devote more space to explaining pluralization because the concept, as we use it, adds an analytical dimension to the social policy field. Both of these trends embody much of what is changing the politics of social policy and shaping the future directions and relations between markets, communities, and states in the early part of the twenty-first century.

Economic Globalization

We have all experienced the rush of globalization. Information travels around the world at the click of a button. Capital can move from one country to another in seconds. We have become part of an international culture and international economy. This rapid flow means that issues spread instantly from country to country – ideas, new products, and medical discoveries travel at the speed of the Internet. Problem-solving social interventions used by one nation are soon on the political agendas of another. Positive and negative events travel at the same split-second pace. Remote famines and wars are part of the regular six o'clock news as the CBC, BBC, and CNN provide worldwide coverage of every conceivable topic, twenty-four hours a day. People are connected in an ever-tightening communications web, and are able to communicate more often and far more quickly than ever before.

The introduction of this new communication and production technology is having a profound effect on the politics of social policy. But before jumping into the effects of globalization it is important to see how it affects the world economy. Thus, we must first examine the three major impacts that the new global technology has on the economy: it increases the ability of corporations to transfer resources and technology from one county to another; it increases the concentration of economic power in the hands of multinational corporations; and it opens domestic markets through the removal of trade barriers.

Increase in Corporations' Ability to Transfer Resources

The introduction of new telecommunications and computing processes has created new organizational connections (Doern, Pal, and Tomlin 1996:3). Corporations have developed a global perspective wherein international markets are as important as national or domestic ones. This new orientation leads corporations to tailor investment and production decisions to take advantage of changing market conditions. Companies segment markets and organize production to benefit from low labour costs and the availability of natural resources. A large pool of non-unionized labour is viewed as a ready asset in the same way the discovery of oil or nickel once inspired corporations to locate production facilities in remote areas.

Globalization makes every corporate decision an interconnected one. A decision to take advantage of low wages in Mexico can hasten the closure of an assembly plant in Nova Scotia, which in turn can alter corporate investment decisions about locating a plant in Nagpur, India. The economic liberty offered by globalization means that more businesses can seek conditions that favour their productive capacities. To maximize profits, companies actively pursue situations that offer the least regulation, the cheapest labour, and the smallest social welfare burden. Corporations will bypass countries that uphold laws and regulations limiting business profitability in their relentless quest for favourable economic and social conditions.

Concentration of Power

Almost weekly it seems we hear of another two large companies merging to form a mega-corporation. The ease with which such mergers is accomplished has been aided in large part by the ease with which resources and capital can be transferred. The concentration of corporate power is staggering. Corporations are so powerful they have more influence on the global economy than most national governments.

There are 40,000 corporations operating on the international level. Of these, 200 control a quarter of the world's economic activity. Sarah Anderson and John Cavanagh (1996) point out that 'instead of creating an integrated global village, these firms are weaving webs of production, consumption, and finance that bring economic benefits to, at most, a third of the world's people.' The activities of these corporations, claim Anderson and Cavanagh, hurt the bottom 20 per cent of the rich countries and the bottom 80 per cent of the poor countries. To support their claim the authors provide a snapshot of the extent of corporate concentration. Of the 100 largest economies in the world, 51 are corporations. The top 200 corporations' combined sales are larger than the combined economies of all countries minus the largest nine. These same corporations have almost twice the economic power of the poorest four-fifths of humanity. The top 200 corporations have been net job destroyers in recent years, and in 1995 had combined revenues of $7.1 trillion. Because these corporations have become so powerful, they can make certain demands as they seek out new areas in which to invest.

Opening of Domestic Markets through Removal of Trade Barriers

Economic globalization increases corporate influence on the public agenda. Companies prod and push governments to introduce legislation that increases privatization, deregulation, the expansion of free markets, and tax reforms that shift burdens from the corporation to the individual. Governments, responding to the mobility of capital, are removing trade barriers, eliminating national standards, and opening domestic markets to free trade. To refuse to take such steps is to risk rejection by corporations looking for new investment opportunities. The global economy appears to reward those states that are open and flexible. A frightening example of the new corporate power is the Multilateral Agreement on Investment (MAI) now being considered (Cohen 1997b). MAI is being negotiated between twenty-nine member countries of the Organization for Economic Co-operation and Development. Some of the new rights contained within the agreement allow corporations to challenge government decisions regarding internal activities of the state. For example, corporations from other countries could challenge a government's provision of public or nonprofit social services. Corporations could also encourage the dismantling of public services and social programs, and the marketization of services provided by public or nonprofit organizations. If a government is unwilling to introduce legislation favourable to corporate interests, a company could sue the government, or, if all else fails, simply hunt for a different investment market.

Figure 1: The Effects of Globalization on Social Policy

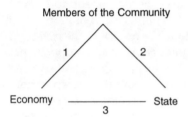

1 Job insecurity and inequality
2 Transformation from citizens to customers
3 Limits on government

The possibility of such agreements puts enormous pressure on governments to change. In response to the flexibility, immense power, and demands of corporations in the new global economy, governments attempt to court corporations by privatizing, deregulating, decentralizing, and downsizing public services, laws, and rights. As a result, governments give up some of their power to solve or even address social problems. Globalization has three effects on the politics of social policy: it undermines job security, it changes the relationship between a citizen and the state, and it limits government influence over the economy. Figure 1 depicts the changing relationships.

Globalization Undermines Job Security and Polarizes Labour Markets

Globalization undermines job security by threatening the employment security of workers. For example, engineering technology allows machines to replace people; new communications technology makes it possible for corporations to shift production from countries with expensive labour and restrictive laws to countries with cheap labour and few regulations; and the opening of domestic markets reduces the need for domestic product, which threatens the jobs of workers involved in its production. The automation of the workplace, the exportation of jobs, and the importation of products mean fewer jobs. The result is a steady increase in unemployment, which has not been below 7 per cent in Canada for the last twenty years. Those who become unemployed are without a job for longer periods. More people in the last ten years have had part-time or temporary jobs without benefits. Canadian wage rates have also fallen in real value over the same period. The result is a growing division between those who have 'good' jobs, with security and benefits, and those who have 'poor' jobs, without security or benefits.

New production processes and distribution systems have also reinforced the forces of globalization, and the combined effect means fewer workers. Jeremy Rifkin, in *The End of Work* (1995:198), points out that 'in every advanced economy, new technologies and management practices are displacing workers, creating a reserve army of contingent labourers, widening the gap between the haves and have-nots, and creating new and dangerous levels of stress.' Those who have been unable to compete have suffered economically and socially; those who have succeeded in expanded global markets have improved their economic well-being. The resulting increase in inequality places the state in a contradictory position: it seeks to keep its economy competitive by harmonizing regulations, tax structures, and welfare policies; it must, however, contend as well with the increasing stress of citizens excluded from the labour market. Keith Banting (1996:32) comments that this 'emphasis on adaptation and flexibility conflicts with the emphasis on security and protection that was embodied in the historic conception of the welfare state.'

Globalization Changes the Relationship between Citizen and State

John Ralston Saul (1995) claims that the growth of corporate power is disfiguring the ideal of the public good. Corporations, whether they are banks, developers, businesses, or producers, are primarily interested in their own bottom line. As Saul (1995:91) describes it, like the corporatist movements in the 1920s they seek to 'shift power directly to economic and social interest groups; push entrepreneurial initiative in areas normally reserved for public bodies; and obliterate the boundaries between pubic and private interests – that is, challenge the idea of the public interest.' The shift in power from the state to the corporation transforms the relationship between the government and the public by turning citizens into customers. This shift is evident in the 'marketization' of social discourse and social programs, a process we examine in Chapter 6. Universities, hospitals, and social service workers, for example, are encouraged to think of students, patients, and clients as consumers. But, while citizens have rights and duties conferred by the state – and benefits that accrue from these rights – customers have only choices that are defined by their purchasing power. This change from citizen to customer has the potential of undermining the social fabric of the community. It undermines and encourages public institutions to abandon their social obligations.

Globalization is reducing governments' ability to solve social problems by limiting their power over the economy. To keep corporations from moving production out of Canada both federal and provincial governments have dismantled parts of their welfare programs, reduced corporate taxes, overlooked or under-enforced environmental regulations, and helped ensure a compliant workforce by allowing growth of the perception that there is general insecurity in the workplace.

Societal Pluralization

If economic globalization generally looks outward from the nation state, societal pluralization looks inward. Pluralization, a trend found in many countries, relates primarily to affairs and circumstances within the nation state and society. The process of pluralization describes the growing divisions within Canada based on the social characteristics of groups of people. It is a multidimensional process that reflects increased diversity in people's cultural, economic, social and political orientations. People with different orientations have different ways of knowing, seeing, understanding, and explaining the way the world operates and they want these differences reflected in the way that the state develops social policies. This means the policy process will become more fraught with tensions and controversies as people struggle to have their needs recognized. On the one hand, pluralization encourages the development of new identities leading to personal empowerment and group recognition for people who have felt excluded from the mainstream of society. On the other hand, the process creates fear and leads to attacks on groups of people because they are seen as different.

As Canadian governments have supported economic globalization, they have also supported pluralization, through their policies on Aboriginal governance, divorce and family law, immigration, official languages, multiculturalism, employment equity, and public funding of nongovernmental groups, as well as the entrenchment of the Charter of Rights and Freedoms in the Constitution. Thus pluralization relates to and is affected by the forces of economic globalism, calls for social protection, and claims for the recognition of diverse identities and life circumstances. As well, social trends such as the aging of the population and cultural trends such as the decline of deference and the growth in the acceptance of differences (Adams 1997; Reid 1997) are factors contributing to this pluralization.

The concept is intrinsically a multidisciplinary idea, and different aspects of pluralization are addressed by different academic disciplines and different practitioners and organizations. As an overarching concept, pluralization encompasses what has been called the politics of difference, identity politics, labour market polarization, and elements of postmodernism. Thus, economists have tended to examine the growing incidence of irregular patterns in employment and careers; gerontologists have traced the decline of age sixty-five as the normal age of retirement from the labour force; demographers and statisticians, among others, have highlighted the shifts in family forms, sizes, and roles in recent times; anthropologists and sociologists have made a distinctive contribution to Canadians' image of their country through studying the ethnic and racial composition of society; critical theorists, feminists, pollsters, and social workers have contributed to the deconstruction of prevailing ways of thinking about and explaining modern society and the political economy; political scientists and legal scholars have assessed the implications of the Charter of Rights and Freedoms and changes in intergovernmental relations as they apply to the distribution of public power and the status of various groups.

We examine the following elements of pluralization in present-day Canadian society: the increasing variation in education, work, and retirement patterns; the expanding forms of family structures and relationships; the changing ethnic, linguistic, and racial composition of the population; the declining consensus on the postwar welfare state and the deconstruction of common ideas and theories; the proliferation and networking of interest groups; the decentralization of governmental authority and program delivery; and the constitutional recognition of several groups and identities.

One important aspect of pluralization is the new way people are approaching education, work, and retirement. Over the last generation, educational careers have become more varied, secure careers have become less common, and employment histories more diverse. A British Social Justice Commission report (1994, 81) commenting on the development of more flexible patterns of life apply also to contemporary Canadian society: 'The linear progression from education to adult life to retirement is being supplanted by more complex processes: education and training take place throughout the life-cycle; employment is mixed with caring responsibilities through the prime working years; retirement is taken early or late.' For many people, at least some of these transitions across the life span do not call for personal choices. As we discuss in Chapters 6 and 8, increasingly jobs are taking nonstandard forms such as contract, part-time, temporary, shared, and self-employment. Part-time workers form a larger share of the employed labour force and there are more nonstandard work hours. These trends have resulted in a polarization of work and earnings between high- and low-skilled jobs in the Canadian labour force. Closely linked is what Grant Schellenberg calls the destandardization of retirement. 'People are leaving the labour force through different pathways and for different reasons than in the past' (1996:151). The ages at which people are retiring from the labour force, as well as the causes and the ways, have become more diverse. Retired people in Canada are not necessarily 'old people' or senior citizens.

A second aspect of pluralism is the diversification of family forms in Canada. The nuclear family – married heterosexual couples with children – once the predominant form of family structure in the country, accounted in 1995 for less than half (45 per cent) of all families, compared to 55 per cent in 1981. Even within this category, there has been a growing number of 'blended families' consisting of couples with the mother's, the father's, or both partners' children from previous marriages or common-law unions. Other types include single parent, joint custody, adoptive, teenage parent, later-life parent, childless couple, and extended families.

In the expansionist era of the Canadian welfare state, from the 1940s into the 1970s, the main reason for being a lone parent was widowhood (Evans 1991). Today the prime reasons are that persons have never (or are not yet) married, are divorced, or separated. The proportion of lone parent families, of which women head over 80 per cent, have increased substantially since the 1970s, and in 1995 represented 14.4 per cent of all families (Statistics Canada 1997). Common-law families jumped in number from 6 per cent in 1981 to 12 per cent of all families in 1995 (most are in Quebec), the strongest increase over this period in the number of children in a particular family form. Common-law unions are also becoming more popular among older as well as younger people. Statistics Canada does not yet track the number of same-sex couples with or without children, but it appears that the number of these family forms are increasing and gaining recognition as laws change and programs are initiated in some Canadian jurisdictions. The growing diversity in family forms has ramifications for household incomes, social care and informal support, child rearing, family law, employment standards legislation, and human rights.

A third dimension of pluralization is the growing racial, ethnic, and linguistic diversities of society. Ethnic differentiation is not new in Canada. In *The Vertical Mosaic*, John Porter observed many years ago: 'If not its one distinctive value, that of the mosaic is Canada's most cherished. Legitimization for the mosaic is sought in the notion of collective or group rights' (1965, 558). What may be relatively new is the pace of change in the Canadian mosaic's design and composition. What remains an important insight in Porter's work is the connection between race and ethnicity on the one hand, and class and power on the other; he carefully documented the vertical or hierarchical relation between Canada's many cultural groups. Another legacy from his work is the insightful reminder that Canadian society is not just pluralistic but is also stratified into groups with unequal power and status. More recent analyses have added the dimensions of age, disability, gender, and sexual orientation, plus others, in exploring the nature of inequality and authority in societies. We consider these issues in various ways in Chapters 4, 6, 7, and 8.

On ethnic diversity, Andrew Armitage (1996:23) observes that 'Canada has become, through immigration, a polyethnic multicultural state in which Aboriginal peoples and peoples of French, British, other European, Asian, and African origins live together using common social institutions.' According to the 1996 census, immigrants represent over 17 per cent of Canada's population, the largest share in over five decades. In addition, for the first time in the twentieth century the majority of immigrants to Canada now come from Asia and the Middle East. Growing shares of immigrants come also from Central and South America, the Caribbean, and Africa. The proportion of immigrants living in Canada who were born in Europe declined from 67 per cent in 1981 to 47 per cent in 1996. This recent immigration-based diversification of the population is concentrated in three provinces and in urban centres. Almost 90 per cent of immigrants live in Ontario, Quebec, and

British Columbia. About one-fifth of the populations of Toronto and Vancouver are immigrants who have come to Canada since the early 1980s.

With growing multilingualism, the linguistic character of the country is changing.[1] In the past decade, the share of the population whose mother tongue is English or French has declined gradually: close to 17 per cent of the population now is allophone – people whose mother tongue is neither of the official languages; and most recent immigrants to Canada, about 80 per cent, report a language other than English or French as their mother tongue, compared to 54 per cent in the 1960s. In the 1990s Chinese surpassed Italian as the most common nonofficial language among Canadians. Among the top ten language groups in Canada, other than English and French, four languages – Chinese, Punjabi, Arabic, and Tagalog (Filipino) – were not on the list twenty-five years ago, and have replaced Greek, Dutch, Hungarian, and Yiddish. Indeed, the 1996 census found that 18.7 per cent of the population describes their ethnic origin as Canadian; 17.1 per cent as from the British Isles; 9.5 per cent as French; 26.3 per cent as some combination of the above groups; 2.7 per cent as Aboriginal; and 25.7 per cent as other ethnicities. Among people with Aboriginal ancestry in Canada, there are 608 First Nations, comprising fifty-two cultural groups and languages.

The 1996 Canada census, for the first time, provided information on the numbers and characteristics of visible minorities, defined by the federal Employment Equity Act as 'persons, other than Aboriginal peoples, who are non-Caucasian in race or non-white in colour.'[2] The census found that 11.3 per cent of the Canadian population, nearly 3.2 million, are people of colour, an increase from an estimated 6.3 per cent in 1986. Statistics Canada forecasts that as a share of the population in Canada, visible minorities could double to about 23 per cent by 2016, a significant change in a relatively short period. In our view, Armitage is correct in concluding that what he calls the paradigm of British/French/Other European discourse, 'no longer represents the basis on which social policy can be developed' (1996:24).

A fourth strand of pluralization is the deconstructing of dominant ideas and conventional wisdom regarding the human condition, social theories, and politics. Public opinion analyst Angus Reid writes of the 'attitudinal mosaic' in the values and beliefs of Canadians (1997). Pollster Michael Adams in *Sex in the Snow: Canadian Social Values at the End of the Millennium* (1997), argues that traditional forms of social consensus and conformity are breaking down and that people now define themselves by their personal priorities and life choices. Adams argues that this goes beyond talking in terms of being members of a particular generation, such as the baby boomers, Generation Xers, or the baby echo cohort. Adams's survey research suggests that Canadians are divided into twelve social value 'tribes' with different demographic characteristics, motivations, values, and philosophies.

As it pertains to social policy, deconstruction involves questioning critically, and perhaps ultimately rejecting, taken-for-granted assumptions of such key concepts as citizenship, universalism, the public interest, and work. It also involves the assertion that alternative perspectives and social relationships are valid and legitimate. As Iris Marion Young (1990:102) has argued, 'reason cannot know the whole and cannot be unified.' In this perspective, claims of impartiality and universality of policies and practices are a fiction. 'No one can adopt a point of view that is completely impersonal and dispassionate, completely separated from any particular context and commitments' (1990:103). Rather, everyday life is a 'plurality of moral subjects and situations' characterized by group affiliations and differences, by needs and desires, by particular perspectives, and by passionate beliefs.

Official expressions of a 'general public good' and a dichotomy between public and private spheres of life are challenged. In their place, postmodernist thinkers advance the idea of the heterogeneous public, emphasizing the particularities of ethnicity, race, gender, culture, age, religion, sexual orientation, ability, social class, and geography. Implicit in the idea of the heterogeneous public, suggests Young (1990:120), are 'two political principles: (a) no persons, actions or aspects of a person's life should be forced into privacy; and (b) no social institutions or practices should be excluded *a priori* from being a proper subject for public discussion and expression.'

The emergence in recent decades of new theoretical approaches to analysing society, the economy, and the state have challenged prevailing notions concerning scientific social knowledge, government planning, and the management of human affairs. Many of the new ways of thinking and theorizing about the welfare state hold a conflict model of society – stressing struggle, coercion, and oppression – rather than a consensus approach which suggests stability and unity over values. Newer theories critique conventional notions of social integration as partial and exclusionary; they also question claims concerning the benefits of industrial growth, pointing out the adverse consequences of industrialism for communities and the natural environment. Such challenges have contributed to weakening the progressive liberal and social democratic, intellectual underpinnings of the postwar welfare state (Mishra 1984, 1990a), as we show in Chapter 4. Moreover, in the domain of policy practice and social provision, ideas on retrenchment, fiscal constraint, and making the welfare state more responsive to market conditions gained predominance in the 1980s and 1990s.

These challenges to ways of thinking about economic and social issues closely connect to a fifth aspect of pluralism: the proliferation of interests within most public policy fields. More groups are forming and claiming a direct interest in public issues and programs, and expecting to participate in policy reviews and consultations. 'In the past two decades,' Canadian political scientist William Coleman (1991:204) has perceived, 'the number of interest groups representing all facets of social, cultural, and economic life has grown more rapidly than at any previous time in Canadian history. There has also been a significant professionalization of interest groups, as these have become institutionalized participants in public policy making.' Types of groups include client-based organizations such as those for pensioners; producer groups such as teacher's federations and nurse's associations; public interest organizations such as anti-poverty groups; think-tanks and social planning councils; voluntary social service agencies, and health advocacy groups. The mainstream political parties in Canada have been partly eclipsed as vehicles for political participation and policy development. A greater range of values and views is brought to bear on policy debates and processes, although a dominant policy focus may still persist. Daniel Drache and Duncan Cameron (1985) apply the phrase 'popular sector groups' to those organizations that express a discourse of politics, economics, and social welfare counter to the dominant view. This alternative approach focuses on human well-being and the needs of the poor and marginalized, supports significant and new roles for government in the economy, and stresses the importance of job creation and full employment.

Alongside the more traditional forms of parliamentary, electoral, linguistic, and intergovernmental politics are newer forms and styles. These include politics of Aboriginal self-determination, ethnicity, gender, sexuality, disability, intergenerational relations, and the Charter of Rights and Freedoms. New social groups represent people from a variety of backgrounds: gays and lesbians, Blacks, single parents, people with disabilities, Aboriginal peoples, and women. There are new religious or faith groups, new movements fighting for the rights of disadvantaged people, ethnic groups struggling for their cultural identities, and new advocacy groups finding ways to strengthen their communities (Fagan and Lee 1997: 143). These new social movements are community-based (Fisher and Kling 1994:8). People do not have to become formal members, but can be loosely federated with the group. Computer bulletin boards and e-mail lists are the new ways of communicating and informing members of the group's activities. The fight to establish identity and raise social status is taking place as much on the street and the Internet, and in the press and courtroom, as it once was through the governmental policy process.

A new context is taking shape as innovative social movements begin to influence the policy-making process (Scott 1990:16). Social movements seek to obtain some of the resources and rights enjoyed by the older, work-oriented collectives. Each group seeks input into the policy process and governments respond in a number of ways: opening up the process, ignoring the groups, or making policy changes. New social movements challenge and can alter more established interest-group structures within policy communities. At one level, governments may find it easier to manage the policy process. With so many contenders in the policy arena, they can play one group off against another, seeking and finding support with one group while rejecting the advance of another. At a deeper level, however, pluralization and the pursuit of cultural recognition seek to redefine, and to democratize, the social contract underpinning both policy and the Canadian welfare state.

The differential retrenchment of social programs, which we examine in later chapters, contributes to the segmentation of not just clientele and other group interests, but also the distribution of authority within the Canadian federation. Divided jurisdiction and regional political identities are longstanding features of Canadian federalism and governance. What is distinctive in the current age, particularly for social policy, are the following developments: the entrenchment of the Charter of Rights in the 1980s; the retreat of the federal government from its postwar (1940s to 1980s) leadership role; the emergence at the federal level in the 1990s of the Bloc Quebecois and the Reform Party, both representing strong regional discontents and resolutely advocating more decentralization; the assertiveness if not aggressiveness of the provinces in the later 1990s towards further delegation of funding and powers; the concerns of municipalities as well as hospital and school boards concerning offloading responsibilities for programs and services from the senior levels of government; the establishment of Nunavut in 1999 as a new territorial government in the eastern and central arctic area, with the transfer of delivering health care, public housing, and other social programs taking place over the 1999–2009 period; and the (re)building of First Nations governments in Aboriginal communities across the country.

We now comment briefly on one of these developments – the introduction of the Charter to Canada's constitutional order – to illustrate the implications for societal pluralization and social policy. In the original British North America Act of 1867, which established Canada as a political union, a few groups such as denominational education schools, Indians, and aliens were identified. In the Constitution Act of 1982, which entrenched the Charter of Rights and Freedoms, many more groups gained constitutional recognition. In addition to Indians, the existing rights of Inuit and Metis peoples were recognized and rights and protections were specifically granted to women, official language minorities, visible ethnic and racial minorities, persons with mental or physical disabilities, and northerners. Our political system, policy discourse, and processes now rest on a far more pronounced, politicized, and constitutionalized form of pluralism.

The conception of citizenship in Canada has deepened and become more complex. The Charter has undoubtedly added to the rise of the individual- and group-oriented rights discourse so evident today. Alan Cairns (1991:173) claims, with considerable reason, that 'the Constitution is now the crucial instrument for defining one's place in Canadian society.' Of course, the paid labour market remains the crucial *economic institution* for defining one's place in society. For groups that do not see themselves in the Charter, such as gays and lesbians, the Constitution remains an exclusionary document, and any subsequent process of reforming the Canadian Constitution has and will prompt groups to advance their claims for recognition.

Conclusions

Economic globalization and community pluralization tend to push and pull societies, economies, and states in unchartered directions. The external forces of globalization draw governments towards an opening up of their domestic economies, push for a retrenching of social and other public programs, and expose communities to market upheavals. International corporations looking for new investments press governments to reorganize the fiscal, monetary, industrial, and social sectors so that they can maximize profits. The internal forces of pluralization are moving countries, we believe, towards increased diversity, fragmentation, and social inclusion. A multiplicity of groups are demanding the reorganization or devolution of public programs and services to better meet their members' needs. These changes are having similar effects on the what constitutes public space or the 'commons.' Globalization encourages corporations to find ways of taking economic control of public space by creating new forms of ownership on such things as air, the use of the sea, and space exploration. At the same time pluralization encourages the transformation of public space into territorial space as particular groups come to control public institutions such as schools, hospitals, and other public organizations.

The classes and interests in support of economic globalization pressure governments to remove social programs in order to create an 'even playing field' for international competition. As corporations shift capital from one country to another, most governments find it difficult to maintain social programs that place real or alleged burdens on the corporate sector. Thomas Courchene (1987:11), an enthusiastic champion of economic liberalism, argues that Canadians 'no longer have the luxury of designing social policy independently of the underlying economic environment.' Policy harmonization encourages the government to relinquish national sovereignty to other political structures by transferring powers through international agreements. Courchene (1987:18) identifies two social policy challenges in this process: 'first, to ensure that the incentives within the social policy network will encourage, rather than inhibit, the required adjustment on the economic front; second, to ensure that the social safety net evolves in a manner that reflects the changing needs of citizens as they adapt to the new economic order.' We explore this and contending views on globalization in Chapter 6, and we offer, in Chapter 10, an alternative vision of the social policy challenges and choices facing Canadians for the new century.

Community pluralization both reflects and reinforces diversities within the Canadian polity and society. This process has created a means for people to express their own needs, which in turn contests and partially alters the beliefs and practices underpinning the social contract. We are therefore witnessing a transformation of the social sphere and the welfare state. To appreciate the scale and significance of this transformation, the history of developing this system of social security is the subject of the next two chapters.

2

Early Developments in Canadian Social Welfare

Histories of welfare states are much more than collections of facts and chronologies of programs. They are also compilations of human memories and myths, of political conflict and struggle, of compassion and sharing, and of aspirations and achievements. They are the stories of community members coming together to protect themselves or organizing and encouraging their governments to create security against unforeseen misfortune. And they can teach us so much.

The most fundamental lesson we can learn from these histories is that today's politics are rooted in yesterday's social policy legislation, and that the principles that were established during the early period of social welfare development can still be found in policies today.

Our intent in this chapter is not to examine the early history of social welfare policy in its entirety, but to highlight major changes in the economy and society, and to note key developments in social policy making.

Colonial Origins of Welfare

Dennis Guest (1985:9) tracks the origins of modern Canadian social policy back in time to the late sixteenth century in England and France. Legacies from the colonial period became reflected in Canada's first constitutional document, the British North America Act of 1867, which regarded matters of social welfare as local and private, and thus under the jurisdiction of the provinces. Colonial arrangements for social welfare included local and provincial jails, penitentiaries, and asylums; government funding and supervising of private charities; and municipal/provincial systems of public relief for the poor and destitute. Most elements of pre-Confederation social policy are captured in the name of the administrative agency, the Board of Inspectors of Prisons, Asylums and Public Charities, created in Upper Canada (Ontario) in 1859. In Quebec, public responsibilities for social welfare were assigned to the church (Guest 1985:13).

Community members saw social problems as the immediate consequences of people's behaviour. Members of the community often assumed that poverty was a symptom of personal weakness and that an inability to take care of oneself was a sign of failure. They believed that families could and should be able to solve their own problems with a little help from the community. There are four principles of social provision that were established in the colonial era that reflected the way people thought about welfare at the time. These principles mirrored the conditions and beliefs of the day and have continued to fundamentally influence the politics of social assistance as we move into the twenty-first century.

The first principle maintained that social assistance should be residual to assistance available from other sources. Private philanthropy, good neighbours, voluntary organizations, and the churches were all looked to as important and legitimate sources of support and help to people in need. Indeed, colonial administrations delegated or contracted out the responsibility to care for the poor and destitute to charities and religious orders. It was only after all other sources of help had been used up that people could legitimately turn to the government for help. Public relief was usually financed and administered by local governments from a rather restricted tax base, and rudimentary bureaucracies provided the services.

The second principle maintained that social assistance should be categorical and targeted to particular groups of people. Public responsibility for support to the poor was for certain impoverished groups – the old, orphans, the mentally ill, and the disabled – groups seen as deserving of aid. If an able-bodied unemployed person (someone Canadian governments now call an 'employable') was an applicant for public assistance, they were expected to perform work duties as a condition for receiving assistance (Guest 1985:37). This was called the workhouse test or work test. For the children of poor families there were apprenticeships.

The third principle stated that assistance should be conditional upon the applicant engaging in certain civic duties or activities, with penalties for those who did not comply. In the colonial years, legislation for relief to the poor included sections on the responsibility of parents to care for their children and for older children to contribute to the care of their parents and grandparents.

Finally, the fourth principle – called the principle of 'less eligibility' – was that assistance should be minimal, not optimal or even average in amount. It held that anyone collecting social assistance should receive an amount less than that of the lowest paid worker so as not to encourage dependency on relief or to undermine the work ethic and low wages. This principle is evident today in discussions of welfare rates, minimum wages, and work (dis)incentives of welfare and unemployment insurance. For observers of welfare reform and debates over 'workfare' in Canada in recent years, this all should sound eerily familiar.

During this period, the dominant ideology stressed the importance of private initiative and individual responsibility, based on a strong belief in the work ethic and in self-improvement. It was widely assumed that successful families were hard working and frugal, while people living in poverty were lazy or unwilling to make sacrifices. Sometimes the poor were thought of as 'down on their luck.' However, those who were indigent and dependent were viewed in the same way as criminals and the mentally ill: responsible for their fate and deserving of their 'lot in life.' The ethos of individualism, the pioneer experience, and later industrial capitalism fostered the notion that the first line of defence against poverty and other needs was the family, and, where that institution failed, charity and voluntary organizations – church groups, missions, child welfare societies, and neighbourhood settlement houses – were expected to respond to the social problems of the day and develop programs for those in need. The word 'relief' appropriately described social welfare in this early stage because it implied the state's limited acceptance of a 'public' responsibility for the care of those who were unable to care for themselves. The belief in self-reliance fostered the notion that governments should not be involved in the private affairs of citizens, and, if necessary, they should do so with as little interference as possible.

Growing Country, Growing Community Needs: 1867 to the Early 1900s

Elisabeth Wallace (1950:383) suggests that the origins of the Canadian welfare state can be traced to the first thirty years or so after Confederation, from 1867 to 1900, 'when the proper function of government was a matter of general concern and wide debate.' During this period, both economic and social conditions and public opinion on social welfare 'underwent a marked transformation.' Governments in Canada, especially municipalities but also the provinces, began intervening more and more in the social sphere. After Confederation, as people left the farm for work opportunities in the growing towns and cities, they found that their lifestyles changed. There was less allegiance to, and reliance on, primary groups. The separation from the family and the farm created new situations, which required new ways of meeting one's needs. Gone or declining were the rural communities with their single, unambiguous social structures. Gone was the sense of community that had seemed to naturally protect the individual or family. Going or gone was the reliance on a self-sufficient environment.

New lifestyles emerged as living patterns changed. Urbanization created new eating and drinking habits. New towns grew, as did urban slums. Spending and consuming patterns changed. Health and sanitary practices were altered and new norms for personal interaction developed. Problems of infant mortality, child neglect, and juvenile delinquency became more evident and serious. In the 1890s and early 1900s there were differences in the way men and women looked at these social problems. Thelma McCormack (1991:31) points out that 'men saw the industrial system, the factories, women saw the slums and households; men saw exploited workers, women saw women exhausted by child-bearing; men saw unemployment, women saw sick and under-fed children; men saw industrial accidents, women saw the impact of alcoholism on the family.' Men pushed for policies about factory legislation, workers' compensation, and pensions. It was not uncommon for women to push for policy measures concerning public health, family planning, mother's pensions, and, later, family allowances.

Over this period, Canadian society became fragmented and differentiated. A wage-labour class emerged that was totally reliant on others for income. Unemployment was always a possibility. As all these changes took place, new stresses and strains were placed on people to find ways to cope and meet their welfare needs. Individuals were forced to turn more and more to the community for help. As J.S. Woodsworth (1972:178) observed in 1911, 'In a small community it is easy to give relief to the occasional needy family. There exists a personal relationship which largely precludes imposition, and which goes far in encouraging thrift. But in the city the situation is quite changed. The well-to-do are separated from their less fortunate neighbours by distance and by social cleavages of many kinds. The very numbers make personal knowledge and sympathy almost an impossibility.'

Table 2.1
Provincial Social Expenditure (Gross), 1871–1977

Year	Social Welfare %		Health %	Education %	Protection %
1871	–	9.5	–	22.5	12.8
1881	–	12.7	–	16.6	8.1
1891	–	13.4	–	16.8	10.8
1901	–	14.7	–	15.1	8.9
1911	–	11.1	–	14.2	7.7
1921	3.9		8.6	20.0	9.2
1931	5.8		8.1	18.0	6.2
1941	10.8		9.6	13.7	B
1951	14.1		17.1	16.1	5.1
1961	11.0		24.8	22.9	3.8
1971	11.3		26.7	26.8	3.4
1977	14.6		24.3	23.6	3.5

Source: Allan Moscovitch and Jim Albert, eds. *The Benevolent State: The Growth of Welfare in Canada* (Toronto: Garamond Press, 1987), 22.

In the later decades of the nineteenth century, public attitudes were shifting as well, and the ideas of 'laissez-faire and individualism were being challenged by notions of social justice, by a concern for the well-being of the group and of the wider interests of the community as a whole' (Guest 1985:24). As people were separated from their family and community by the process of industrialization they found it more difficult to meet their needs. There was growing cultural disorganization, secularization, and individualism.

The provinces became increasingly involved in social welfare. Table 2.1 shows that from the beginning of Confederation the four provinces were spending more than 40 per cent of their budgets on social welfare, health, education, and protection. While the figures fluctuated as new provinces joined Confederation and the country lived through two world wars, they did not fall below a third of all provincial government expenditures. These figures are contrary to the common idea portrayed in some history texts and the modern press – that provinces played a minimal part in addressing social issues during the formation of the country and that 'rugged individuals' took care of themselves.

As industrialization transformed Canadian society, old structures and processes were found inadequate. Citizens encouraged the provinces to take major responsibility for certain groups of people: the aged, the sick, children, and people with mental disabilities. The provinces provided an ever-expanding range of institutions, tuberculosis hospitals, homes for the aged and infirm, child welfare services, and other specialized programs. In 1874 Ontario passed the Charity Aid Act, putting the practice of government grants to voluntary social welfare organizations on a more uniform basis. The law intended to determine grants in accordance with the services actually performed and the amount of funds received from other sources. Another key principle in the legislation was that voluntary agencies receiving provincial grants would be subject to provincial supervision or monitoring of their activities. In effect, the Charity Aid Act represented a political recognition of the continuing role that voluntary agencies were to play, partly as instruments of provincial social policy.

'Although it was not until the twentieth century that the phrase "social security" was invented, and emphasis placed upon the need for prevention as more important than cure in attacking social problems, the germ of the idea may be found well before 1900' (Wallace 1950:387). By 1893, 32.4 per cent of the Ontario budget was devoted to social welfare spending, and Splane (1965) suggests that this increase in expenditures through the 1880s and 1890s indicates the emergence of a philosophy of prevention. The prevention of illness, disability, and dependency was the essence of the new provincial public health program and the measures for the inspection of factories. Beginning with Ontario in 1884, followed by Quebec in 1885, Manitoba in 1900, and the other provinces later, the provinces enacted Factory Acts regulating the working conditions of industry. A child welfare program 'represented the willingness of the province to launch a new non-institutional type of programme aimed at preventing crime and dependency through timely assistance to the neglected and dependent child' (Splane 1965). A philosophy of prevention and increasing provincial action on social welfare was prompted in part by the work of pioneer social researchers and reformers, as well as the advocacy of Canadian trade unions, the urban reform movement, and the social gospel movement.

In addition, by the beginning of the 1900s provincial and municipal governments and school boards were providing free, widely available public education with compulsory attendance; free public libraries in many towns and cities across Canada; and playgrounds, parks, community centres, and art galleries (Wallace 1950; Cassidy 1947; Manzer 1985).

The Shift to Provincial and Federal Responsibility for Income Security Policy: 1914 to the 1930s

Growing industrialization and urbanization created many new problems for families in Canada. There was increased risk of industrial accidents, sickness from living in an urban setting, and unemployment from volatile changes in the economy; increased likelihood of mental illness due to social stress; and rising threats to the family from crime. The market mechanism was unable to provide employment for all Canadians, and welfare needed to be provided through government activity. But municipalities were unable to create needed programs in any systematic and effective way, which forced people to turn to higher levels of government. Both the provincial and federal governments responded to the demand. Thus we now examine the role of both the provincial and federal governments especially with regard to income security reforms.

Provincial Responsibility

The provinces agreed to take over more responsibilities. They had to expand the programs they offered and the services they provided. New programs and organizational structures introduced in one province were soon copied or adapted in several other provinces and then followed by the rest, often with a lag of ten to twenty years. This pattern of social policy innovation, diffusion, time lag, and convergence was to be repeated numerous times throughout the twentieth century. There were four major developments that reflected this changing pattern of welfare provision with respect to income support between 1914 and 1939 – changes that represented a modernization of income security policy in Canada. Each of these developments is examined at some length in the literature, so we need only briefly note them here.

First, workers' compensation was introduced, initially in Ontario in 1914 and followed soon after by Nova Scotia (1915), British Columbia (1916), Alberta and New Brunswick (1918), and Manitoba (1920). About a decade later Saskatchewan (1929) and Quebec (1931) enacted comparable legislation, and much later Prince Edward Island (1949) and Newfoundland (1950) did the same. Workers' Compensation was based on the principle of insurance, rooted in the rights of workers under the common law. The insurance principle fitted well with the ethos of industrial capitalism. It was an accepted market mechanism, even though it altered the employment contract by creating new obligations between worker and employer. It brought the state further into the worker-employer relationship by making the government party to the contract.

Second, most provinces introduced mothers' pensions or allowances, beginning in western Canada with Manitoba (1916), Saskatchewan (1917), Alberta (1919), and British Columbia (1920). Ontario closely followed (1920), and there was then a lag until Nova Scotia (1930), Quebec (1937), New Brunswick (1943), and Prince Edward Island (1949) introduced similar programs. Program design varied across provinces in terms of the range of single-mother situations covered; residence requirements, if any, and other eligibility criteria. All of the mothers' allowance programs, however, provided means-tested public assistance to certain indigent mothers with children. Private charities and voluntary agencies, for the most part, were still strong believers in individualism and self-reliance, charities and agencies were suspicious that government aid weakened people's will to work and bred dependency, and were unsympathetic if not hostile to the idea of income support for needy mothers (Guest 1985:52–61).

Third, provincial minimum-wage laws were another advance in income security policy. The early wave of legislation began with British Columbia and Manitoba (1918), then Quebec and Saskatchewan (1919), Ontario (1920), and Alberta (1922). Nova Scotia enacted a law in 1920 but it was not implemented until 1930. Other provinces introduced minimum wage laws even later.

Fourth is the provision for old age pensions (examined in detail later in this chapter). The Old Age Pensions Act was passed in 1927. The four western provinces and Ontario quickly accepted the plan within a year or two, then it took nearly ten years until the Maritime provinces and Quebec entered into the agreement (Bryden 1974).

These four reforms represented a modernization of the concept of social assistance. Social assistance changed from the traditional private practices of poor relief by private charities, churches, and municipalities to a public responsibility addressed in legislation and administered by trained civil servants. The four program reforms provincialized income support. They were provincially financed in whole or in part, with some costs shared with employers, as in the case of workers' compensation and minimum wage rates, or, in the case of old age pensions, with municipalities and the federal government.

The Federal Government's Expanding Social Policy Role

The British North America Act of 1867 gave the provinces major responsibility for much of what today we call social policy. Thus the story
typically told of the rise of state social welfare in Canada over the first
sixty years of Confederation emphasizes the role of the provinces and
local governments. The limitation of this approach is that it overlooks
key social roles of the federal government and leads to a narrow view of
what constitutes social welfare and whom social policies and programs
have affected.

Under the Constitution, the original legislative powers of the Canadian Parliament on social welfare included responsibility for the military, and hence veterans; marine hospitals; the census and statistics;
regulatory powers over trade and commerce, weights and measures;
immigration, naturalization, and aliens; Indians and lands reserved for
Indians; marriage and divorce; and the criminal law and penitentiaries.
These functional responsibilities were underpinned by fiscal powers
giving Ottawa authority for the raising of money by any mode of
taxation, and the borrowing of money on public credit.

Deficit financing was pursued by successive federal governments
from the 1870s to 1890s in the face of three economic recessions and the
imperatives of nation building (Gillespie 1991; Wallace 1950). Over the
period 1917 to 1923, the personal income tax, the corporate income tax,
and the manufacturers' sales tax (predecessor to the Goods and Services Tax – GST – introduced in the late 1980s) were inaugurated. Over
the next decades, these taxes became the major sources of revenue for
the federal government.

The composition of a political cabinet tells us something about the
policy functions and priorities of a government, as well as about the
times in which they govern. In 1867 the federal public service contained
thirteen ministerial departments, two of which were concerned with
social policy: Justice and Agriculture, the latter having responsibilities
for health and for immigrants. The Department of the Interior, created
in 1873, was responsible for Canada's Indian populations. Indian Acts
were passed in 1876, 1880, and 1884. In 1880 the ministerial position of
Superintendent General of Indian Affairs was established. The federal
Department of Labour was formed in 1900. A small number of new
federal social ministries were created at or near the end of the First
World War, specifically the Departments of Immigration and
Colonialization in 1917, Soldiers Civil Re-establishment in 1918, and

Health in 1919. The latter two marked relatively new fields of activity for the federal government (Hodgetts 1973), though the Department of Health did bring together health services from a number of other federal departments, along with the Dominion Council of Health, which was formed at the same time. An early example of administrative federalism with an element of citizen participation, the council consisted of the federal deputy minister of health as chair, the deputy minister or executive director of each provincial department of health or board of health, and up to five other people appointed by the federal cabinet. In 1928 the Health and Soldiers' Civil Re-establishment departments were merged to form the Department of Pensions and National Health to provide veterans with pensions, medical treatment, and sheltered employment. So over the course of twenty years the federal government moved from two to six ministerial departments dedicated to social policy.

But the federal government was not limited to the policy side alone. It also, like the provinces, became involved in income security. The federal government's earliest meaningful entry into income security came with the introduction of financial benefits for veterans.[1] As Andrew Armitage (1996:197) explains: 'federal involvement was a product of high regard for veterans but also of social unrest, including the Winnipeg General Strike. Returning veterans were not assured work and found a marked contrast between the society's rhetoric and their destitute circumstances.' Over the period from 1916 to 1939, the federal government was quite active in veterans' policy development, passing two orders-in-council and five key pieces of legislation, plus another dozen acts amending legislation. In 1916 the federal cabinet instituted a Board of Pension Commissioners to award and administer pensions to veterans of the First World War. Pension regulations were established which replaced the pay and allowance regulations of the Department of Defence: whereas under the previous rules a disability or death had to be directly due to service to qualify for payments, the new regulations introduced the insurance principle.

In 1918, just after the end of the war, the cabinet amended the regulations to introduce the principle of prospective dependency for parents of deceased members of the armed forces. Earlier that year, legislation establishing the Department of Soldiers' Civil Re-establishment had been passed and the department was given responsibility to help re-establish First World War veterans into civilian life, and offer care to their dependants. The 1919 the Soldier Settlement Act defined as a 'settler' any person who, at any time during the 1914–18 war, had been engaged in active service with a military force from Canada, Britain, or any British dominion or colony; and the widow of any person who would have been eligible if he had lived. A Soldier Settlement Board was created and authorized to issue free land of up to 160 acres to any settler; to make provision for instruction in agriculture and economics for settlers; and, among other benefits, to make cash advances of up to $1,000 for permanent improvements to land.

The Pension Act of 1919 was the other major legislation for veterans in the aftermath of the war. Under this measure, the federal government committed itself to providing pensions for disabled members of the armed forces and their dependants, on a scale based on the degree of disability and the military rank of the veteran. Pensions were also provided for dependants on the death of a veteran, the amount geared to military rank. Here, for the first time, the principle of income support as partial compensation for disability or death was introduced into federal policy. Equally noteworthy, disability pensions awarded under the Pension Act were the first *universal* income benefit in Canadian social policy, as the entitlement to a pension or the amount of a pension was not determined by the financial circumstances of the veteran. (We discuss the topic of universality and selectivity in social programs fully in Chapter 7.) Through the 1920s and 1930s, the Pension Act was amended several times in the direction of expanding eligibility of benefits, increasing benefit amounts, and establishing and reorganizing the structures that would allow hearings and decisions on appeals when such pensions were refused.

Despite all the social security measures for veterans, the programs did not 'deal adequately with the problem of the prematurely old ("burnt out") veteran, and, in 1930, under considerable pressure from veterans' organizations, Parliament passed the War Veterans' Allowance Act' (Bryden 1974:79). This program provided for means-tested allowances for veterans aged sixty or over, or veterans who were permanently unemployable because of a physical or mental disability, and for allowances on behalf of their wives and dependants. The basic benefit was the same as under the Old Age Pension Act of 1927, but was available at a younger age. Under the old age pension law, benefits were payable to certain individuals seventy years of age or over, while the war veterans' allowance was available to certain veterans at age sixty.[2] Next we examine old age pensions as an example of the federal governments commitment to income security.

Old Age Pensions: A Brief Case Study

With the introduction of the Old Age Pensions Act in 1927, the federal government formally entered the social security arena in a major way for the second time. The legislation authorized federal reimbursement of 50 per cent to any participating province for pensions to British subjects (Canada did not pass a citizenship law until 1947) aged seventy or over who had resided in Canada for at least twenty years and in the province for at least five years. Indians were excluded from the program. The maximum pension, which was means tested, was initially $240 a year, an amount unchanged until the 1940s.

It is informative to examine the particular politics of the introduction of this federal-provincial income security initiative and agreement, because the same issues have reappeared many times up to the present time.[3] The examination also provides an opportunity to indicate the differences between the larger sociopolitical questions and the more immediate electoral and parliamentary politics of social security. At the larger sociopolitical level, the public pensions issue developed as a result of social dislocations created by industrialization and urbanization, and the inability of many of the elderly to save for their retirement. At the more immediate electoral level, like many social policy issues, the introduction of the Old Age Pensions program came about as a way of solving an immediate *political* problem: the federal election of 1926.

The pensions issue had been around in Canada for some time (Bryden 1974). The Trades and Labour Congress of Canada (TLC) had called for legislation in 1905 and 1907, had sent delegations to petition the prime minister and members of Parliament in 1910, and had put forward specific proposals to the government in 1922 and again in 1925. A select committee of the House of Commons examined the need for a public pension plan in 1912, and concluded it was premature. A special parliamentary committee examined the topic again in 1926 and felt pensions were outside the constitutional jurisdiction of the federal government and were too expensive as well. Prime Minister Mackenzie King faced the prospect of resigning after the 1925 election because his Liberals had won fewer seats than the Conservatives had. However, he sought a way of retaining power by offering opposition members J.S. Woodsworth and A.A. Heaps cabinet positions. Both declined and instead wrote to King suggesting the introduction of legislation regarding the development of an old age pension. Knowing that labour, particularly the TLC, supported the idea of a public pension and that there was no organized business lobby against it, King put the bill through the House of Commons in exchange for the political support of Heaps and Woodsworth. The Senate, however, defeated the bill on the grounds that it was an unwarranted intrusion into provincial jurisdiction.

In the ensuing political fight, King asked for the dissolution of the House, yet the governor general, Lord Byng, refused. The Conservatives, under Arthur Meighen, then formed the government but were defeated three days later, resulting in a federal general election. King took the pensions issue to the public, as part of the famous King-Byng constitutional affair, and won a majority government committed to introducing a public pension plan. While the constitutional drama of the proper authority relationship between a governor general and a prime minister is unique to this case, the related events were not. Parliamentary opposition politics (especially in a minority government context), party policies, and the style and philosophy of a prime minister, as well as interest groups and public opinion, have great influence.

The Old Age Pensions Act was passed by the new Parliament and instantly faced another issue which was to become common in the politics of social policy: opposition from provincial governments. From the beginning it was clear that federal social welfare initiatives, with the exception of immigrants, Indians, and veterans, would have to be worked out with the provincial governments. The provinces, and in particular Quebec, opposed any legislation that directly allowed the federal government access to what was considered provincial responsibility. To deal with both the provincial resistance and the constitutional problems caused by the division of powers in the BNA Act, the federal government offered to finance an old age pension in the form of a conditional grant. Each province was encouraged to develop and operate its own pension program with the aid of a conditional federal grant for 50 per cent of incurred program costs. The legislation represented 'an ingenious compromise between provincial responsibility and federal initiative' (Bryden 1974:77). The federal government established the conditions under which it would reimburse the provinces, and the latter operated and co-financed the programs. In 1931 the program was amended, increasing the federal share of pensions from 50 to 75 per cent to attract all provinces to enter the plan. By 1936 all provinces had taken advantage of the federal policy and developed public pension programs for low-income seniors.

The 'ingenious compromise' of the old age pensions contained two fundamental difficulties which have haunted federal-provincial relations ever since. First, the federal government had no way of supervising the administration of the provincial pension programs aside from expenditure audits; and, second, the provinces varied significantly in the way each interpreted and implemented the federal legislation. The first problem led to misgivings on the federal government's part that money could be used in ways contrary to the conditions laid down in the legislation. The second problem created concerns on the provinces' part that the federal government, in trying to achieve conformity, would encroach upon provincial authority. Provincial fears that after introducing a program the federal government would withdraw funding were addressed by a provision in the legislation which compelled the federal government to provide ten years' notice of any plan to discontinue the agreement.

In addition to concerns about staying in power, winning elections, and designing programs to meet with constitutional rules and provincial approval, federal governments must incorporate into their policies the dominant ideas of the day if they are to remain in power. The design of the old age pension reflected the residual belief that normally the elderly should be responsible for saving for their own retirement. If the elderly were unable to meet their income needs, a public pension should provide minimum benefits – after ensuring by a means test that there existed insufficient personal income, property, or other resources, including, in some cases, the ability of adult children to provide support for their parents. This policy also reflected the interests of labour and business. A balance was achieved by closely following the recommendations of a 1924 special committee, which included two labour representatives but at the same time served business interests by reinforcing the work ethic through low benefit levels and limited eligibility.

The responsibilities of both the federal and provincial governments for old age pensions, acknowledged in the legislation and implemented by conditional grants, meant that there was no politically easy way to alter existing programs in the short term; both levels of government had to agree on the problems and the solutions. Guest (1985:79) claims that as far as early pensions were concerned, this was an unintended benefit. Difficulties in altering the agreement by either party 'achieved a degree of stability from the beginning which enhanced the programme's worth, particularly during the depression of the 1930s when many government programmes had to be severely curtailed.'

The 1930s: The Depression Decade

The Great Depression profoundly effected many Canadians and deeply influenced the way governments and the public thought about social policies. The economics, ideas, and politics that had influenced the development of the Old Age Pension and other federal, provincial, and municipal programs were dramatically altered by the depression, which spanned the entire decade of the 1930s with worldwide consequences. By 1933, in the depth of the depression, the Canadian economy had shrunk by one-third from its level in 1929. Over the same period, the official unemployment rate rose from about 3 per cent to 25 to 30 per cent of the working force (Goffman 1968; Marsh 1975). Industrial production was cut in half, exports fell by two-thirds, and construction dropped to one-tenth of its previous level. With hundreds of thousands out of work, family dislocation, social unrest, and political dissatisfaction were heightened. Canadians increasingly came to believe that unemployment and poverty were not the result of individual characteristics or failures, but rather of larger social and economic forces, both domestic and international.

The social and economic chaos of the depression forced individuals, families, and communities to look for new ways of protecting themselves from economic instability and other risks. The search for security undermined the old ideas of self-sufficient individualism. A wider range of ideologies became popular in various segments of society: socialism, communism, and fascism, to name a few. There was, too, rapid growth in alternative political organizations: the Social Credit Party, the Co-operative Commonwealth Federation (CCF), precursor to the New Democratic Party, the Union Nationale, farmers unions and co-operatives. Each organization sought to protect the individual from the uncertainties of unbridled capitalism. There was growing belief and claim that government had to provide some form of protection and assistance for those who could not protect themselves against unemployment and other risks. These beliefs and demands shaped a new 'social contract' under which people were prepared to live and work.

The costs for relief programs had to be met by the provincial governments, whose sources of tax revenue were declining in the 1930s. Local municipalities, the traditional level of government to respond to such needs, could not deal with the magnitude of the problem and so the provision of relief shifted in large part to the provinces. This centraliz-

ing tendency was not to be reversed. The change in social policy structures and resources can be seen in the shifting shares of social welfare
expenditures by municipalities and provinces. In 1913 local expenditures on health and welfare were twice that of provinces. In just twenty-
five years the situation was more than reversed. By the end of the 1930s
the provinces were spending over twice as much on social welfare as
were municipalities.[4] As harsh economic conditions persisted through
the decade, the costs of unemployment relief hopelessly exceeded the
financial resources of municipal and provincial governments. The federal government was required to provide substantial assistance to the
provinces. Through a series of special grants, federal help was delivered while the constitutional responsibilities of the provinces for welfare matters were respected. Harry Cassidy (1947:52) called these relief
arrangements the first nationwide service of economic security for the
Canadian population: 'The result was a great emergency system of
unemployment relief administered mainly by the municipalities according to traditional poor-law methods but financed largely by the
Dominion Government and the provinces through grants-in-aid. This
system lasted ten years, from 1931 to 1941; involved total expenditures
of about one billion dollars, and at its peak (in April 1933) supported
nearly 1,600,00 persons, about 15 per cent of the total population.'

The Department of National Defence also established relief camps for
the unemployed and indigent, but these were immensely unpopular.
The intent was to offer some relief and work as well as to maintain
public order. The camps were located in remote areas and unemployed
men lived in bunkhouses and were paid a dollar a week to do menial
labour. As Leonard Marsh (1975:xiv) reported many years later about
these camps, 'growing resentment culminated in the March to Ottawa,
and the confrontation with the police in Regina, in 1935. Following a
change of (federal) government in that year, they were discontinued.'

Besides providing grants-in-aid to the provinces for unemployment
relief, the federal government undertook other social policy initiatives
during this decade, some successfully, others dramatically not. For
example, we have already mentioned legislative measures with respect
to veterans and old age pensioners made in the 1930s that extended
benefits. Another related measure was an amendment in 1937 to the
Old Age Pensions Act which provided for pensions to blind persons
aged forty and over, with a maximum monthly payment equal to that
of the old age pension. A third policy initiative developed in response
to the prolonged drought conditions in western Canada, the Prairie

Farm Assistance Act, was passed in 1939. The Canadian Wheat Board also was formed in this period.

Along with the above examples, the federal government also entered the housing policy field.[5] The Dominion Housing Act of 1935 authorized federal assistance in the construction of houses for persons with moderate incomes, by making loans available through private lending institutions. The National Housing Act of 1938 replaced the earlier legislation and extended the scope of assistance to include the improvement of housing conditions and to stimulate the construction and building-materials industries. The new legislation, administered by the minister of finance, also enabled the federal government to make direct loans to local housing authorities to assist in the construction of low-rental housing to be leased to families with low incomes. This legislation began the trend of using housing policy as a tool of economic stimulation and development (Prince 1995).

The above are all examples of successful social policy initiatives. We now turn to the ones that failed. The most ambitious policy effort at federal intervention in social and economic affairs, and the most dramatic failure, was the Employment and Social Insurance Act, passed at the end of the mandate of R.B. Bennett's Conservative government in 1935. The legislation was revolutionary in the Canadian context given the broad scope of planned new public programs and the potential extent of intervention by Ottawa into what were provincial, local, and private-sector domains. The legislation provided for action on unemployment insurance and on health care. An employment and social insurance commission was to be formed to administer a national employment service and a program of unemployment insurance for certain classes of workers. Insurance contributions were to be made by both employees and employers. For persons excluded from insurance coverage, assistance would be provided during periods of unemployment. As well, training would be offered, in cooperation with educational institutions, to rehabilitate unemployed persons. On health care, the legislation charged the commission with collecting information and submitting to cabinet implementation proposals to provide – in cooperation with the provinces, municipalities, corporations, and other groups – benefits for medical, dental and surgical care, including medicines, drugs, appliances, or hospitalization; or compensation for loss of earnings arising out of ill-health, accident, or disease. Bennett also promised improvements to old age pensions, a federal minimum wage, and a shorter work week. Mackenzie King returned to power in the

1935 federal election, and, in the face of sharp provincial attacks on Bennett's 'New Deal' legislation, referred the law to the courts for a ruling on its constitutionality.[6] In 1937 the Judicial Committee of the Privy Council in Britain (at that time the final court of appeal for Canada) declared the Employment and Social Insurance Act *ultra vires*, or beyond the powers of the federal government as granted under the Constitution.

This constitutional ruling presented the country with a fundamental impasse. On the one hand, most authority for social policy resided with the provinces and the municipalities. Yet the staggering events of the thirties showed that these governments were unable financially to provide the programs and services clearly needed to prevent starvation, offer relief and hope, and proffer a modicum of economic security. On the other hand, the federal government may have had sufficient resources and even the inclination to become more greatly involved in the social security of Canadians. But key provinces were unwilling to relinquish jurisdiction to Ottawa, and the King government was loath to intervene in these areas without provincial support. In true Canadian political fashion, then, 'This complex constitutional issue was referred in 1937 to the Royal Commission on Dominion-Provincial Relations (the Rowell-Sirois Commission), which did not submit its report until the beginning of the war. By then the needs for relief had greatly diminished, and the Dominion-provincial controversy regarding the social services was, temporarily, at least, subordinated to other issues' (Cassidy 1947:53). Thus the most ambitious social policy initiatives of the time were never implemented.

Conclusions

As we have seen throughout this chapter, social welfare as a communal and governmental activity predates the rise of the welfare state in the 1940s as well as the academic discipline of social policy. The origins and extent of public intervention in social welfare are found perhaps unexpectedly early in Canadian history.

Over the period surveyed, from the colonial era to the end of the 1930s, social policy emerged and changed along many dimensions, four of which we observe here. First, the *sponsorship of social care and control* began shifting from the private and charitable sectors to the state sector, and public bodies took on responsibility for child welfare, public health, education, and the income needs of injured workers, single mothers, soldiers, and seniors. Second, within the Canadian state, the *level of government(s) involved in social programs* changed from a heavy reliance on municipalities to a reliance on the provinces and on federal initiatives and federal-provincial arrangements. Local bodies kept an important role outside of income support, however, in matters such as education, public libraries, policing, parks, and recreation. Third, the *structures for administering and providing services* changed from a local and nonprofessional nature to relatively more centralized, provincial/ federal and professional in nature (Cassidy 1947; Rice 1979). Fourth, the *policy instruments and processes* used by governments for designing and implementing social programs changed over this period. Several innovations took place: early emphasis, not simply on remedial measures but also on preventive services; the first social insurance program with Workers' Compensation; the first universal income benefit with disability pensions for war veterans; and federal-provincial cost sharing agreements on health matters, old age pensions, and unemployment relief.

Social welfare policy in Canada has developed in response to, and in interaction with, several factors. At one level are broad socioeconomic trends and political events: the rise of industrial capitalism, urbanization, immigration, and the profound effects of the First World War, the depressions of the late 1800s, and the Great Depression of the 1930s. We discussed how these forces impacted on individuals' lives, on family and community structures, and on the economy and the labour market. At a second level are the role of ideas and beliefs, which of course intermingle with material circumstances. By the 1890s 'social and economic conditions had so altered that public opinion was demanding government action on matters held in 1867 to be primarily personal and of no concern to the state' (Wallace 1950:384). Liberal individualism, Christian charity, private altruism, trade unionism, and socialist thought all influenced, in different degrees and ways, the development of social welfare policy. The prevailing philosophy of public finance and government budgeting was also significant. This was a view of the state as modestly active, influenced by a concern for balanced budgets. The state was like the household and should live within its means (Maslove, Prince, and Doern 1986; Gillespie 1991). International experiences were important, a factor we give attention to in the next chapter. Finally, at a third level are political forces and governmental factors. These include the impact of the Constitution, judicial rulings, and the evolution of intergovernmental relations; the role of social movements, businesses, and interest groups; the limited tax base of municipalities, and the later development of local government in Newfoundland and the western provinces; and processes of social policy experimentation and dispersion across Canadian jurisdictions. In practice, woven together, these three levels of factors constitute the political context within which the social welfare and diswelfare of people is experienced. This context simultaneously displays changes and continuities, and embodies forces that both support and resist the development of social programs and services.

3

Envisaging and Establishing a System of Social Security for Canadians

Having reviewed early developments in social welfare, we now examine the first period of modern social policy and the formation of a welfare state in Canada from approximately 1940 to the early 1970s. We begin by looking at what community activists and politicians came to think about social issues, and their ideas concerning how to solve some of the social problems facing Canadians. Thinkers such as Leonard Marsh, Harry Cassidy, Charlotte Whitton, C.A. Curtis, and J.J. Heagerty wrote important reports or chaired important committees, while federal civil servants such as Joseph Willard, George Davidson, and Robert Bryce helped design the systems. We then describe how many of these ideas were put into practice between 1940 and the early 1970s, our purpose being to identify the thinking behind social security proposals and to discuss the forces that affected the major social policy developments over this period.

Envisaging a Social Security System

Envisaging a social security system for Canadians began in the 1930s and intensified during the 1940s. Social researchers and government bodies gathered information and drew lessons from the harsh experiences of the Great Depression, and they looked at the social risks, needs, and hopes of Canadians during the Second World War (1939–1945). They contemplated better ways of addressing each of these in the planning for the postwar reconstruction of Canada's economy, federal system, and society. As Leonard Marsh (1975) remarked at the end of this period, whatever the war represented in death and destruction, it was a time of political agitation and fundamental rethinking of economic management and social policy making. The events of the 1940s were epoch-making for social security in many countries. The term 'welfare state,' itself coined during the war, generally referred to government responsibility for the provision of a range of services, benefits, rights, and duties for citizens. The idea of a welfare state or system of social security meant that government financed, organized, and delivered varying levels and forms of health care, housing, education, income support, and social services. Government also had an active role in managing the economy towards the goals of high and stable levels of income and employment. In Canada, governments, especially the federal government, were seen as providing leadership in developing a comprehensive, national social security system.

A community of reformers, intellectuals, and public administrators, the 'government generation' (Owram 1986) played an energetic part in redefining the social role of the Canadian state. New ideas concerning the relation between state and citizen and the design and purpose of social programs were conceived and considered. The initial wave of envisaging a social security system for Canada may be said to have taken place between about 1937, from the appointment of the Rowell-Sirois Royal Commission, to 1945, when federal proposals for postwar reconstruction were presented at a federal-provincial conference. A second wave of taking stock and contemplating the future of social policy occurred during the late 1960s and early 1970s, at the end of this period of establishment and expansion.

How important were ideas in directing the formation of social policy in Canada? One view is that they were not that influential. Alan Cairns and Cynthia Williams (1985:16) have argued that 'The Canadian welfare state is a classic example of incrementalism. Its development was ad hoc and subject to the complexities of the division of powers. No articulate philosophy guided its halting early development and subsequent consolidation.' A different view holds that beside economic and social forces, visions of the welfare state had 'powerfully shaped' the evolution of Canadian social policy. Keith Banting (1987:147) has argued that 'Social policy making inevitably proceeds within a broad conceptual framework that defines the critical problems facing society, the goals that should guide government action, and the range of relevant policy alternatives. These underlying assumptions about the domain of social policy need not always be comprehensive, internally consistent, or explicitly elaborated. Nonetheless, they are critical; decision making is inevitably guided by a general conception of the social role of the state.'

Looking back from today's vantage point, it is true that the Canadian network of social programs took thirty years or more to build. It was built program by program in response to various needs. It was conditioned by the politics of federalism, including at times provincial pressures for federal action. It was an incremental process. Yet if there was no articulate philosophy, there was a set of ideas, expounded in an intelligible fashion to the public and to politicians, about a new economic and social role for the state. These ideas reflected the growing belief that governments could solve some of the problems facing Canadians. Richard Splane (1987:246) has written of what he refers to as 'the initial agenda for the development of a comprehensive social security system for Canada,' a hypothetical agenda 'conceived and nurtured by the findings of royal commissions and comparable studies conducted from the 1930s into the 1960s.' Here, we will examine the thinkers and the documents that set this agenda.

The Ideas of Keynes and Beveridge: Intellectual Foundations of the Welfare State

Two seminal works came out of Britain in the late 1930s and early 1940s: John Maynard Keynes's *The General Theory of Employment Interest and Money* (1936) and Sir William Beveridge's report, *Social Insurance and Allied Services* (1942). Both had a dramatic influence on the development of social policy in Canada and elsewhere. Prior to the publication of Keynes's book, economic theorists claimed that full employment was assumed to be part of the natural order of things. Periodic unemployment and recessions were considered aberrations that would be solved through natural market processes. Any person wanting to work would be able to find employment if they looked for it and were willing to accept the wage rate of the day. The theories at the time claimed that high unemployment would only result when wages were kept at unnaturally high levels. The mass unemployment of the 1930s, however, was difficult to explain using accepted economic theory. A million or more individuals were certainly willing to work for any wage in Canada, but there were no jobs for them. The message from economists was to wait for the downswing to flatten out, as this would eventually turn into an upswing on its own accord.

Keynes argued against this perspective, calling for government spending to stimulate the economy. He contended that the level of unemployment is determined by the level of output, which in turn is determined by the level of effective demand. Effective demand is affected by expenditure, which is affected by the supply of income. Keynes divided income into consumption and investment, and demonstrated that individual decisions made about consumption and investment would not necessarily create full employment. The policy implication was that if the community wanted full employment, then their governments would have to take steps to modify the levels of consumption and investment.

The importance of Keynes's critique and prescription for social policy was clear. Up to this point social policy was seen as a means of providing relief to those who were unable to provide for themselves. It was now evident that environmental conditions had a large part to play in one's ability to find and keep work. It also became evident that social policy could play a much larger role than just that of welfare – it could be used as a major tool for economic management. Keynesian economics postulated a direct link between social policy and economic development. Although each area may have its own goals, achievement in the one area was believed to have positive outcomes in the other. By encouraging consumer demand through public expenditures, the government could promote full employment – a goal of economic policy. The government could sustain economic growth by fuelling the economy, and yet, if prices became inflationary, it could withdraw expenditures and thereby cut back on economic stimulation. Politically, this happy marriage of the welfare function and the economic management function decreased the hostility towards the introduction of large-scale social programs (Rice 1979).

The emergence and at least partial acceptance of Keynesian thinking by governments in Canada and other industrial countries in the 1940s changed the language of social policy. The debate was no longer described in terms of a struggle between capitalism and socialism, or between the exploitation of workers and the sanctity of unregulated private enterprise, but rather as the economic necessity of stabilization, regulation, and stimulation. Social welfare programs became countercyclical benefits rather than anti-capitalist intrusions in the economy. From Keynes's perspective, mass unemployment was the result of economic conditions and was a public issue to be addressed through public policies, not just a private trouble families had to endure on their own. Aided by the fresh memories of the depression, the realities of wartime mobilization with strong central government intervention, and the desire to avoid another economic downturn after the war, Keynesian concepts provided a practical blueprint for government involvement in the management of the economy and society.

The Beveridge Report aroused great attention on both sides of the Atlantic. Beveridge is widely regarded as a prime architect of much of British social legislation in the 1940s, including the 1944 Education Act, the 1945 Family Allowance Act, the 1946 National Insurance and National Health Service Acts, and the 1948 National Assistance Act. He believed the need for public assistance and means-tested relief would dwindle to a minor role with the introduction a system of social security. Though the record of the next decades fell short of this intent, Canada adopted the social security model as the primary foundation of the welfare state.

In 1940 Beveridge chaired an interdepartmental committee of civil servants established by the British government to undertake a comprehensive survey of existing national schemes of social insurance and affiliated services, including workers' compensation, and to consider adding health benefits to any other risks not covered by social programs. Unlike Canada, Britain by the early 1940s had a fairly extensive system of social security programs in place. A good part of the Beveridge report therefore entailed extensions of existing policies and the integration of various administrative arrangements. A main proposal, for instance, was the unification of social insurance and public assistance programs with respect to contributions and administration. Beveridge described a plan for social security that would attack what he called the five giants facing modern society – want, disease, ignorance, squalor, and idleness – all of them great obstacles on the path of social progress. The principal reforms Beveridge recommended included a universal national health service; a system of universal children's allowance; a comprehensive social insurance plan to address interruptions or loss of earning power due to unemployment, disability, old age, or sickness; and maternity and funeral grants.

Canadian Thinking on Social Security

The flow of international ideas had a profound affect on Canada. Canadians came to believe that governments should become more involved in the management of the economy and in the provision of social programs. Just how the governments were to become involved was a matter of public debate, which was fuelled by six key documents published between 1940 and 1945. These documents, which represented a critical turning point in the development of the larger politics of social policy, proposed a range of mechanisms for transforming ideas and lessons into concrete programs that were to become the foundation of the social security system in Canada. The ideas proposed by each report follow.

The Rowell-Sirois Royal Commission
When Prime Minister King announced the formation of the Royal Commission on Dominion-Provincial Relations in 1937, Canadian federalism was in fiscal crisis. The provincial governments of Manitoba and Saskatchewan, battered by the depression and severe droughts, were financially unable to provide essential public services and meet their budgetary commitments. The commission's major task was to reexamine the economic and financial basis of Confederation and the distribution of legislative powers in light of economic and social developments of the past seventy years. The commission was asked to examine the constitutional allocation of revenue sources and governmental burdens placed on the federal and provincial governments; to determine whether the allocation of taxation, public expenditure, and public debt was as equitable and efficient as can be devised; and to investigate federal subsidies and grants to the provincial governments to meet needs. The supplementary reports to the commission, known as the 'Red Books,' reviewed all existing social programs: social services, old age pensions, widows' pensions, mothers' allowances, health care, social insurance, and education.

Despite serious financial problems facing the provinces, the commission argued that Canada, as a population with diverse origins, traditions, and goals, should remain a federal state. The report noted that most legislative powers dealing with 'pressing social questions' rested with the provinces and should so continue. The report recognized, however, that the provinces were unable to finance their social welfare responsibilities without financial assistance from the federal government, and recommended that a system of unconditional adjustment grants be provided to the poorer provinces so that they might provide adequate public services without excessive taxation. The commission also recommended that the federal government take over responsibility for personal and corporate income taxes and assume responsibility for the unemployed, the elderly, and provincial debts arising from the depression. However, the provinces rejected these recommendations.

What did come out of the Rowell-Sirois report was the argument for a national standard for social programs and a national system for equalizing the fiscal capacity of the provinces. The report warned that if provincial governments were unduly limited in spending on education or social services, disparities would open that could have critical implications for general welfare and national unity. This idea has reverberated through the politics and practices of Canadian federalism ever since, symbolized by the principle of equalization payments which was enshrined in the Constitution in 1982. Contemporary debate about the social union and national standards in social policy can also be traced back to this landmark study of public finance and Canadian federalism.

The Marsh Report

The *Report on Social Security for Canada,* authored by Leonard Marsh and presented to the House of Commons Special Committee on Social Security in 1943, has been called 'The most important single document in the history of the development of the welfare state in Canada ... a pivotal document in the development of war and postwar social security programs, the equivalent in Canada of the Beveridge Report in Great Britain' (Bliss 1975, ix). Like Beveridge's report, the Marsh Report contemplated a comprehensive package of social programs for Canadians. Unlike Beveridge's, however, Marsh's report was a preliminary appraisal, not a final blueprint with all the details included on matters such as rates of benefits or levels of contributions.

The three central ideas of Marsh's report were social insurances, children's allowances, and national investment. The Marsh Report argued for greater use of the social insurance technique in place of the public assistance method, and set out the rationale for, and the elements of, an extensive system of social security. The principle of social insurance held many advantages over the public assistance method of relief and means testing: it held the recipient partly responsible for meeting the costs of the program through mandatory contributions and/or general taxation; encouraged a feeling of self-dependence; identified who was eligible to receive benefits; ensured a broad financial base through the shared pooling of risks and funds; and was a policy mechanism which did not have the 'flavour of charity.' As Marsh (1943:14) expressed it, 'The genius of social insurance is that it enlists the direct support of the classes most likely to benefit, and enlists equally the participation and controlling influence of the state, at the same time as it avoids the evil of pauperization, and the undemocratic influence of excessive state philanthropy.'

Marsh distinguished in his scheme between 'universal risks,' applicable to all persons, or to all persons of a working age; and 'employment risks,' which are applicable to and insurable for wage earners only. Under the employment group of risks, Marsh recommended a national investment program that, while not a part of the ordinary social security structure, was included to complete the postwar employment strategy. In contrast to Beveridge, who favoured flat-rate benefits, Marsh proposed that employment-related benefits be largely related to prevailing wage scales. On the other hand, income maintenance benefits for meeting universal risks would principally be at a standard rate, rather than dependent on past income or wages or the actual amount of the premium or contribution paid. Here again, as discussed in Chapter 2 with respect to veterans' disability pensions, is the principle of universality in income support.

The Marsh Report envisaged a federally financed and administered children's allowance for all children, whether or not there were one or two parents and regardless of whether the parents worked or were unemployed.[1] Together, these two categories of benefits would lay the base for a national minimum, provided as a right, still leaving considerable leeway for individual insurance provision and for additional social services. Marsh estimated that the full application of his scheme would cost something approaching $1 billion. This was about four times the total of direct expenditure spent by all three levels of government in Canada on public welfare in the late 1930s, and represented about 20 per cent of the federal budget for 1942–43.

As part of a 'grand economic strategy,' Marsh recommended a government-sponsored program of peacetime investment and social and economic development, perhaps lasting for three years or more. Such a national investment program would make work available, and, by offering wages rather than subsistence support, would be a positive measure in providing social security for Canadians. There was a great range of enterprises, which would almost certainly, Marsh believed, only be undertaken through public initiative, such as the redevelopment of blighted city areas that would remove 'wastes, eyesores, and social costs.' Reflecting the influence of Keynesian economics, Marsh (1975:83) reminded those worried about the cost of reforms that 'the creation of a social security system brings about directly a stronger demand for what might be called collective consumer goods or social utilities – housing, hospitals, schools, libraries, urban and rural recreation facilities, and so forth.'

The federal government's initial official reaction to the Marsh Report was not encouraging. According to one social policy historian, the government ignored the report and it was never tabled in Parliament (Guest 1985:124). Fairly or not, critics said the report's scheme was too interventionist, too expensive, and, within Canadian federalism, too centralizing. Nonetheless, a universal family allowance program was introduced in 1945. The Marsh Report's impact over the next few decades was far more significant. Angela Djao (1983:25) has observed, 'Not all of Marsh's recommendations were followed or implemented in the ways he suggested. But the general contours of Canada's social welfare programs since the Second World War were sketched out in his grand plan, and, in the main, the same rationale was used.'

The Heagerty Report
On the day the Marsh Report was released, the *Health Insurance Report* (1943, Heagerty Report) on health insurance was also published. This report set out the plans for a joint federal-provincial health and medical insurance scheme that would be administered by the provinces with financial assistance from the federal government. The report 'envisaged the whole population being covered for a full range of benefits in kind, including medical, dental, pharmaceutical, hospital and nursing services' (Guest 1985:138). The recommendations were based, like the Marsh proposals, on the social insurance principle, with annual premiums sufficiently low so that the program would be universal. After considerable alterations the proposals were included in the recommendations made by Ottawa to the Dominion-Provincial Conference on Reconstruction in 1945.

The Curtis Report
The Marsh and Heagerty Reports were followed the next year by the Curtis Report on Housing and Community Planning, which recommended massive federal intervention in the housing market and in town planning. The report contended that an adequate and modern housing policy demanded bold action by the public, private, and cooperative sectors in the financing and operation of housing schemes. Within what was a comprehensive approach, the report said special attention should be given to low-rental housing, farm housing, and home and farm improvements.

The Curtis Report was a milestone in the enunciation of social responsibility by the federal government in the housing field. The view of housing policy expressed by Curtis was a thorough mix of market-assisted and social-based housing (Prince 1989). While the vision of the

Curtis plan was breathtaking in its scope, the report's impact was perhaps inevitably disappointing. Marsh (1975:xxxi) himself noted thirty years later that 'few of the recommendations were followed with any dispatch, in spite of its documentation of the urgency of the situation.'

A new National Housing Act, passed in 1944, was designed to promote the construction of new houses, the modernization of existing ones, and the expansion of employment in the postwar period. The Central Mortgage and Housing Corporation was created and began operating in 1946, and rental housing program for veterans was introduced in 1947. However, many of the branches of housing policy discussed by Curtis were largely ignored. There was no strong federal leadership in town planning, little action on slum clearance, and no priority attention to low-rental housing until the mid-1960s, or to cooperative housing associations until the mid-1970s.

These first four reports – the Rowell/Sirois Royal Commission, the Marsh Report, the Heagerty Report, and the Curtis Report – were all written by advisory committees. Running through these reports were a number of themes reflecting the shifting context and politics of social policy: the economy was not self-regulating, and if left unattended would collapse, leading to social upheaval; individual self-reliance had been dramatically altered by urbanization and industrialization, and in dire economic circumstances people could no longer count on family members, charity, or the market to meet their needs; the federal and provincial governments separately and cooperatively would have to become dominant actors in providing protection against income disruption; and social policy instruments and administrative organizations had developed to the point where they could be used to provide comprehensive social security. These themes found voice in the claim that the state should accept three fundamental responsibilities: the stabilization of the economy so that the overall risk to wage income would be diminished; the creation of high levels of employment; and the development of a social safety net.

The wartime cabinet of Prime Minister Mackenzie King was aware of the growing popularity of these themes and ideas, as demonstrated in the public support for the CCF, which became the official opposition in Ontario in 1944. King's Liberals knew that in the long run steps had to be taken to capture the political support generated by these new ideas. The politicians were not alone; there existed also a number of influential people within the civil service, intellectual allies of the authors of these reports who were prepared to translate them into a language and programs that was ideologically acceptable to the governing party. Thus the Canadian government, as distinct from the advisory committees, released two federal documents in 1945: the White Paper on Employment and Income and the Green Book Proposals to the Dominion-Provincial Conference on Reconstruction.

The White Paper
Ideas in the White Paper were previewed in earlier Speeches from the Throne, which spoke of the government's intent to prevent unemployment after the war, and, more positively, to secure adequate incomes and full employment for Canadians. Robert Campbell (1987:3) accurately depicts the White Paper as 'a precise Keynesian statement of the government's plan to respond to the new socioeconomic public expectations in a particular way.' The government's particular Keynesian policy response was economically optimistic, politically restrained, and generally explained in the technocratic language of economics. David Wolfe (1985:129) claims the White Paper provided the basis for a substantial degree of ideological consensus, for the next three decades, over the conduct of public finance. The White Paper declared that the government had adopted as a major aim of employment policy the creation and maintenance of 'a high and stable level of employment and income.' The White Paper conveyed the King government's optimism about the capacity of private sector investment and enterprise to create sufficient jobs, and stated that the government did not think it desirable or practicable to expect that further expansion of government would provide the additional employment required.

Thus the White Paper did not call for a significant extension of public ownership; it proposed only a modest program of public works, and signalled the government's intent to reduce taxation as rapidly as possible. Further, the transition from wartime to peacetime economy would involve the substitution of private sector expenditure for a large part of public sector expenditure. Other ideas in the Marsh Report, however, were apparent in the federal government's Green Book submissions to the Dominion-Provincial Conference on Reconstruction just a few months after the release of the White Paper.

The Green Book
The federal submission to the reconstruction conference outlined Ottawa's goals as a high and stable level of employment and income,

support of national minimum standards of social services, and a greater degree of public responsibility for economic and social security. The main federal proposals concerned public investment, major reform of intergovernmental financial arrangements, and several social security initiatives. The social security proposals sought to provide small, regular payments as a protection against the risks and hazards of unemployment, sickness, and old age. The federal proposals were designed to fill three main gaps in the Canadian social security system: health insurance, national old age pensions, and unemployment assistance. More specifically, the federal government offered grants for a national health insurance plan, hospital construction, and a range of public health services. It assumed 100 per cent of the cost of a universal old age pension for those aged seventy and over, and contributed 50 per cent of the cost of a provincially administered means-tested old age pension for those between the ages of sixty-five and sixty-nine. It assumed responsibility for the able-bodied unemployed not covered under unemployment insurance, through an unemployment assistance program. It offered grant-in-aid programs for community planning, housing projects, and slum clearance, and it extended training services and unemployment insurance coverage and benefits. We can see here some, but by no means all or even most, of the recommendations of the Curtis, Marsh, and Heagerty reports. In relation to the Rowell-Sirois Report, the Green Book 'rejected the equalization principles and the concept of effective provincial autonomy' (Black 1975:53), but did embrace the notion of national standards for certain public services. While Rowell-Sirois conveyed a view of cooperative federalism, the Green Book communicated a centralist concept that would place greater powers at the federal level.

Compared to the comprehensive social security plans envisaged by policy specialists and social workers in Canada as well as in other countries, the social security proposals of the King government were fairly limited in scope and were based far less upon the principle of social insurance. Dennis Guest (1985:137–8) suggests that this distinctive and meagre policy agenda was the result, in part, of the government's real priorities: reducing spending and taxes, and balancing the budget. Guest also suggests that the proposals were not framed primarily on their intrinsic merits or welfare considerations. Instead, they were regarded as inducements for the provinces to agree to open their personal and corporate income tax fields and succession duties to Ottawa in return for some form of unconditional grants. In part, too, they were viewed as an economic tool for maintaining consumer demand. Finally, by choosing public assistance and universal income policy instruments, the federal government was hoping to sidestep the challenging process of securing agreements to amend the Constitution. In one sense, the 1945 conference on reconstruction ended in failure because of the federal and provincial governments' inability to come to agreement on tax rental arrangements. Consequently, the federal government's modest plans for reforming the social security system were put aside, but were not, however, off the national policy agenda for long. For although the ideas and recommendations of these six documents were not all acted upon immediately, they did fuel the debate about how governments should be involved in the management of the economy and the provision of social programs for years to come. We next discuss some of the programs that were developed over the years in response to the ideas generated by the reports.

Establishing a Comprehensive Social Security System / Implementing an Ordered Series of Measures: 1945 to the Early 1970s

Close to the end of the Marsh Report (1975:260) the question was raised 'whether comprehensive social security should be inaugurated completely or as an ordered series of measures over a period.' The report itself offered possible priorities concerning which categories of social need should be given earlier consideration than others. The chronicle of the Canadian welfare state clearly shows that a comprehensive social security system was not set up in the space of one government's mandate. Instead, it took over ten mandates, from the end of the war to the early 1970s, before virtually all of the social security proposals made by the federal government to the provinces at the reconstruction conference had been introduced through a series of measures. Thus the history of social policy in this period is less about sweeping reform than about ordered change; not so much about disjointed incrementalism as *directed incrementalism*, a sequence of actions by governments implemented one by one over time, but guided and connected by a general conception of, and policy agenda for, the social role of the state. Given the expanse of program areas in the field of social security we can discuss only some areas. For the most part, the following review considers the six categories of social need identified by the Marsh Report;

specifically, unemployment, sickness, and medical care; disability; old age and retirement; premature death; and family needs.[2] And as it had the largest impact, we will focus on Marsh's Report as the body of ideas that were acted upon.

Unemployment Insurance

In relation to unemployment insurance, the UI program was amended six times in the nine years from 1946 to 1954, in response to pressures for coverage to be extended to those groups of workers hitherto excluded. Coverage was extended by adding particular sectors under the program, such as loggers and nurses, and by raising the annual earnings ceiling to include more middle-income employees. Contribution rates and benefit rates were also both increased. In 1945 the federal government introduced a vocational school assistance program and in 1948 the Vocational Training Act was passed, which led to agreements with the provinces over the next decade (Campbell 1987). Perhaps the most significant change to UI in this period was the introduction in 1950 of extended or supplementary benefits, worth about 80 per cent of regular benefits, to reflect the greater difficulty of finding work during the winter months. Supplementary benefits were originally set for the months of January through March; by 1957 they spanned the period from December to mid-May. A new Unemployment Insurance Act in 1955 replaced the original 1940 legislation. The new act contained a mix of cuts in some areas and enrichments in others. For instance, the maximum duration of benefits was reduced from fifty-one weeks to thirty-six weeks, while the supplementary benefits were replaced with seasonal benefits of the same value as regular benefits. Coverage was again extended to include municipal police forces and certain types of work in agriculture, horticulture, and forestry. Whereas the 1940 act covered 42 per cent of the labour force, the 1955 legislation applied to 75 per cent of workers (Pal 1988). In 1957 coverage was further extended to include employment in fishing.

From 1946 to 1956 the national unemployment rate in Canada averaged 3.2 per cent, but then went from 4.6 per cent in 1957 to 7 per cent in 1958, and stayed around that level for the next three years. In 1959 the UI program was amended to increase the maximum duration of benefits from thirty-six weeks to fifty-two weeks, reversing the change made in 1955. The earnings ceiling and contribution rates were also raised. From the early to mid-1960s, the Canadian unemployment rate continued to decline, and only a few modest changes were made to UI in that decade.

A major reform to Unemployment Insurance program took place in the early 1970s, when the 1955 act was replaced by new legislation in 1971. The new act expanded coverage of the workforce, increased benefits and introduced new ones, eased the eligibility qualifications, and consolidated regional elements in the program's design. The earnings ceiling was eliminated and coverage was extended to nearly all people in an employee-employer relationship, over 96 per cent of the labour force. The benefit rate for UI was increased to two-thirds of average insured earnings, and the maximum weekly benefit was now automatically indexed to changes in the wage rates. New sickness, maternity, and retirement benefits were added to the program for persons with twenty or more weeks of insured earnings. Another innovation was that benefit duration for regular benefits was now to be determined by the number of weeks of insurable employment, as well as by regional and national unemployment levels. Moreover, the 1971 policy provided that employer and employee contributions would cover the cost of the new benefits and the regular benefits when the national unemployment rate was lower than 4 per cent, and the federal government would pay the cost of regular benefits when the national unemployment rate was over 4 per cent.

Even with the extensions in coverage made to UI since the early 1940s, many of the unemployed were not insured and thus ineligible for benefits. In the Green Book proposals, besides promising to extend the unemployment insurance system, Ottawa offered to assume responsibility for able-bodied unemployed workers not covered by UI and to create a national scheme of unemployment assistance. To permit such a scheme, in 1956 the Unemployment Assistance Act was approved. Rather than being delivered under federal auspices as the Marsh Report (1943) favoured, the plan relied on the existing provincial and local welfare bureaucracies. The federal government was authorized to reimburse a province 50 per cent of the amount spent by provincial and municipal authorities on financial assistance to unemployed persons in need. Activities and programs not cost-shareable included mothers' allowances, payments to inmates in public and charitable institutions, health care costs, and payments to clients of other federal and federal-provincial income benefits. Within three years all ten provinces had signed agreements with the federal government.

In 1965 the federal government offered to the provinces tax abatements in return for the provinces' taking full responsibility for the administration and financing of unemployment assistance and related welfare programs. In 1966 much of the Unemployment Assistance Act was replaced by the Canada Assistance Plan (CAP), a significant needs-tested social welfare measure. The parts remaining of the Unemployment Assistance Act included programs which were means tested rather than needs tested, and thus not covered under CAP. The Unemployment Assistance Act was also amended that year to allow for the cost sharing of provincial mothers' allowances programs.

Hospital and Medical Care

Ottawa's reconstruction proposals included a federal-provincial system of medical care for the whole population, and federal grants to assist the provinces in mental health and public health. In 1948 a national health grants program was established to assist the provinces in building their health services and infrastructure. Grants were available for health surveys; research and professional training; hospital construction; crippled children, mental health, and general public health; and for the control of cancer, tuberculosis, and venereal disease. In 1953 the program was extended to allow grants for child and maternal health, laboratory and radiological services, and medical rehabilitation. The impetus for introducing the health grants program apparently was a threat by a prominent Canadian neurosurgeon that if federal support on health care was not forthcoming he would be forced to close his institute and move to the United States (Guest 1985:141).

This modest health initiative was followed by the Hospital Insurance and Diagnostic Services Act of 1957, a far more ambitious and extensive health policy measure. The legislation authorized federal payments, from general revenues to provincially administered programs of hospital insurance and laboratory and other diagnostic services. Exceptions included mental hospitals, nursing homes, and tuberculosis sanatoria already publicly funded in most provinces. Heedful that health care was primarily a provincial jurisdiction under the Constitution, the legislation stipulated that federal contributions would not commence until at least six provinces, representing at least half the population of Canada, had entered into agreements with Ottawa (a 6 and 50 consensus threshold).

After nearly twenty-two years in power, the Liberals were defeated in 1957 by the Progressive Conservatives led by John Diefenbaker of Saskatchewan, a province that had and was pioneering many innovations in health care and social services. On the health insurance issue, Diefenbaker acted quickly, amending the legislation in 1958 and withdrawing the provision that no federal contributions would be paid until a new cost-sharing program was developed (Johnson 1987:40). By 1961 agreements were in place between the federal government and the provincial governments. As a universal social program, the intent was that hospital care would now be available to all residents of a province, and on the same terms and conditions.

In 1962 Saskatchewan again was the policy pioneer in introducing the first universal medical insurance plan in Canada, in the midst of a harsh and distressing doctor's strike (Badgley and Wolfe 1967). Despite the conflict, the plan proved to be immediately popular and of great interest in other provinces as well as at the federal level of party politics. Ottawa established the Health Resources Fund, with $500 million available over the 1966 to 1980 period. Like the earlier health grants program, the new fund was for cost-sharing with the provinces, on a fifty-fifty basis, for construction, acquisition, and renovation of health facilities and equipment. In 1966 the Medical Care Act was passed, taking effect two years later due to budgetary concerns of the federal finance minister. In introducing the legislation, the responsible minister described the purpose of the legislation thus: 'to insure access to medical care to all of our people regardless of means, of pre-existing conditions, of age or other circumstances which my have barred such access in the past.' To receive federal contributions, provincial and territorial medical care plans had to meet certain criteria or principles. The five key criteria were that the coverage reach and be maintained at 95 per cent or more of each province's population; that the plans include all the benefits deemed to be medically necessary services provided by physicians; that the plans be portable from one jurisdiction to another within the country; that plans be nonprofit and administered by a provincial or territorial public authority accountable to the legislature; and that services be available on reasonably equal terms and conditions to all insurable residents by ensuring that any health insurance premiums paid by residents did not financially impede or preclude access to medically necessary services. By 1972 all provinces and territories had entered into agreements. Through the Medical Care Act, the federal government positioned itself as a continuing and major actor in health care policy, and Canadians had a universal medical care system with access to insured services regardless of ability to pay.

Social Programs for People with Disabilities

Aside from workers' compensation and veterans' programs, until the 1940s few provincial or federal policies recognized disability as a category of social need. People with various kinds of disabilities were seen as 'worthy poor,' yet often they were given public or private charity rather than granted regular citizenship rights (Bach and Rioux 1996). The Marsh Report, however, regarded nonindustrial disability as a universal risk facing Canadians, a risk calling for special provisions as part of the social security system. The income support needs of blind persons had been addressed under the Old Age Pensions legislation since the late 1930s and increases were made to pension for the blind four times throughout the 1940s. Further, the eligibility age for such pensions was lowered from forty to twenty-one.

Marsh's vision of a comprehensive, national social insurance program for disability was not followed. Instead, a group of categorical, means-tested programs for people with disabilities was instituted. Michael Bach and Marcia Rioux (1996:318) describe the pattern and consequences of this policy approach as follows: 'Investment in institutional facilities, special education, segregated vocational training, and employment and community services exclusively for persons with disabilities grew substantially in the postwar period. In this way the postwar framework for securing the welfare and well-being of Canadians ironically institutionalized exclusion for people with disabilities.'

For persons with visual impairment, for instance, the Blind Persons Act of 1951 offered allowances to blind persons aged twenty-one to sixty-nine, cost-shared with the provinces on a 75 per cent federal – 25 per cent provincial basis. The residency requirement of twenty years under the previous Old Age Pensions Act was changed to ten years, and the earlier provision excluding Indians was dropped. The maximum allowance of $480 a year was the same as for a blind person under the repealed old age pensions law, although the total allowable income for a recipient, including the allowance, was initially raised an average of $10 a month, and then raised again in 1955, and twice in 1957. The eligibility age for a blind allowance was lowered from age twenty-one to eighteen in 1955, and the allowance itself was twice raised in 1957, by the Liberals before the federal election and by the victorious Conservatives after the election. The allowance was next raised around the 1962 and 1963 federal elections.[3] The Blind Persons Act was amended in 1966, allowing provinces to switch the financing and administration of the program under the new CAP legislation. That reform, coupled with the transfer of federal tax points to the provinces, under fiscal arrangements for financing this and other welfare programs, essentially removed the blind persons' allowance from the federal agenda.[4]

The 1950s also saw initiatives on income support for persons with total and permanent disabilities, and on the vocational rehabilitation of disabled persons. In 1951 the federal government formed the National Advisory Committee on the Rehabilitation of Disabled Persons. The committee had thirty-seven members, comprising representatives from the federal and provincial governments, health and welfare voluntary agencies, the medical profession, employers, organized labour, and universities. Representatives from disability groups themselves were not specified as interests deserving designated membership on the committee.[5] In 1953 medical rehabilitation was added to the list of services funded under the National Health Grants Program. Also that year, the federal cabinet authorized the minister of labour to enter into agreements with the provinces to develop activities for the rehabilitation of disabled persons.

Under the Disabled Persons Act of 1954, the federal government offered to share, on a fifty-fifty basis with the provinces the cost of allowances to permanently and totally disabled persons aged eighteen to sixty-nine. A person was deemed totally and permanently disabled if he or she were suffering from a major impairment, one likely to continue without substantial improvement over the person's life, and severely limiting their ability to handle self-care and daily activities. There was a ten-year residence requirement and the allowance was not payable to a recipient of other federal and provincial income benefits. By the end of 1956, agreements had been made between the federal government and all the provinces. This program was also means-tested rather based on the social insurance principle. The subsequent story of the disabled persons program is the same as for blind persons in terms of periodic increases around federal elections in the late 1950s and early 1960s; the influence of new intergovernmental fiscal arrangements and the CAP in the mid-1960s; and the eventual cancellation of the legislation in the 1980s.

The Vocational Rehabilitation of Disabled Persons Act, passed in

1961, offered agreements to the provinces and territories of federal sharing of 50 per cent of the costs for a range of vocational rehabilitation services designed to help people with physical or mental disabilities become capable of pursuing a gainful occupation. The federal government's financial obligation was open-ended, a function of how much provinces wished to spend on these services. Except for Quebec (which eventually did participate by the late 1980s), all the provinces entered into two- or three-year agreements with Ottawa which were regularly renewed over the years (Prince 1992).

Old Age Pensions and Retirement Insurance Provisions

'The universality of old age' in the human condition, observed the Marsh Report (1943:153), 'is evidenced by the fact that only in the case of old age pensions is there a full acknowledgment of social responsibility by all nine provincial governments [Newfoundland did not join Canada until 1949] and the federal government as well.' Marsh went on to argue, however, that none of the provincial pension programs were an adequate response to the income or service needs of aged persons. The report discussed possible improvements to old age assistance and recommended the introduction of a compulsory contributory retirement insurance scheme. The trend internationally was away from means-tested old age assistance towards social insurance-based retirement plans, a trend that to Marsh seemed irreversible and desirable. 'Individuals prefer to get their retirement income as a right, on a basis consistent with their idea of human dignity. Means-test procedures, however lightly applied, violate to some extent this conception of the right to retirement income' (Marsh 1943:171). The Green Book proposals included, as we noted earlier, a new old age pension and a revamped old age assistance scheme. Action on both these ideas happened fairly rapidly.

In 1947 the federal government amended the Old Age Pensions Act, making three changes along the lines proposed by Marsh. To relax the system of eligibility conditions, the provincial residence requirement of five years and the British citizenship requirement were eliminated. To raise the pension payable, the maximum pension was increased from $25 to $30 a month and the total allowable income was also increased. In 1949 the maximum pension was raised to $40 monthly. These were minor repairs to the legislation since the age limit of seventy, the means-testing of benefits, and the practice of holding adult children responsible for aged parents were all retained.

More fundamental changes to old age pension policy came with the Old Age Security and Old Age Assistance Acts in 1951, and the revocation of the Old Age Pensions Act. These measures were preceded by a constitutional amendment approved earlier that year giving the Canadian Parliament authority to make laws in relation to old age pensions. The Old Age Security (OAS) Act introduced Canada's third universal income benefit, the one that would eventually be the largest in terms of clientele and program expenditures. A monthly flat-rate pension of $40 was offered to persons aged seventy and over regardless of their financial or family circumstances. The exclusion of Indians under the previous policy was removed. One of the old design features that remained, though, was the residence requirement of twenty years; furthermore, pensioners had their OAS benefit suspended if they left the country even for a few months. The financing for the program, the '2–2–2 formula' was unique: revenues derived from an OAS tax comprising 2 per cent on personal income, 2 per cent on corporate income, and 2 per cent from general budgetary revenue, all to be deposited in a special OAS Fund. The intended political function of the tax and fund was to make the public aware of the apparent costs and taxes associated with the new universal benefit, and therefore curb public demands for increases. The tax mix was raised to a 3–3–3 formula in 1959, to 4–3–3 in 1964, and altered again in later years (Bryden 1974). The OAS tax was formally abolished in 1972 while the fund continued until 1975. Since in practice the OAS program has always been financed from federal general revenues, Bryden (1974:205) maintains that talk of an OAS tax and fund 'was a purely metaphorical way of describing it.' However, as we will show in the next chapter, many seniors and pensioner groups reacted sharply to proposed cuts to the OAS during the 1980s, arguing that they were entitled to the benefits because they had specifically paid for them from the early 1950s to the early 1970s.

Along with the universal OAS for those aged seventy and over, the 1951 Old Age Assistance legislation introduced a revamped means-tested selective program for persons aged sixty-five to sixty-nine. The federal government would cost-share the program on a fifty-fifty basis with the provinces. Recipients of the blind persons' allowances and war veterans' allowances were excluded, and there was a residence requirement of twenty years. The maximum level of assistance of $40 a month was the same as under the repealed Old Age Pensions Act. Some of the more undesirable features of the earlier law were not continued, such as excluding Indians, making recoveries from the estates of deceased pensioners, or suspending benefits when a pensioner was in a public mental institution.

In 1965, with the introduction of the Canada Pension Plan (CPP), a contributory retirement insurance plan for people age sixty-five and older, the universal OAS program was amended. Beginning in 1966, the eligible age for the OAS pension was lowered, one year at a time, to age sixty-five.[6] The previous residence requirement was once again extended to include 40 years in Canada after age eighteen. From 1968 annual increases in the OAS benefit were indexed to the Consumer Price Index (a measure of cost of living) subject to a 2 per cent limit.

The introduction of the Guaranteed Income Supplement in 1967 marked an innovation in public pension policy, and, some commentators believed, foreshadowed a guaranteed annual income program. The GIS was an income tested benefit for OAS pensioners with a low income, determined on a family basis. The GIS was conceived as an alternative to yet another increase in the universal OAS pension (Johnson 1987:44), and the GIS maximum benefit was set at 40 per cent of the OAS pension. The GIS was originally thought of as a transitional program which would fade away as the CPP matured and as more Canadians secured their retirement savings through that program as well as through occupational plans, investments, and private savings. Experience since then demonstrates that these were heroic assumptions, especially on the expansion of private pension plans, resulting in the GIS playing a large role in the retirement income system to the end of the 1990s (Prince 1997).

The story of the debate over, competing design ideas and actual implementation of the Canada and Quebec Pension Plans (C/QPP) has been well chronicled elsewhere (Bryden 1974; Johnson 1987). A constitutional amendment in 1964, the third in twenty-four years, was passed enabling Parliament to make laws in relation to supplementary benefits, including survivors' and disability benefits irrespective of age, in addition to the old age pensions authorized by the 1951 amendment. The CPP came into effect in 1966 with the collection of contributions. Benefits were phased in over the next four years: retirement pensions became payable in 1967, survivors' benefits in 1968, and disability benefits in 1970. Though nearly a quarter of a century had elapsed, many of the ideas of the Marsh Report were evident in the design of the CPP. The CPP embodies, as Marsh had argued, the principles of a compulsory, contributory, social insurance retirement program, covering most of the working population. The CPP covers employees and self-employed persons between the ages of eighteen and seventy with pensionable earnings in all provinces and territories except Quebec, which has its own parallel plan. At the outset (and continuing to 1986, in fact) contributions of employees and employers was 1.8 per cent of pensionable earnings, and 3.6 per cent for the self-employed. The retirement age for eligibility began at age sixty-eight in 1967, and was reduced, one year at a time, to age sixty-five in 1970. The basic retirement pension is graduated, dependent on earnings, and set at 25 per cent of average adjusted earnings. As a result, the CPP offers a basic minimum public pension allowing room for occupational plans.

Marsh (1943:174) had endorsed this approach, saying, 'there is something to be said of regarding a retirement pension as a small nucleus to which private and industrial provisions may be added.' In discussing family needs, Marsh had examined the issues of widowhood, survivors' insurance, and funeral benefits. The CPP addressed these issues in part by providing pensions for widows and disabled widowers under sixty-five; flat-rate benefits for children of deceased contributors and children of disabled contributors; and a lump sum death benefit paid to the estate of a deceased contributor. All monthly benefits were initially indexed to changes in the Consumer Price Index, subject to a 2 per cent ceiling to maintain something of the purchasing power of the benefits. In 1974 the retirement and other benefits became indexed to the full annual increase in the price index.

These cycles of reforms indicate pension politique – the inseparability of politics and policy making (Prince 1996b). For instance, during the minority and majority federal governments of Lester Pearson's Liberals and John Diefenbaker's Conservatives, both the universal and selective old age maximum benefits were increased four times by the same amounts, rising from $40 a month in 1957 to $75 a month by 1963. In addition, the limits on total allowable income was raised while the residence requirement for both programs was lowered to ten years. During the minority government of Pierre Trudeau from 1972 to 1975, with the NDP holding the balance of power, the basic OAS pension was increased from $80 to $100 monthly and the GIS raised from $55 to $67 monthly. The benefit payments of both programs were to increase quarterly by the annual rise in the Consumer Price Index. In 1975 another selective, family based, income tested program for seniors was introduced, the Spouse's Allowance. The maximum monthly Spouse's Allowance was set at an amount equal to the monthly OAS pension plus the maximum monthly GIS. At the outset, this program was designed for persons aged sixty to sixty-four inclusive, and thus ineligible for the CPP or the OAS or GIS, who were married to and living with a pensioner, that is, someone age sixty-five or older.

Family Income Maintenance

The reports of Beveridge, Marsh, and others stressed the risk of personal and societal insecurity that can arise when earnings and income are interrupted or are insufficient for the needs of families with children. A prime recommendation in this regard was a family allowance, a version of which was introduced in Canada in 1945. Several notable changes were made to the Family Allowances program over the next thirty years: Indian and Inuit children were no longer excluded from receiving benefits (1947); the residence requirement for a child not born in Canada was lowered from three years to one year (1949); reductions in allowances for the fifth and succeeding children were abolished (1949); the program was extended to the children of Newfoundland upon that province's entry into Confederation (1949); benefits were increased for children age five and under and for those aged ten to twelve, by one dollar a month (1957); a standard monthly allowance of $12 was set in 1973 and then enriched in 1974 to $20 a month. The 1974 reform also allowed provinces to vary federal allowances according to the ages of children and/or the number of children in the family, an option taken up by Alberta and Quebec. The 1973 Family Allowances Act was the first overhaul of the legislation since the original law. Age eligibility was extended to children under eighteen and special allowances were provided for children under eighteen who were living in foster homes or public institutions. Both types of allowances were to be fully indexed to the Consumer Price Index, and family allowances became taxable as income.

Other family income programs during this period included family assistance, youth allowances, and mothers' allowances, all patchwork programs. Family assistance was a program begun in 1956, which paid to families not eligible for Family Allowances (Canadians resettling in Canada and recent immigrants) a monthly benefit of $5 for each child under age sixteen. Following on a similar initiative by the Quebec government a few years earlier, a federal youth allowances program was begun in 1964 offering monthly benefits of $10 to parents of youths aged sixteen and seventeen, so not covered by the Family Allowances program, who attended school or university but could not continue because of serious illness. Guest (1985:150) describes the program as a 'recognition of the increasing years of dependency of the young as the requirements of Canada's technological society called for greater educational preparation.' The Youth Allowances Program was a short-lived universal program for a narrow age group as both it and the Family Assistance Program were repealed and subsumed by the comprehensive 1974 reforms of the Family Allowances Program. Mothers' Allowances, as discussed in the previous chapter, were among the earliest income programs in Canada, and wholly financed and administered by provinces. This pattern continued in the postwar period. It was not until 1966 that Mothers' Allowances Program was included for federal cost-sharing purposes under the Unemployment Assistance program.

A Vision of Comprehensive Reform Realized

By the early 1970s the consensus was that the Canadian welfare state was finally complete. All the categories of social, need and risk enumerated by the Marsh Report and others were provided for in some way by federal, provincial, and intergovernmental social programs. According to Johnson (1987:50), with the introduction of Medicare in 1968, 'the grand design of 1945' was in place, 'not always tidily, not always peacefully, but it was there. There had been some embellishments; there had been some shifts in the balance between elements of the system; there had even been some harbingers of new directions for the future (notably the Guaranteed Income Supplement).' Splane (1987:246) writes of 'the initial agenda for the development of a comprehensive social security system for Canada being completed by the early 1970s.' For Splane the completion date was the passage of the 1971 Unemployment Insurance Act with its extension of coverage to nearly the entire labour force, and the introduction of sickness, retirement, and maternity benefits.

Whether called a grand design, a long-term national social policy agenda, or a Keynesian welfare consensus, there was in effect from the 1940s to the 1970s a broadly shared set of beliefs on building a progressive system of social security. Forged in the experiences and aspirations of Canadians, these beliefs were reflected in the administrative culture of federal and provincial social welfare departments and related portfolios. Outside government, beliefs were reinforced as well as challenged by researchers and academics, client groups, professional associations, and other interests. For Splane, who was one of these reformist bureau-

crats, as indeed was Johnson, the overarching objectives were introducing new programs, making improvements in coverage and benefits,
and developing a comprehensive, nationwide system of social security.
The credo of these reformist bureaucrats included strong support for
the concept of public responsibility for social welfare, an agreed-upon
recognition of unmet social needs and contingencies facing Canadians,
engagement in policy analysis and advice, 'and an interest in finding
workable solutions to common problems' (Splane 1987:235). Continuity
in implementing the agenda was facilitated at the federal level by the
fact that from 1944 to 1972, the Department of National Health and
Welfare had only two deputy ministers on the welfare side, both of
whom were specialists in social administration with links to the provinces, voluntary sector, and international welfare agencies.[7] The expectation was that social policy measures would significantly reduce
insecurity and poverty. Research has shown that social programs have
created a level of protection against unemployment, injury, sickness,
old age, and disability; and, along with other public policies and the tax
system, have mitigated market-generated income inequalities, although
poverty persists.

While we have reviewed in quick succession many of the key programs put in place during this period of social policy ascendancy, we
want to emphasize that the particular political histories of each program are different. Different needs, interest groups, political factors,
and social events influenced the formation of each program. In general,
the ability to implement the vision of a comprehensive social security
system was shaped by the interplay of many forces. These included the
skill and determination of individual ministers and their deputies;
support from the prime minister and other members of cabinet, especially the finance minister; interdepartmental relations, whether it was
a majority or minority government; the level and nature of public
knowledge and concern; the lobbying efforts of interest groups; the
state of the domestic and world economies, and the fiscal health of
governments; the state of federal-provincial relations and issues of
national unity; and any other major issues that were on the public
policy agenda preoccupying leaders (Splane 1987). Behind these there
were deeper forces at work, such as the impact of the depression and
world war, and the further industrialization and urbanization of Canada
(Johnson 1987). As examples, consider that the populist Diefenbaker
government helped to entrench equalization payments for the less-
well-off provinces in an effort to overcome the centralist biases of the

previous Liberal government; the same Liberal party adopted left-of-centre policies during the Pearson minority government in which the NDP was able to exercise some influence; and the architects of social programs were able to argue that new programs were not only just but affordable during the economic expansion of the 1960s.

Conclusions

Envisaging and establishing a national system of social security from the 1940s to 1970s transformed social welfare in Canada from a system of allocating benefits on the basis of relief and means testing, to one based more on the principles of universal entitlement, public service, and social insurance. Needs testing, income testing and the automatic indexation of benefits also emerged near the end of this era as new social policy instruments. Old Age Security, Family Allowances, and Medicare are examples of universal programs providing benefits to the eligible population as a social right. Unemployment Insurance, Workers' Compensation, and the Canada and Quebec Pension Plans are examples of programs designed so that provision was limited to those who paid a social insurance premium. Relief and means-testing devices were maintained for social assistance programs such as Mothers' Allowances, Unemployment Assistance, and Old Age Assistance Program. The Canada Assistance Plan was based on a needs test and the Guaranteed Income Supplement for seniors introduced the device of income testing to federal income security. By the early 1970s several federal programs were indexed to the Consumer Price Index.

Social reforms take time and are made in various parts of the state. This review reveals that while the policy ideas of a report may be rejected or ignored in the short term, many are adopted in one form or another in later years. Social policy making occurs through many forums: the legislative process of parliament; cabinet orders and departmental regulations; key court decisions; constitutional amendments; and intergovernmental arrangements. This analysis also reveals that the evolution of Canada's social security system was a mixture of minor reforms and marginal measures on the one hand, and fundamental structural changes on the other. Much of postwar social policy was created incrementally – that is not surprising. Given the constraints of limited resources and parliamentary time, and competing issues and interests, each governmental mandate allows only a few social policy initiatives, if that. What is noteworthy, we believe, is that the overall process was not disjointed, but rather one directed to a general direction of social reform and a set of values concerning the role of the state in society.

Another important trend in this period was the centralization, or, perhaps more aptly, the federalization of the income security system. Most of the major cash benefit programs designed after 1940 were delivered by the federal government. In other social policy areas, such as hospital insurance and human rights, for instance, the pattern was one of provincial innovation and diffusion, as in the pre-welfare state era. Together, both levels of government were involved in collaborative decision making and financial responsibilities for social programs. This was called the era of cooperative federalism, explained in part by public acceptance of the role of social policies in the development of a stable and growing economy. Although there was not always easy agreement on specific arrangements, and in many instances the provinces protested that the federal government was encroaching on their constitutional territory, the social policy process developed a system with a greater degree of shared responsibility than any other policy field (Rice 1985).

The analysis in this chapter has shown that the growth of an extensive system of social security recasts the character of politics and governing in Canada in several ways. With the entrance of Keynesian economics into public budgeting and policy making, even if a modest version (Campbell 1987), the historic strain between social welfare and 'free enterprise' was diminished. Keynes demonstrated that it was possible through social policies to achieve both welfare functions and economic management functions. A new set of rationales and terms for debating and justifying social policy arose, and the reduction of the existing tension cleared the way for the introduction of a wide variety of social policies. On the constitutional front, amendments were made granting powers to the federal government on matters of income security – exclusive powers in the case of unemployment insurance, and concurrent powers with provincial paramountcy in the case of old age pensions and contributory pensions. Despite these amendments, most legislative powers on social questions remained with the provinces as the Rowell-Sirois Royal Commission had urged. In public finance, a complex array of fiscal arrangements developed between the federal and provincial governments on tax rental and sharing, equalization payments, and shared-cost programs. In terms of the distribution of expenditures on health and social security by level of government, the federal share jumped dramatically during the war, from about 49 per cent in 1940 to nearly 72 per cent in 1945, and stayed near that level into the 1960s, declining gradually to about 65 per cent in the early 1970s.

The share of social spending by the provinces continually grew over the postwar period, from 21 per cent in 1945 to 34 per cent in the 1970s, while the share by municipalities declined over the whole period, from a substantial 17 per cent in 1940 to 7 per cent in 1945, down to less than 2 per cent by the mid-1970s (Guest 1985:242). Finally, while acknowledging that the state did not have a monopoly with respect to social policy formation and provision, the vision and discourse tended to concentrate on the state. A state-centred conception of social care and social intervention became apparent in the Canadian literature in political science, sociology, social work, and public administration, among other disciplines. As the next chapter shows, the crisis politics of social policy in the later 1970s and 1980s directly and profoundly challenged both the effectiveness and desirability of this focus on the welfare state.

4

The Crisis of the Welfare State: Canadian Perspectives and Critiques

No sooner had the Canadian postwar social policy agenda been seemingly completed than critics began lamenting its effects on public and private budgets, the economy and community, the status of women, and clients and service providers. As a federal Royal Commission observed in the mid-1980s: 'With the major elements of the welfare state in place, a loss of momentum and a growing uncertainty about the next steps were perhaps inevitable. But this hesitancy was reinforced by economic difficulties of the last decade and the criticisms from both right and left' (Canada 1985:578). Viewed historically and comparatively, these economic difficulties were neither minor nor exclusive to Canada; they were unprecedented in the postwar period and struck industrialized economies around the world. Over the 1973–75 period, 'The combined GNP of the Organization for Economic Co-operation and Development (OECD) countries fell by 5 per cent, industrial output plummeted, and world trade declined by 14 per cent. Unemployment climbed to a staggering 15 million in all OECD countries combined. At the same time, inflation accelerated' (Gough 1979:132).

From this period onwards, complaints arose that the economic system could no longer function with ever-increasing levels of taxation to support the welfare state apparatus constructed over the previous several decades. The business community charged that governments were adding to inflation by borrowing money to finance social policy, and that greater numbers of people were actually becoming dependent upon the welfare system. The list of denunciations grew: commentators soundly deplored the infusion of welfare programs with monies that could be better spent on economic investment. Criticisms were reinforced by the view that the social policy agenda, in any case, was failing to address problems effectively and with due speed. Pressure mounting under these attacks became known as the crisis of the welfare state, a period in Canada that roughly spanned the mid-1970s to the late 1980s.

Perspectives outside and inside the welfare system defined and influenced the nature of the welfare crisis. Here, we survey five main perspectives on Canadian social policy during this period – Left, Right, feminist, communities, and insiders – and we examine a number of critiques each raised. Left-leaning academics and politicians expressed disappointment with the persistence of inequality and poverty amidst the obvious prosperity. Right-leaning academics and politicians were concerned with contradictions between social programs and economic structures. Feminist critiques, which we examine more fully in Chapter 8, questioned the function of social policies and their role in marginalizing women, keeping women 'in place,' and concealing the burden women bear as governments abandon policy initiatives. Community members voiced their opposition to the welfare system's disregard for clients trapped in bureaucratic organizations. People within the system – service providers, caregivers, and clients – questioned the manner in which welfare programs institutionalize recipients, the way discretionary administrative power was exercised in determining who should receive benefits, and the way the system forced people to live in poverty.

The analysis does not provide an overview of the crisis period, or even a detailed review of the central tenets of each argument. These have been thoroughly analyzed in the literature.[1] Rather, here we make the case that the welfare crisis as articulated in Canada during this period comprised a series of contending ideas, issues, and developments that significantly challenged and strained the consensus upon which the social security system was built.

Critique from the Left

The political Left – a mixture of community activists, welfare-oriented liberals, social democrats, labour leaders, Marxist thinkers, and other critics – developed penetrating analyses of the welfare state. In the Canadian context, it was the Left initially, starting in the early 1970s, that argued that many social programs were no longer meeting the needs of people, if they ever did. Thus the Left called for a review of the social security system. This was part of the background of the 1973–75 social security review by the Trudeau Liberal government, as well as of the social security review by the Chrétien Liberal government in

1994–95. The Right's interest in restructuring social programs, beyond the simple mantra of rollback benefits and regulating clients, came later (Lightman 1995:356).

Ranging from concerns about the plight of people forced to work in the secondary labour market to claims about the impending collapse of capitalism, three themes help illustrate the Left's critique of the welfare state: the way governments used welfare systems to control and blame the poor; the effect of economic contradictions on the welfare state; and the impact of new forms of capitalism on the state's ability to solve social problems.

The first theme, about the way governments used welfare systems to control and blame the poor, examines the damaging ways in which governments employed social policies to address social issues. Frances Piven and Richard Cloward (1971:40), early critics of welfare, studied how the system maintains social and economic inequalities while forcing people to take low-paying jobs. Their research showed how governments use welfare programs to regulate the poor during periods of social upheaval. They argued that governments introduce social policies, or an increase in benefits, to quash civil disorder during periods of mass unemployment. These same programs are then restricted during times of economic growth. Equally important to Piven and Cloward was the fact that governments abandon programs and services designed to support the poor during periods of economic growth in favour of programs supporting workers and the middle class. Far from providing liberal benefits, the welfare system is 'periodically expanding and contracting relief rolls as the system performs its two main functions: maintaining civil order and enforcing work' (Piven and Cloward 1971:xv). Through the 1970s and 1980s, this cyclical nature of social welfare could be observed in Canada.[2] The ideals of full employment, the war on poverty and support for the development of Trudeau's just society were declining; social spending was increasingly viewed as a burden; and, despite several social policy reviews at the federal and provincial levels, concrete reforms were insubstantial compared to expectations and achievements of earlier decades. With respect to the redistribution of income and wealth, the Canadian welfare state was not the Robin Hood many thought it was meant to be or perceived it to be in practice (Gillespie 1978; Osberg 1981), due, in part, to regressive features and gaps in the tax system.

Other critics on the Left claimed that when governments introduced welfare programs, they constructed them in a way that blamed the victim. William Ryan examined the process of victim-blaming, disguised often as kindness and concern. Unlike the conservative ideologies that dismiss welfare recipients as 'inferior, genetically defective, or morally unfit,' blaming the victim allows the humanitarian to have it both ways: 'He can all at the same time concentrate his charitable interests on the defects of the victim, condemn the vague social and environmental stresses that produced the defect (some time ago), and ignore the continuing effect of victimizing social forces (right now)' (Ryan 1971:7). Ryan's criticism stressed that welfare programs blame the victim by failing to take into account social stratification, political struggle, inequalities of power and distribution of income, and ethnic and racial group conflict.

In examining the ideology of the welfare state in Canada, Angela Wei Djao (1979: 301–2) did an empirical study of public perceptions and beliefs. She discovered that 'the ideology comprised some factual statements about the welfare system for the poor, some misconceptions about those dependent on the welfare system for the poor, and general concealment of the welfare system for the non-poor.' Djao concluded that 'the ideology of the welfare state is based on individualism in the liberal tradition. Its key components are desirability of state intervention in promoting social welfare and suspicion towards the poor. State intervention should, however, be interpreted with caution. The official goal of state intervention is to reduce income inequality in society; in practice, state intervention amounts to a few programs providing subsistence income to the poor. The ideology masks the real workings of the welfare state, so that the structure of inequalities in society is left intact' (1979:314).

Over this period of crisis politics, many on the Left began drawing attention both polemically and analytically to the welfare system of tax breaks, subsidies, and grants for corporations (Lewis 1972; Clement 1975; Calvert 1984; Tudiver 1987), as well as to the hidden welfare system of tax expenditures, cash transfers, and services for the well-to-do in Canada (National Council of Welfare 1976, 1978).

A second theme from the Left concerned the underlying and contradictory nature of the welfare system. Internationally, James O'Connor (1973), Ian Gough (1979), Ramesh Mishra (1984), and Claus Offe (1984) all raised theoretical questions about the state's ability to support ongoing welfare. Their book titles indicate, respectively, the direction of this critique: *The Fiscal Crisis of the State*, *The Political Economy of the Welfare State*, *The Welfare State in Crisis*, and *Contradictions of the Welfare State*. In

Canada, edited works by Leo Panitch (1977), Allan Moscovitch and Glenn Drover (1981), and Allan Moscovitch and Jim Albert (1987) provided similar critical assessments of the welfare state's viability within a political economy approach.[3]

These writings suggested that the crisis of the welfare state was actually a crisis of the capitalist state in maintaining a comprehensive welfare function. For the moderate Left in Canada – social democrats and welfare liberals – the relationship between social programs and market economics was not contradictory at root, but rather a tension that could, with a judicious mix of policy instruments, be managed. The more radical Left's position, vividly articulated by O'Connor, described the crisis as a basic contradiction between the rising expenses of social welfare and the declining ability of the state to meet these costs. According to O'Connor, every capitalist state has two central functions: ensuring the private accumulation of wealth, and legitimizing the capitalist social structure in a way that maintains social order. To achieve these functions, governments develop policies supporting social investments and social consumption on the one hand, and social expenses of production on the other. Social investments such as cheap electricity, highways, education, or training of the working class are meant to increase labour productivity. Social consumption expenditures on projects and services such as social insurance are meant to lower the costs of labour. Such programs include tax credits for children, child care, and income support programs for families. Finally, governments try to ensure social stability by providing support for people who must leave or are left out of the labour market in the form of unemployment benefits, pensions, and compensation for injured workers.

O'Connor argues that the more programs government creates, and the more services it provides, the greater will be the numbers of people wanting access to them. This growth of the welfare system requires additional resources to finance new programs. At some point the government comes to the limit of its ability to find new resources; it can no longer manage both the growth of welfare and the growth of the economy – the deep contradiction between the two reflecting the welfare state's crisis.

Canadian academics and activists quickly took up O'Connor's framework. They used his categories and arguments to evaluate taxation policies, the status of public employees, regional economic underdevelopment, and social spending (Deaton 1973; Armstrong 1977; Kuusisto and Williams 1981; Moscovitch and Drover 1987). Data on the functions and levels of expenditures and on tax revenue sources confirmed O'Connor's thesis of a fiscal crisis for Canadians. In an analysis of public expenditures, Allan Moscovitch and Glen Drover (1987:37) found that there was 'a trade-off between transfers to persons and aid to business and industry. In the postwar period, when transfers to persons increased, spending on capital declined. Conversely, when spending on capital increased, transfers to persons declined.' On the tax side, they found that 'During a downturn, it has become easier for government to reduce taxes on capital than to increase public expenditures, producing the net effect of continuously shifting the tax burden from corporations to persons.'

The contradictions exposed by O'Connor created a new language to describe the welfare system: *a fiscal crisis*; that is, there was a large structural gap between what governments were spending on programs and what they were raising from taxes. This criticism allowed elites to blame welfare for the large deficits of the 1980s slow or no-growth period. The fiscal crisis analysis undermined the notion that protective welfare systems create political conditions to encourage the rapid movement of resources that finance economic growth. In our view, the analysis failed to see that large-scale social and economic transformations have taken place without social upheaval, that urbanization, industrialization, commercialization, and dramatic labour-force changes have revolutionized society. These transformations were only possible because of the security offered by the social welfare state.

A third theme dealt with the impact of new forms of capitalism on the state's ability to solve social problems. Offe and other critics suggested that the conditions of capitalism altered as the economy shifted from organized capitalism to disorganized capitalism (Offe 1985:6; Lash and Urry 1987). Organized capitalism reflected a period of mass production of standardized goods, often called Fordism.[4] Large vertically integrated companies employed many semi-skilled workers to make products for largely undifferentiated markets. This coincided with the development of large unions engaged in collective bargaining for workers. These structural conditions supported the development of the welfare state. The welfare state grew from the 1920s into the 1970s because there were organized political parties, labour unions, and, to a limited extent, interest groups. These structures provided ways for the working class to fight for rights and social security within the context of a capitalist society (Offe 1985:7).

Changing economic conditions – with increased competition between companies, a growing division between highly skilled and unskilled workers, and a declining role of state intervention – disorganized capitalism. New forms of capitalism began to take shape with the introduction of new production processes which quickly spread from the United States to Japan and other parts of the world. These changes included the weakening, even the destruction, of the union movement, the introduction of robotics, the development of small-batch production, the expansion of horizontal integration between producers, and the introduction of multipurpose production strategies. Corporate activities became more targeted, with an increase in local production designed for niche markets. Just-in-time processes eliminated the need for vast stockpiling of products; specialization in production allowed parts to come from all over the world to low-cost assembly plants. These new processes led to a fragmenting of the production process and declining demand for semi-skilled labour.

The restructuring of the economy led to a decline in the role of labour unions and in labour protection practices. Similarly, governmental regulation of markets began to weaken as producers searched for the least expensive places to produce their goods. The effect of these changes was to engender conditions in which government found it much more difficult to address internal issues. As the economy changed, a 'coalition of neo-liberal politicians, internationally competitive industries, finance ministries, central banks and private financial institutions emerged within and across states and sought to reduce the size and scope of government' (Bernard 1994:225).

In exploring the changes that were taking place, some on the Canadian Left challenged their colleagues to reassess the continued validity of Keynesian prescriptions and to alter their policy agendas to new economic circumstances. In 1984 James Laxer, a prominent member of the New Democratic Party (NDP), in *Rethinking the Economy*, pointed out that the world was moving 'towards a new international division of labour and a basic technological transformation.' Laxer argued that social democrats in Canada needed to shift their attitudes concerning the economy. They needed to change their preferred policy tools while maintaining their goals of full employment and fair social programs. Laxer's proposals included an abandonment of traditional Keynesianism towards more concern with production, especially in the manufacturing sector, renewed economic nationalism, and the democratization of the workplace. Laxer's analysis was controversial, and, at the time, quite divisive within the NDP.

Drawn together, the control of the poor, the contradictions within the welfare state, and the changing nature of the economy highlighted the larger context of tensions or contradictions between the demands of social investment and economic investment. This tension is further explored in Chapter 6. The changing politics of social policy reflect this division between social and economic spheres.

Critique from the Right

The enormous expansion of the welfare state in all industrial democracies has brought forward many conservative and neo-conservative critics who question the government's role in creating large social programs. While accepting the need for some forms of government intervention, these commentators are sceptical of the range and impact of ever-expanding government social programs. In particular, their Right-leaning fingers are pointed at the welfare system. In the 1970s some new groups on the Right appeared in Canada. The Canadian Federation of Independent Business and the Business Council on National Issues joined traditional business groups such as the Canadian Chamber of Commerce and the Canadian Manufacturers' Association. These new business associations were public policy oriented, spoke out on matters of social programs, among other issues, and actively lobbied governments (Doern and Phidd 1983:85). Right-wing policy institutes, or think-tanks were also established in this period. Most notable was the formation of the moderately conservative C.D. Howe Institute and the more radical Fraser Institute. The Fraser Institute's vision was and is to achieve a society based upon free markets, private property rights, individual responsibility, and limited government. All of these groups, in one form or another, believe in market solutions for social problems, and in the context of 1970s and 1980s, were seeking 'to redirect public attention to the role markets can play in providing for the economic and social well being of Canadians.'[5]

Three themes capture the nature of the neo-conservative critique: the evolution of Canadian social policy and changed economic context; the notion that the welfare system infringes upon individual liberty and creates dependency in the recipient population; and that social policy provided by the state commonly uses resources inefficiently.

The first theme of the evolution of Canadian social policy and changed economic context is based on a particular interpretation of the development and nature of the Canadian welfare state. In a series of writings,

Thomas Courchene (1980, 1987, 1994) has argued that the welfare state supplanted traditional sources of protection and support, such as the family and local communities, and politicized economic affairs. Moreover, the welfare state as it was built in Canada conferred a comprehensive range of generous social benefits and rights. According to this view of our history, social policy moved substantially away from selective programs to universal programs. Most significantly, this network of social programs assumed a life of its own because of the steady flow of tax revenues from the sustained economic growth of the 1950s and 1960s. Social policy making became detached from the discipline of the market and the imperative of wealth creation. Michael Walker, the director of the Fraser Institute, called the Canadian welfare state a fiction in that 'the state does not create welfare or wealth or economic production of any kind' (1985:21). An 'explosion' in the expansion of social programs was virtually costless in political terms, Courchene claims, because of the growing economy and fiscal surpluses. In addition, 'the nature of demands on government in the name of "social policy" altered rather dramatically' from economic security and human needs to economic compensation and human wants (Courchene 1987:8–9).[6]

Conservative critics emphasized that the good old days of easy growth were gone and social programs therefore had to adapt to a much different and harsher economic context. To quote Courchene (1987:11) again: 'The 1980s are very different form the 1960s. Productivity has been flat for the better part of the past decade, and unemployment has been unacceptably high. Fiscal deficits are nothing short of staggering. In addition, the world economy is anything but tranquil. Economies everywhere are restructuring, and the new world trading environment is becoming more, not less competitive.' As a consequence of these new economic, fiscal, and global realities, 'social policy has to facilitate and assist the occupational, industrial, and often geographic relocation that the new economics requires of the current generation of Canadians. We no longer have the luxury of designing social policy independently of the underlying economic environment.'

A second line of criticism by the Right was that the welfare state infringed upon personal freedom and created dependency. Some critics on the Right dismissed the welfare state on principle: governments have little or no place in regulating the economy, and social programs deter people from making choices about their own lives. The Fraser Institute created the idea of 'Tax Freedom Day,' reporting annually for each province how many days and months of the year an average worker's total income was needed to pay for all the taxes to all the various levels of government. In effect, the message was that for the first five or six months each year, Canadians' incomes were going entirely to the tax collectors. Taxes were portrayed as a necessary evil at best, the public confiscation of private wealth, and at excessively high levels. Walker described the welfare state as 'a coercive system of paying for things' (1985:35). Since taxation is mandatory and automatic, individuals do not get to decide if they will 'participate as sponsors of the welfare state.' Transfers of wealth through social programs are not voluntary nor personal in contact. Walker expressed doubt that people would willingly support the overall welfare state apparatus if they had the choice, and pointed to tax evasion and the growth of the underground economy as evidence of such resistance to tax burdens.

Critics from the Right asserted that welfare assistance encouraged people to rely on social programs rather than take care of themselves. Impoverishment came from pathological behaviours, part of a 'culture of poverty,' where the poor take on different values and norms from those of mainstream society. Anthropologists and sociologists writing in the 1960s used the concept of the culture of poverty to describe the *effects* of poverty on the beliefs and lifestyles of families and communities. Neo-conservatives over the next few decades used the term as a causal *explanation* of poverty. In its original meaning, the culture of poverty referred to the reaction and adaptation of people to high rates of unemployment and underemployment, low wages and lack of property, inadequate social benefits, and marginalization from mainstream social institutions and government agencies. A culture of poverty became the way of life for many of the poor caught in these structural features of the market economy and society. Those on the Right twisted the concept, arguing that a subculture of poverty with dysfunctional work values and family structures was created and perpetuated by the welfare programs themselves.

Welfare as a way of life was claimed to be transmitted from parent(s) to children as a result of repeated or long-term reliance on social assistance or unemployment insurance.[7] In the United States, more so than in Canada, neo-conservative writers blamed welfare for poor parenting and the breakdown of the traditional family, a weakening of the work ethic, and defeatist attitudes among the poor. Charles Murray (1984) argued that the rules governing availability of welfare made it profitable for the poor to behave, in the short-term, in ways that are destructive in the long-term. Murray claimed that the welfare system ignored three premises: that people respond to incentives and disincentives – sticks and carrots do work; that people are not inherently hardworking or moral – in the absence of countervailing influences, they will avoid work and be amoral; and that people must be held accountable for their actions (1984:146). By disregarding these premises, the welfare system created dependency.

In the late 1960s and early 1970s, a federal task force report on urban issues, and Senate committee reports on poverty and on aging demonstrated to the Right (and indeed to some other Canadians) the problems of the welfare system. The documents demonstrated that social housing produced ghettos, income maintenance programs failed the poor and reduced people's willingness to work, and public pensions encouraged citizens to spend and not save for their old age. But for neo-conservatives especially, the poor were seen as rejecting the work ethic, accepting instead a life based on handouts and transfer payments. When social policies are needed to address social problems, Right-leaning critics advocated selective benefits so as not to encourage people into welfare. Those arguing for limited government involvement believed in having the poor arm themselves for the future through educational and/or training programs. The poor needed to be forced into work by reducing social welfare benefits; the more stringent the benefits, the more rapidly people would return to taking care of themselves. Workfare in particular, and the emphasis on duties and obligations more generally, are favoured reforms by the Right to counter the welfare state's emphasis on rights and entitlements.

A third theme was the assertion that welfare programs should not be allowed to interfere with the economy and are an inefficient use of resources. Rightist critics rejected the notion of the state trying to create full employment, that by doing so the government disrupts the natural workings of the market, creating greater unemployment. For the capitalist system to work, workers must be obliged to sell their labour at the prevailing market price. In this way, the capitalist can use labour in the production of wealth. Neo-conservative critics maintained that governments spent vast sums of taxpayers' money without achieving many results; their evidence for this view was that welfare programs had not changed the living conditions of the poor, nor had large-scale programs affected the distribution of income in capitalist countries. The Right contended that the costs of social programs placed an unfair burden on taxpayers, creating disincentives for investment; encouraged people not to work; and that the structure of the programs allowed government to intrude upon people's lives in ways that threatened their liberty. Conservatives rejected many aspects of the welfare state: universal programs such as education and health care, as well as social insurance programs such as public pensions and employment insurance. The introduction of these kinds of social programs reduced the choices of individuals while simultaneously requiring massive tax burdens that undermined the economy's vitality. In essence, this was a public-burden model of welfare, with the Right depicting social policy expenditures as a drain on the productive capacity of the economy.

For Walker (1985:24), inefficiency was a central flaw of the Canadian welfare state in that 'of the income taken from them [the public] allegedly to support people whose means are less than their own, only one dollar in five is used to that end.' He contended that some Canadians at the poverty line were contributing to the support of other, more fortunate citizens, that the universality of income programs financed by general taxation results in the poor transferring some of their income through the tax system to the rich. Many health and social services, he argued, are inefficient 'because the government sector often operates under conditions of monopoly' and so 'there is no efficiency-inducing competition for the production of the service' (1985:35).

The social policy prescriptions offered by the Canadian Right in this period can be briefly summarized. Major reform of the welfare state was needed for economic, fiscal, and sociocultural reasons. At the core of this critique was the notion that social well-being can be furnished through deregulated markets in which individuals compete for jobs, income, and social status. Collective interests are undermined by the idea that competition is healthy and desirable. All collective action – unionization, consumer or community groups, environmental regulations – is seen as counterproductive to individual well-being. The boundaries of social policy and public intervention need to be reduced, and the content of social programming needs to move away from entitlements and towards assistance. The Right accepted some level of a safety net, but one far more residual than the social security system established during the 1940s through 1970s expansionist era. Income security programs required more targeting, and little if no universality of benefits. A selective, means-tested negative income tax (or tax credit) was considered a way to restructure the multitude of income programs.

The Right called for greater 'welfare pluralism' in the sense of retrenching the role of the federal government and public sector in social policy, while increasing the roles of the provinces, the market, the voluntary sector, and families (Courchene 1980, 1987; Walker 1985). In particular, the market was the sector which could be expanded in a number of ways: by introducing and increasing user charges for social services; by terminating certain public policies such as rent controls; by allowing private sector firms to enter the education field; by contracting out services in the health care field to firms; and by transferring public sector activities such as social housing to the private sector. In addition, social policy needed to be coordinated with, or even subordinated to economic, industrial, and trade policy considerations. In short, the Right was calling for a dramatic retrenchment of Canadian social policy in terms of programs, the overall system, and even the paradigm of the postwar welfare state. Courchene (1987:16) appreciated the controversial nature of this call, predicting that 'there will be organized resistance to these initiatives, at least initially, since they represent a turning back from the philosophy that dominated the expansionist era in Canadian social policy.'

Feminist Critiques

The emergence of second-wave feminism in the 1960s and early 1970s coincided with the final years of the expansionist era of welfare states in Canada and other countries. A crucial event and process in the Canadian context was the creation in 1967 of the Royal Commission on the Status of Women (RCSW), which reported in 1970. As Heather MacIvor (1996:80) notes, 'the commission travelled across Canada, listening to women in shopping malls and church basements as well as hotel ballrooms and legislatures. Women who read or heard about these meetings in the media were astonished to hear their own personal experiences in the words of others. The RCSW was a gigantic national consciousness-raising exercise. It helped to build a bridge between the older, more traditional feminists of the YWCA (Young Women's Christian Association) and VOW (Victoria Order of Women), and the younger, more radical feminists emerging from the campuses and the new social movements.'

The RCSW had several effects on the women's movement and the politics of social policy (Brodie 1995:42–4). It provided an agenda of issues and strategies for popular mobilization and policy advocacy by women, which continues today. It threw attention onto the state as the primary sector in society for addressing many of the concerns and claims of women for equality and equity. The RCSW provided a rationale for the formation of bureaus for women inside federal, provincial, and even some municipal public service bureaucracies. These included the establishment of the Canadian Advisory Council on the Status of Women within the federal government. The RCSW also prompted the formation and consolidation of women's organizations outside of government.

From 1972 to 1976, in what may be called the transition years between the expansionist and crisis phases of the welfare state, eight national women's organizations were established: the National Action Committee on the Status of Women (NAC); the Canadian Abortion Rights Action League; the Native Women's Association of Canada; the Canadian Teachers' Federation; the Canadian Association of Women Executives; the National Association of Women and the Law; the Canadian Research Institute on the Advancement of Women; and the Women's Bureau of the Canadian Labour Congress.

The NAC was created initially to track and assess the implementation of the RCSW's recommendations, particularly by the federal government. It evolved into a multi–issue, multi-perspective umbrella association for the Canadian women's movement, with 570 affiliated groups by the later 1980s (MacIvor 1996:328). In the 1980s, several other national women's organizations were formed, most representing the interests of various groups of minority women: the Congress of Black Women; the Canadian Congress of Learning Opportunities for Women; the Inuit Women's Association of Canada; the Disabled Women's Network; and the National Organization of Immigrant and Visible Minority Women (Burt 1994:213). There was, then, a growing organization and pluralization of feminist views in Canada.

In addition to the RCSW, events such as the International Women's Year in 1975 and the constitutional reform process of the early 1980s, in which, after considerable lobbying by women, a sexual equality clause was entrenched in the new Charter of Rights and Freedoms, mobilized and expanded the women's movement. Thus over the course of the crisis period, while the welfare state was coming under increasing attack, the women's movement grew in size, complexity, and influence. Marjorie Cohen (1992:217) recalls that 'in the 1980s government and employers had accepted women's intervention in issues like equal pay, maternity leave, and the movement of women out of traditional occupations. They also accepted our right to speak on daycare, reproductive choice, pornography – anything that could be seen as a women's issue.' Efforts, however, to speak out on issues beyond traditionally understood notions of social policy and women's issues, such as trade policy or fiscal and monetary policy, were challenged by governments and business interest groups as outside the expertise and mandate of women's groups.

Feminist critiques of the welfare state are but one part of a larger feminist analysis of all institutions of contemporary society: the community, the education system, the family, the legal system, the mass media, the political system, the religious orders, and the wage system of the labour force. Feminists argue that all social policies reflect stereotypes about family, the role of women, the raising of children, and the nature of relationships between men and women (Abramovitz 1988). The three themes from the feminist critique demonstrate this concern about stereotypes; the government's use of the policy process to marginalize women's issues, the way policies keep women 'in place,' and the way policy initiatives conceal gender issues by using apparently neutral terms.[8]

Feminists claim that governments develop most social programs in ways that marginalize women's issues by maintaining the dominance of patriarchal structures. In *Women and the Welfare State*, perhaps the first book approaching modern social policy from a feminist perspective, Elizabeth Wilson (1977:9) stated that 'social welfare policies amount to no less than the *state organization of domestic life*. Women encounter State repression within the very bosom of the family.' Wilson and other critics argued that welfare systems marginalize women within the social, political, and economic spheres (Williams 1989; Firestone 1979). Welfare policies encouraged women to assume roles based on reproduction and reproductive relations. As such, these policies heightened the importance of maternal relations based on birth, nurturing, and the rearing of children that are the crux of how welfare treats the family. In the political arena, the welfare system divided women into subgroups as defined by conditions of eligibility. Policies upheld specific categories: unmarried women, welfare mothers, divorced women, single women, and female lone parents. In the economic sphere, social policy reinforced the unequal division of labour in the workplace: women are not accorded the same rights and benefits as men; instead they are treated as a reserve of cheap labour (Abramovitz 1988).

When examining the marginalization of women's issues, feminist analysts asked who benefits from the dependence of women and the domestic division of labour. They explored the ways in which policies are used to support the relationship between patriarchal domination and capitalist social relations. Their critique provides a theoretical explanation of why the state supports such activities as child care for stay-at-home mothers, family benefit programs, and social assistance. Dorothy Miller (1990:21) suggested that 'social welfare's treatment of men primarily functions to uphold and serve the economy and its treatment of women, albeit not exclusively, in service to patriarchy.' This 'patriarchal necessity,' as Miller defines it, is the 'need among the collectivity of men to separate the sexes and devalue and control women.'

The second theme from feminist critiques is that many social policies function in a way that keeps women in place. Feminist writers criticized the traditional vision and practice of the welfare state, as well as the Left and Right, for downplaying or ignoring the position and experiences of women. Feminists pointed to how governmental welfare policies perpetuated the idea that women are caregivers, their primary role being that of mother and wife. Feminists believe that policy makers assume married women are dependent upon their partners – a construction of welfare that locked women into historical roles dependent upon male-dominated social systems. Feminist theory drew attention to, and then sought to challenge the ideology behind, and the practice of, the division between the public and private spheres of life. Men dominate the public domain, women the private domain. The private domain 'covers not only the process of bearing children, but also the physical, emotional, ideological, and material process involved in caring for and sustaining others – not just children' (Williams 1989:42). Social policies are one way for men to extend the public domain into the private one, thereby controlling women. Feminists noted that laws developed by men controlled the availability and use of contraceptives; male-dominated medicine controlled the process of childbearing and birth; educational systems structured the process of child rearing; and employment policies influenced women's relationships with the labour market (Pascall 1986:25).

A third theme concerns the gendered impact of language and problem formulation in policy making. Risks and needs of women were inadequately envisaged, if not totally excluded in some cases, in the postwar vision and development of the social security system. The social evil of abuse and violence against women needed to be added to the national agenda. Reproductive rights were a category of social citizenship that was then not part of mainstream social policy studies or political discourse. A national child care program went beyond the grand design of 1945 examined in Chapter 3; that is, it was not part of the Marsh Report or other government studies on the postwar reconstruction of Canada. The Keynesian welfare consensus was essentially a consensus among male-dominated institutions of government, business, and organized labour, with notions of full employment premised on a male breadwinner model of the family. Feminist thinking and advocacy did share with the postwar design, however, a state-centred conception of social care and provision.

Feminists have expressed scepticism about policy reforms that sought to shift responsibility for providing support from the government onto the family and community. Such activities hide the fact that shifting responsibility means placing the burden on women. When policies described 'home care' as an alternative to institutional care, feminists pointed out that they really mean low-paid or unpaid care by women. When policies suggested the expansion of 'community care,' it really meant that the burden is shifted back onto women. These seemingly gender-neutral descriptions of policy initiatives concealed the fact that the greatest burden within formal community or informal systems of care is borne by women. Concepts such as the 'welfare state' and the 'public interest' were seen to mystify the discriminatory impacts of social laws, transfers, and services on women. Similarly, feminists deplored classifications of social problems that disguised issues that affected women more than men. For instance the term 'elderly' – used in almost all social research – concealed the fact that most elderly people are women, especially over age eighty. Likewise, the term 'child abuse' also did not identify men as the major perpetrators. The terms 'domestic violence' and 'spousal abuse' also blurred the harsh reality of wife battering and male violence. Social policies that discussed 'lone parent' problems ignored the reality that these were, and still are, mainly women's families.

Second-wave feminism in Canada began challenging these ideas in the 1960s and 1970s. For feminists, new concepts and categories had to be developed that were inclusive, less hierarchical, and more sensitive to power relationships between men and women. Women's groups were no longer willing to be marginalized or kept in place by the development of social policy. Feminism demanded equal rights and opportunities, if not results, in the labour force, the law, politics, and the family. In contrast to the Right, activities by the women's movement called for a renewed and expanded welfare state.

Critiques from the Community

In relation to the welfare state and social policy, 'community' refers to formally organized groups based on a common place (locality) and/or a common interest (affinity/identity). Community groups associated with Canadian social welfare traditionally included charitable and philanthropic organizations, churches and other religious groups, co-operatives, service clubs, and social action groups. Starting in the 1960s with poverty groups and social planning councils, and increasingly through the crisis years of the welfare state, the array of community-based social service and policy groups expanded greatly. This expansion was prompted by social movement developments in the United States and domestic policy initiatives. These domestic initiatives included the Canadian war on poverty of the mid-1960s, including the 1966 Canada Assistance Plan (CAP), the 1967–70 RCSW, the 1969 official languages legislation, the misguided attempt at abolishing the Indian Act in 1969–70, the 1971 multiculturalism policy, community employment programs of the mid-1970s, the co-operative housing movement of the 1970s and 1980s, the 1977 Canada Human Rights Act, the 1982 Charter of Rights and Freedoms, and the 1986 Employment Equity Act. These federal government initiatives sought to address claims for social protection and/or cultural recognition.

During the crisis period of the Canadian welfare state, there were three major issues expressed by community groups: the failure of policy makers to recognize their differences and properly include them in policy development structures and processes; their alienation from mainstream professional service bureaucracies; and the inappropriate and inadequate conception of groups, their experiences, and their contributions to society and the economy.

Community groups come together to promote or resist change. They seek influence in the policy process so that new social initiatives can create equality fairness, or impartiality while attending to issues of diversity and difference. It is not uncommon for members of these groups to be hostile to professionals, whom, they claim, regulate the lives of those receiving benefits or services (Wharf 1979, 1990, 1992). These groups almost always find it difficult to directly influence policy making unless they can demonstrate significant political support.

Community groups interested in social policy were critical of the unwillingness of those in power to take their issues seriously – issues such as sexism, racism, homophobia, and the struggle of disabled people in the policy process. They argued that legislators failed to recognize the economic and cultural conditions under which groups of people live, and therefore failed to include those groups in policy making; as an example, gays and lesbians were routinely excluded from adopting children or receiving spousal benefits from government programs. Many community groups lacked formal representation in social policy processes, continually having to struggle to have their identities recognized and their views heard. Offe (1985) believes that many such groups spun off from existing interest groups and government structures because their communities were excluded in some way from the mainstream concerns of industrial growth and economic development. With less power and influence, new social movements lacked the clout of larger, more established interest groups, and their ambitions for recognition and support were constantly thwarted by the formal structures of the policy-making process. At times, this prompted more virulent attacks upon the legitimacy of that process – as exclusionary, racist, sexist, and homophobic.

A second major criticism from community groups was that the welfare state did not meet the needs of disadvantaged people. Governments failed in developing policies that took into account a whole array of new needs. Part of this critique centred on the bureaucratic structure of the welfare state, with its reliance on professionals, and centralized planning and control of services (Davies and Shragge 1990). For many groups, mainstream social policies provided general benefits that did not acknowledge adequately the diversity of populations in need of help from the social welfare system. Nor did these policies allow for the contradictory needs of different groups. People with developmental needs, for instance, have other requirements than those of their parents, who may be more concerned with security than with encouraging their children to live independently in the community. We return to this issue in Chapter 7.

Andrew Armitage describes an important social policy failure by Ottawa to institutionalize support for community social services, which certainly had consequences for community groups across the country:

> Towards the end of the 1970s an attempt was made by the federal government to consolidate this pattern [of community-based services] through the establishment of an overall framework for the financing of social services throughout Canada as part of the social security review. If it had succeeded, it would have established an institutional commitment to community social services as a Canadian citizenship right. It failed, however, partly for financial reasons (the first wave of financial restructuring) but also because of provincial opposition to the further extension of federal authority. It is also possible that these government social services were

beginning to be affected by the lack of informed community participation and by the alienation that their size and bureaucratization were causing. (1996:105)

Although a federal social services act had been agreed upon through intergovernmental discussions by 1976, and federal legislation tabled in 1977, this was withdrawn. So, too, was a subsequent federal proposal to replace the legislation with a block funding approach to social services. After five years of effort, financing for personal and community social services remained under the Canada Assistance Plan.

A third critical theme was that community groups generally conceived of social policies as interventions from above, that those with political clout were in a position to influence the policy process while those in the community had to accept policy dictates as they arrived (Lee and Raban 1988). Community activists in groups like the gay movement, civil liberties and human rights, anti-poverty, and anti-racist groups thought (and frequently still think) of themselves in constant struggle with dominant groups in society. The results of these criticisms from community groups led to a reconstruction of the way in which social problems were framed and talked about. Many deaf people no longer considered deafness a problem but rather a culture with its own language and means of communication. Gays and lesbians reconstructed their way of life as a right rather than a deviance from the norm. People with disabilities started taking control of the organizations that represented them, seeking to shift community understanding of disability away from the medical model towards a social one. Disability groups pointed out that an inability to walk, see, or speak was an impairment which only became a disability if there were barriers to access, no facilities to assist locomotion, nor technical aids to promote communication, that the impairment resides with the individual but the disability is an interaction between the individual and the community. Any disability, then, was reframed as a shared responsibility requiring community action as a human right (Prince 1992).

Community groups began to explore new work and income opportunities in response to growing unemployment, persistent poverty, and the crisis of the welfare state. As David Ross (1986:8–9) put it: 'At the centre of this crisis is the quality and quantity of employment opportunities. No longer able to assume that the traditional mixed economy can provide full employment and sustain welfare state activity at expected levels, we must now seek new ways to attain both full employment and provide income security. One promising avenue is local economic initiative.' Organizations like the Vanier Institute of the Family (1979) and the Canadian Council on Social Development (Cameron and Sharpe 1988), among others, explored the relation between the formal and informal sectors of the economy, the viability of community-oriented economic initiatives, and other concrete measures for job creation. Community groups also lobbied governments for stable funding of core administrative activities, plus advocacy, along with program and service provision functions.

Critiques from Insiders

'If we look more closely at the "crisis of the welfare state,"' Lois Bryson (1992:229) has written, 'we find that it by no means affects all sections of the population equally. The benefits and the advantages of the better-off have largely been maintained and even enhanced. Most of the belt-tightening has been done by those who are at the bottom of the social hierarchy.' With the rediscovery of poverty in Canada and other welfare states in the 1960s, early 1970s, and later in the 1990s, we could add that this is the same as it ever was.

The most morally damning, though not the most politically influential criticisms of the welfare state, came from within the system. People working close to or inside the social welfare system raised many concerns about the impact programs had on recipients. The insider's view provides a description of programs and services from the perspectives of front-line workers and recipients. It reflects personal views of the way the system actually operates for people. Unlike so-called expert perspectives on whether the system provided adequate compensation or sufficient protection, insiders' views described the way the system affected providers and clients, whether it allowed them to live a better life or forced them to live in degrading circumstances.[9]

People who receive welfare benefits know that Canadian social programs have made important differences to their lives. Employment Insurance, Workers' Compensation, Medicare, Old Age Security, provincial social assistance, and the Canada/Quebec Pension Plans improve the lives of people who receive benefits, but they have done so at a cost to these people. These costs are reflected in the three themes we examine from inside the system: the way social programs create stigma for recipients, the difficulty recipients have in dealing with the complexity of welfare programs, and the loss of hope that many people feel once they become part of the system.

In the first theme, social welfare programs have always tended to stigmatize recipients, largely because welfare support is seen as a sign of some deficiency in the recipient. Recipients feel they have been branded a failure, their reputation damaged by the process of becoming dependent upon the state. At a deeper level, becoming a welfare recipient creates feelings of shame. The amount of stigma a person feels depends upon the way social programs assess them for eligibility. Some programs, such as provincial social assistance, are based on needs, are highly selective, and therefore create the greatest stigma. Other programs, such as Employment Insurance, are based on contributions, and benefits are limited to those who pay premiums. People receiving these benefits feel they have a right to support and the programs are less stigmatizing, although there is still a negative connotation. Finally, there are programs such as Medicare, which are universal and available to all Canadians. These programs are the least stigmatizing.

The question Can we afford our social programs? has a stigmatizing ring to it. Those on social benefits increasingly heard it in the politically charged atmosphere of the welfare crisis politics of the 1970s and 1980s. It spoke to them of their value and the contribution they made to society. Every answer of No from the media, the business community, or taxpayers undermined the confidence recipients had in their own worth and ability. They not only thought badly of themselves but they thought badly of other welfare recipients. Every time they read the headlines 'welfare fraud' or 'welfare cheat' they felt like cheaters and fraud artists, even though they complied with every regulation. Similarly, every time they heard the phrase 'get a job' they were made to feel inferior and dysfunctional even though the unemployment rate was at 8, 9, 10 per cent or higher. The question of stigma changed as governments altered classification systems. An example was the reclassification of women with children as 'employable' in terms of social assistance benefits. Mothers, who once were thought of as contributing to society by caring for their young children, were now considered employable. Such changes altered the way such mothers were portrayed: they went from deserving government support to being considered dependent and in some ways undeserving. For those who were defined as employable but could not find work because there were no jobs or no available child care there was increased stigma.

A second theme raised by insiders concerned the level of complexity in the system. *Welfare in Canada: The Tangled Safety Net* (1987:16), a report by the National Council of Welfare, has documented 'a complex of rules to determine who would be eligible for social assistance, how much they were entitled to receive and how the status of recipients could be monitored on an ongoing basis.' In part, the complexity arose because of the piecemeal way the system had evolved. As Chapters 2 and 3 showed, governments developed new social programs, changed old programs, added or took away benefits, created new categories of recipients, and altered eligibility requirements. Not surprisingly, it became difficult to know who could or could not get benefits, or the level of support they could receive if they were eligible. Different jurisdictions continue to have different rules, and there is no uniformity in the system. Recipients and front-line workers struggle in understanding the maze of policies, rules, and procedures.

Michael Lipsky, in *Street-level Bureaucracy* (1980), examined the experiences and dilemmas faced by individual citizens and professional workers in schools, police departments, welfare and social work agencies, lower courts, and legal aid clinics. Lipsky's analysis was of the American welfare state, but it resonated with workers, clients, social policy academics, and advocates in Canada. Lipsky documented how legal aid lawyers, police officers, teachers, and social workers experienced work realities that imposed sharp limits on their aspirations and intentions as service providers and caregivers. The structure of their work typically involved top-down policy directives and hierarchical reporting requirements, large classes or caseloads and seemingly limitless needs, inadequate resources and insufficient time due to budget constraints and cutbacks, uncertainties of work methods, the unpredictability of clients, and constant pressures from the public. These work realities resulted in frustration and alienation by workers, if not burnout, because of inevitable gaps between personal and work limitations on the one side, and service ideals on the other. Lipsky found that workers developed survival mechanisms to cope with the pressures and gaps between the intentions and realities they confronted. Survival mechanisms included establishing routines and stereotypes of clients, simplifying problems and views of clients, and lowering their expectations of themselves and their clients to bridge the gap between work and service ideals.

For the consumers of these public services, there was a loss of individualized service. Citizens as applicants became clients who, in turn, became bureaucratic subjects. In many cases, front-line workers had to interpret the complex rules governing eligibility. It is only natural that these workers differed in their subjective assessment of a situation since the rules governing the case were so complicated. This gave the worker broad discretionary powers in deciding who would and who would not get benefits. This may 'enable the system to respond to individual situations and diverse local conditions ... [but] it also gives rise to inequities' (National Council of Welfare 1987:22). Many people requiring support from the welfare system, and this includes more than just social assistance, found applying confusing and difficult. They did not know where to go or what to ask. The system was structured so that if a person did not ask the right questions he or she could not get the right answers. People in similar circumstances were often treated differently depending upon who they asked and what they asked. Another example from *Welfare in Canada: The Tangled Safety Net* provides an insider's view: 'Now that I have a new worker, I walked in to see her two weeks ago. She said as she was handing me my support payments for the month: "You know, considering that you are unemployable, I don't think it's fair that you should take such a loss. I will go and talk to Mr. M." She left the office, came back and said, "You will get an additional $196." Now I had previously been denied that amount. I walk across the hall and I'm given it from another worker. These are rules I don't understand.' (1987:15)

The welfare system is not really a system. People living in the same conditions can be treated differently depending on where you go within it. Insiders and outsiders agree that there are no unifying principles that hold the programs together. While the government may appear to be providing income protection in one part of the program, it may be punishing recipients as a way of encouraging them back into the work force in another. It is not uncommon for people to find that one section of a program contradicts another. There are hundreds of social programs and laws in Canada, some offered by the federal government, others offered by provincial or territorial governments, still others by municipal governments, health boards, and school boards. Every program has its own set of eligibility criteria and one set does not seem to relate to another. Rather than a system functioning as a whole, it appears to many insiders as a bewildering hodgepodge of programs.

A third theme from the insider's critique concerned the lack of hope created by existing programs. Many clients and workers inside the system think welfare is a poverty trap. Two features contribute to making it a trap: first, the rules and regulations make it difficult to regain independence; and, second, people inside the system begin to feel despondent and lose hope of finding a way out. The basic rules for receiving welfare use a budget-deficit assessment method which calculates the differences between needs and the resources, including assets and income available to meet those needs. This assessment method assumes the person applying for social assistance, will deplete most or all of their assets before seeking help (depending upon the provincial regulations). To meet the requirements of such a process a person must be reduced to a state of impoverishment before they are considered eligible for income assistance. Once all of the resources are gone, it is difficult for welfare recipients to become self-supporting again. The level of benefits provided by social assistance, and regulations regarding how these benefits may be used, mean it is impossible to save enough to get off welfare.

In sharp contrast, in other segments of the Canadian welfare state through the 1970s and 1980s there was a growing militancy by associations and unions representing nurses, physicians, police officers, public servants, and teachers, among other professions and occupations. This trend underscored the power differences that existed between the insiders of the social policy system, specifically between clients (especially welfare recipients) and providers (especially human services professionals). In the health care system, for instance, public and political concerns were growing that extra billing by physicians and the increasing use of hospital user fees were threatening reasonable access to Medicare. These concerns led to studies by a federal Royal Commission in 1979–80, a parliamentary task force in 1981, and a task force by the Canadian Medical Association on the allocation of health resources. In a move to preserve universal health care, the federal government enacted the Canada Health Act in 1984, with all-party support in Parliament. The act consolidated earlier federal laws on hospital and diagnostic services and medical care passed in the 1950s and 1960s, and added a sanction of financial penalties to any provincial or territorial government which allowed hospital user fees.

Conclusions

The period from the mid-1970s to the late 1980s was the era of the 'crisis of the welfare state' in Canada and elsewhere. For some the crisis was the manifestation of inherent contradictions between capital accumulation and social legitimation. For others the crisis was about regulating the poor and blaming victims. For others still the crisis involved concepts such as culture of poverty and workfare and the impact of both. The welfare state in Canada became the object of considerable criticism by several segments of society, yet there were signs that not all was lost.

Indeed, there was some expansion in social provisions and in the number of policy stakeholders over this period. In the area of legislating and extending social rights, there was the enactment of the Canadian Human Rights Act and the Human Rights Commission, the entrenchment of the Charter of Rights and Freedoms in the Constitution, and the passage of the Employment Equity and Canadian Multiculturalism Acts. Yasmeen Abu-Laban (1994) has described the 1971–81 decade as an era of consolidation and the 1981–89 period as one of growth for the development of multiculturalism policy in Canada. On income security for seniors, the Spouse's Allowance program was introduced in 1975 and expanded in 1985, and the Guaranteed Income Supplement was enriched a number of times.

Within the social policy community, we have noted the creation of many new organizations and alliances. The crisis period also had some key defining events that resulted in social policy failures or marginal results. These included the ambitious but largely doomed Social Security Review of 1973–76, the aborted 1977 Social Services Act, and what was called the Great Canadian Pension Debate over the years 1979 to 1984, which yielded less than great reforms.

In a similarly positive way, the final report of the Royal Commission on the Economic Union and Development Prospects of Canada in 1985 rejected the view that the broad postwar consensus on social policy was disintegrating or seriously eroding. The commissioners did concede, however, that political consensus had weakened and ideological debate had become stronger (Canada 1985:577). There was general support from both the Left and Right for the basic principles of market economies; for the need to ensure that people lived healthy, secure lives; and for the provision of education and work opportunities. The critics disagreed, however, on the manner of achieving goals. The Left remained confident that the state could and should intervene in market activities in ways that ensured social justice and human rights. The Right opposed government interference in the workings of the market (save in exceptional cases) in the belief that markets provided the best method of ensuring welfare. Most of the perspectives, while critical of government's role in social policy, wanted the welfare state to be maintained or enlarged, even if reformed and reconfigured in some fashion. Through their critiques, many groups were actually widening traditional conceptions of social policy, with ideas on 'corporate welfare bums,' the informal economy, the hidden welfare system of tax benefits, and the message from second-wave feminism that the personal is political.

Despite the resiliency of the welfare system, political, business, and media elites increasingly interpreted the crisis as a fiscal crisis of the state. There was a rightward shift in the dominant discourse of politics and policy making generally towards promoting markets. Faith in the redistributive capacities of the welfare state declined. There was less agreement on the merit or feasibility of expanding government budgets on health and social service systems. It was argued that the state needed to expand, not constrain the market's role. Liberal and Conservative federal governments began acting as if social programs were a hindrance to economic growth and financial responsibility. Federal transfers to provinces for health and education were restrained. From about 1975 onwards, unemployment insurance programs underwent a succession of cutbacks. The indexation of the universal Family Allowance and Old Age Security benefits, was frozen or capped. Provinces began trimming welfare benefits, and minimum-wage rates were either not raised or only periodically, and then marginally so. In the early 1980s food banks began appearing in cities across the country. Ultimately the crisis was about (re)defining social policy in terms of how many resources should be allocated through the state sector, by what means, and to address what range and types of human needs and social issues.

We next examine at length the different ways that social policy and the welfare system are redefined and changed, and how the forces of globalization and pluralization affect the debate. For although the criticisms from the five main perspectives examined in this chapter deeply strained the underlying consensus upon which the welfare system was constructed, they were not the only forces at work. In hindsight, the crisis was also partly a turning point from the apparent completion of the postwar social policy agenda to the realization that longstanding problems of poverty remained. Looking to the future with the looming problems of globalization and pluralization only increased the concern about the form in which the welfare system would survive.

5

Response to the Crisis: Retrenching the Welfare State and Changing Responsibilities for Social Protection

In the 1990s, governments no longer took for granted their role as the dominant providers of social welfare programs. In response to growing criticism, and given the pressure of the forces of globalization and pluralization, all governments were reexamining their role and taking action. Some governments dismantled their welfare system by eliminating programs and services. Other governments maintained their systems by making incremental adjustments to programs and services. Still other governments remixed social policy, retrenching some parts of the system while leaving other parts relatively untouched (Mishra 1990b; Splane 1987:246). Here we examine the three broad policy strategies used by governments to respond to changing conditions, and how all three strategies have been used in Canada.

As these three strategies reflect the traditional classifications of welfare programs – residual, integrated, and institutional – we will use these terms to discuss the different strategies. Governments that dismantle their welfare systems are moving back towards a residual model of welfare. They want welfare systems that only come into effect as a last resort after the family and private markets fail to meet social needs. Residual welfare systems provide only temporary support in ways that do not confer social rights. Often these programs are means tested and provide only modest benefits. Governments that maintain most aspects of their welfare systems but want to deliver programs in new ways use an integrated model of welfare. They are interested in maintaining an integrated welfare system that uses benefits as a way of supporting their economy. While these governments wish to maintain a clear connection between the economy and the provision of social services, they are looking for ways to share the responsibilities with other sectors of society. Finally, governments that seek to maintain their welfare system as a central function of their society use an institutional model of welfare. These governments take an institutional approach by providing welfare as a right based on the notion of universal need. They consciously use the welfare system as an instrument for social inclusion and cohesion. Changes to social welfare systems can be categorized as primarily fitting into one of these policy responses and corresponding welfare models (although different types of changes may reflect varying degrees of conformity to the model).

Dismantling the Welfare System: Abandoning Policy Goals, Abolishing Programs, and Changing the Context

Dismantling the welfare system, the most severe response a government can make to the welfare crisis, is based on the assumption that government intervention no longer meets the goals for which it was designed. Governments wanting to dismantle their welfare systems must believe that the private sector, families, or the local community can provide social supports in a more effective way than the state can. These governments are turning to the private and nonprofit sectors to take responsibility for solving social problems. Canada, the United States, Britain, and Australia, among other nations, are introducing changes that are generally pushing their systems in residual directions. These countries are deregulating industry, opening trade, and eliminating or tightening existing welfare programs. There are three strategies that the government can use to dismantle the welfare state: programmatic retrenchment, systematic retrenchment, and paradigmatic retrenchment. We now examine each of them.

The first two strategies are described by Paul Pierson (1994). *Programmatic retrenchment* refers to cutting the size and expenditures of social programs, building greater restrictions into the design of programs, and generally shifting policies in a residual direction. This strategy involves direct assaults, in the short-term, on programs and services by cutting and eliminating them. *Systemic retrenchment* focuses on institutional and fiscal practices, but with longer-term effects on the politics and nature of the welfare state. Systemic retrenchment alters the broader political environment, including public opinion, interest groups, intergovernmental relations, and government finances, in ways that yield future cutbacks and a residualization of the social policy system. While Pierson sees this political environment as lying outside the welfare state, in Canada the welfare state is embedded in society and the economy. Because our society is fragmented and politicized, and our welfare state is federalized and dispersed, state and society are intertwined in many ways (Cairns 1986).

We add a third strategy of dismantling called *paradigmatic retrenchment*. This strategy involves weakening or dropping support for guiding principles that serve as the basis for policy action. As discussed in chapters 3 and 4, Keynesianism was a policy paradigm offering a rationale for state intervention in the economy and in society.

Whether the strategy is programmatic, systemic, or paradigmatic retrenchment, the goal of each is to eliminate considerable public responsibility for addressing social evils, needs, and risks.

Programmatic Retrenchment

As stated earlier, programmatic retrenchment refers to cutting the size and expenditures of social programs, building greater restrictions into the design of programs, and generally shifting policies in a residual direction. In Canada both federal and provincial governments have taken steps to dismantle or reduce large parts of their welfare systems and such programmatic retrenchment has had a serious impact on community organizations. Here we outline the cuts to social programs and how they affect community organizations, and we use the example of the deinstitutionalization of the mentally ill as an example of programmatic retrenchment.

The cuts to social programs have been both large – cutting entire programs – and small – abandoning certain aspects of programs. The large cuts, of course, have had the most impact. At the federal level, in 1993, Brian Mulroney's Conservative government eliminated the universal Family Allowance, claiming they had to fight the deficit. They replaced it with the income-tested Child Tax Credit and introduced the Working Income Supplement, consequently abandoning the principle that all families raising children, regardless of income, deserve recognition of this fundamental responsibility.

At the provincial level, the Conservative government of Ralph Klein in Alberta, in 1993, scrapped the existing social assistance program and introduced the Supports for Independence program, which stopped more than 54,000 people from receiving social assistance over the next four years (Azmier and Roach 1997). The new program forces people to use all other forms of support before they turn to the government for help. It is more difficult for people to get on the system and benefits are not allowed to exceed the earnings of low-income workers. The effects of these and other public expenditure cuts in Alberta has been to undermine public support for social programs (Taft 1997).

The Mike Harris Conservative government did much the same in Ontario. In 1993, it cut social assistance benefits by 21.6 per cent and then did away with General Welfare Assistance and the Family Benefits Programs altogether, replacing them with the Ontario Disability Support Program and the Ontario Works policy on workfare. These programs divide welfare recipients into the deserving and undeserving poor. By tightening eligibility requirements, increasing anti-fraud measures, and creating barriers to receiving welfare, the Harris government fundamentally altered the welfare system. For community activists and progressive scholars, the 'common sense revolution' of the Harris government has meant that Ontario is open for business but closed to people (Ralph, St-Amand, and Regimbald 1997).

Such large cuts to social programs are echoed in the many smaller steps the provinces have taken to dismantle welfare. In Newfoundland the government cut 200 seats it sponsored in adult basic education. Alberta has dismantled its school-bus inspection process and turned the responsibility over to the owner/operators. In British Columbia 27,000 people were removed from their unemployable list unless those individuals could obtain special needs status by providing evidence that they were mentally or physically unable to work. Ontario cut the Advocacy Committee, which provided advocacy for psychiatric patients. In Nova Scotia the government reduced transportation allowances, prescription drug co-payment charges, and clothing allowances for those on welfare, and reduced child care allowances for disabled and single-parent students (Fay 1997:92).

Whether through large or small cuts, government dismantling has profoundly affected community organizations. The cuts have reduced the capacity for voluntary agencies to provide services. A study carried out in Metropolitan Toronto in 1995 asked 1,862 community-based agencies how government cuts were affecting their plans and programs. The agencies reported that 106 programs were likely to be eliminated in 1996 and 301 were under review for cancellation (Kitchen 1996:165). The termination of these health and social service programs weaken a community's capacity to respond to social problems.

In addition to reducing the service provision capacity of voluntary agencies, funding cuts have had at least four other serious consequences:

they have weakened the infrastructure, debilitated communication, forced commercialization, and drowned the political voice of these agencies. First, cutbacks often result in the loss of a paid position for managing volunteers, squeezing the already limited infrastructure of most agencies and weakening their ability to recruit, train, and oversee a group of volunteer staff. Thus the entire infrastructure that the voluntary agency is based upon is weakened. Second, cuts in grants can increase competition for funding within the voluntary sector, with agencies chasing a limited number of donors, corporations, and foundations; agencies thus may become less apt to share information and ideas with other groups in their community. Third, community agencies can experience the commercialization of their activities and even their mission, by the introduction of user fees and market pricing for services and goods they provide, putting them perhaps in direct competition with private sector organizations. Such commercialization undermines the foundations the voluntary organizations were built upon. Fourth, in cutting grants to voluntary groups, governments have typically targeted non-service functions such as advocacy activities and administrative support for federations and umbrella associations. This effectively reduces the ability of community groups to network and engage in democratic politics, drowning the agency's political voice. Consequently, the future role and vitality of the voluntary sector in Canada is in some doubt, like love in a cold world (Browne 1996). These serious consequences expose the long-standing myth that voluntarism is independent of government support.

The cutting of welfare programs has long historical roots. Canadians had their first hint of what could happen when governments dramatically altered social policies affecting people with mental illnesses. What began with the best of intentions after the publication of *More for the Mind*, by James Tyhurst, in 1963 turned into the deinstitutionalization of large numbers of seriously mentally ill people. The deinstitutionalization process, which included the closing of psychiatric institutions, discharging patients, and preventing new admissions was meant to move people out of institutions and into the community (Piat 1992:202). In the late 1960s and early 1970s, governments in Canada closed about three-quarters of inpatient beds for people with mental illnesses (Trainor, Pape, and Pomeroy 1997). Patients were shifted to local hospitals and outpatient care, and for many, this meant abandonment. Over time, many could not find a place to live and were slowly pushed onto the city streets. Myra Piat (1992:204) points out that poor housing conditions, financial problems, ghettoization, and dependency on drugs has resulted in the emergence of recent social problems such as increasing numbers of homeless persons and the incarceration of psychiatric patients within the criminal justice system. For those who could find housing in the large boarding houses, it turned out to be not too different from the large institutions, except that they had much less service and no protection from institutional abuse (Murphy, Pennee, and Luchins 1972).

Dismantling programs and services for people who had been deinstitutionalized encouraged the private sector to respond by providing profit-making residential services. Provincial governments allowed the private sector maximum flexibility in developing and operating lucrative boarding homes in which the mentally ill were housed. Governments also encouraged the private sector to keep the boarding houses self-regulating and out of the public domain. The deinstitutionalization of people with mental illness also had a profound effect on the community. Community groups were not consulted, informed, or educated in preparation for the arrival of people who were discharged from institutions (Piat, 205). The community response has been documented by Michael Dear and Jennifer Wolch (1987), who describe the emergence of the 'not in my back yard' (NIMBY) syndrome. This response reflects the deep concern people have about social problems being pushed back into the community. Negative attitudes about government downloading have come to infect every social issue, from developing accommodations for low-income people to providing services for the homeless. Every issue now faces NIMBY resistance as community members express their fear of changes to their local communities.

Systemic Retrenchment

Focusing on institutional and fiscal practices, systemic retrenchment measures 'alter the broader political economy and consequently alter welfare state politics' (Pierson 1994:15). Within this type of retrenchment – which happens primarily at the federal level – governments try to dismantle the welfare system by weakening the policy context in which social policies are made. Here we will outline the different ways that various countries have weakened policy-making process, and explore how such activities take place.

The British governments of Margaret Thatcher did so by weakening the labour union movement. Thatcher introduced legislation that limited the unions' ability to represent workers, and fought unions by supporting plant owners during important strikes (Marsh 1991:301). The British government also deregulated the labour market by introducing eight employment acts with the intent of changing working conditions and increasing the influence of market forces (Pratt 1997:49).

The American administrations of Ronald Reagan changed the context of social policy making by limiting the amount of money governments could borrow to support welfare programs. At the same time, the government lowered taxes on high income earners, leading to a reduction in revenue which put increased pressure on paying down the deficit (White and Wildavsky 1989).

In Canada the Mulroney and Chrétien governments changed the context of social policy by limiting the amount of financial support the federal government gave the provinces for health care, post-secondary education, social services, and social assistance programs. They also then turned a number of cost-shared programs into block grants, thereby limiting the growth of welfare programs. By changing the context of social policy, governments do not appear to be attacking the welfare system directly; nonetheless, such actions undermine the conditions for making social policy.

On the whole, dismantling the welfare state is publicly controversial and therefore politically difficult. Every program develops constituents over time, people with commitments to existing programs and prepared to lobby to ensure that their programs survive. Clientele receive direct benefits from the existence of the programs, while those who seek to dismantle them have only indirect benefits, such as a small reduction in taxes. Even the most strident anti-welfare writers recognize that people support existing systems, and governments face deep political resistance if they attempt dramatic change. David Marsland (1996: 159) suggests hiding the fact that the welfare system is being dismantled. He believes dramatic change would create a political backlash that would stop governments from using this strategy. Rather, he suggests, the dismantling must be phased in so that people have time to save enough to pay for what they need and adjust to the changes. That, in our view, is a flawed strategy, because how can those who have no money save it?

Governments wanting to hide policy changes often alter the way policy decisions are made. When the Conservative government in

Ontario began dismantling the welfare system, they chose a path that would allow them to conceal what they were doing. The Social Assistance Reform Act, which came into effect in 1998, gave the provincial cabinet sweeping powers to make radical changes without going through legislative review, public input, or appeal (Torjman 1997a). The law gives cabinet the power to make regulations concerning every detail of the new welfare system, from determining eligibility criteria to setting benefit levels. The Ontario government can now govern through regulation rather than legislation across a broad welfare front, assuming a vast array of powers while limiting public scrutiny. The result is to avoid community input and remove from the legislature any ability by the public to directly influence the retrenchment agenda. Governments can also restructure the policy domain by shifting the *level* at which decisions are made. In countries with federated states it is possible for the central government to either centralize or decentralize authority depending upon which tactic will help achieve their goal. By shifting decision-making responsibilities (and blame) for cutbacks to local administrators, it is more difficult for future governments to coordinate welfare interventions and/or introduce social policies.

Paradigmatic Retrenchment: Abandoning the Goal of Full Employment

Paradigmatic retrenchment involves lowering support for the underlying principles guiding policy development. Probably the most important case of welfare state dismantling has been the abandonment of 'full employment' as a central goal of public policy. The goal of full employment was closely associated with Keynesian thinking, the dominant paradigm in macro-economic policy, and a major influence on social security policy from the 1940s to the 1970s. Maintaining full employment means the government will adopt fiscal and economic policies to foster job creation and community development; it will also spend tax money on programs and services or capital expenditures to keep people employed during economic slumps, and on education and training. By ensuring a high level of employment, governments offer opportunities and hope, and reduce demands on the welfare system. Once a government abandons the idea of full employment, it allows the forces of the market to determine the level of unemployment.

We need to understand the potential meaning of the goal of full employment, and not simply lament the passing of the historical expression of a policy. During the era of envisaging and establishing the welfare state, the idea of full employment in Canada was actually spoken of by government leaders in terms of 'high and stable levels of employment.' In practice, this referred to full-time paid work for men, with the expectation of a career or job mobility in relatively secure industrial and resource sectors of the economy. *Even in the expansionist era of social welfare, Canada's policy commitment to full employment rested on residualist thinking;* that is, employment was, first and foremost, to be generated by the market economy. The role of government was to create a favourable climate for business, introduce public works projects when the economy slowed or slumped, and have in place public welfare and unemployment insurance programs as safety nets. While a full employment policy was only partially pursued by Canadian governments, through the 1950s and into the 1970s a range of programs, laws, and institutions was established which accompanied and supported economic growth, rising incomes, and tax bases, and a growing standard of living (Campbell 1987; Gonick 1987, McBride 1992).

During the crisis period of the 1970s and 1980s, in the face of a global oil-price shock, along with rising inflation and no growth simultaneously troubling economies, the Right effectively challenged the belief that national governments could manage their economies and maintain a policy of full employment. The goal of full employment dropped off the platforms of Liberal and Conservative political parties as well as the agendas of successive governments in Ottawa. The official discourse of policy makers and most mainstream economists increasingly spoke of a natural rate of unemployment. Definitions of what constituted full employment in the Canadian economy continually lowered the target from 97 to 95 to 93 per cent or lower, of the labour force, as the average rate of unemployment for each decade continually rose.

In the contemporary economy the world of work has changed, and so must the concept of full employment. The Commission on Social Justice has written, 'in the 1990s and beyond, it will involve for both men and women frequent changes of occupation, part-time as well as full-time work, self-employment as well as employment, time spent caring for children or elderly relatives as well as or instead of employment, and periods spent in further education and training. Forty years ago the typical worker was a man working full-time in industry; today the typical worker is increasingly likely to be a woman working part-time in a service job' (1994:154). We examine these trends and their implications for gender and communities in Chapters 8 and 9.

Social Economy of Welfare: Remixing the Provision of Social Care

The mixed or social economy of welfare describes an old practice with a new name. The old practice where social welfare programs are delivered by government agencies, nonprofit organizations, and private corporations (see Chapters 2 and 3) is now referred to as the mixed, or social, economy of welfare. This approach has been used in varying degrees in all liberal-democratic countries. Germany, France, Netherlands, and Italy are currently taking this middle-of-the-road approach to welfare change. Their approach has focused on managing the labour supply through early retirement while keeping their commitment to major welfare programs.

Governments moving to a mixed welfare approach generally believe that welfare systems provide important supports to the economy. They want to alter the provision rather than destroy the principle of the existing system. They believe there are better ways of delivering programs and services than just public sector agencies. In taking this approach, governments assume the social welfare system will work more effectively if there are other organizations involved in developing and delivering programs. Policy makers therefore seek to forge new linkages and expand on existing partnerships with other sectors of society. Governments can mix welfare programs and services between the different sectors in a number of ways. All such tactics entail the changing and sharing of responsibility for welfare between governments and other sectors of society.[1] Here we look at two primary ways that a mix is attained: by changing the governing body responsible and by contracting out with other sectors. But first, a quick look at the different domains within the Canadian mix will help us understand how the mixed economy of welfare works.

The term 'mixed economy of welfare' captures the pluralistic nature of the provision of social benefits and the allocation of resources. In the mixed model of welfare within Canada there are five primary domains: the public sector, the voluntary sector, the private-for-profit sector, the Aboriginal sector, and the informal sector of families and local communities. Each sector has different attributes. In the public sector, benefits and services are normally funded through the general tax system and provided by public servants working in government agencies. In the voluntary sector, programs are normally funded through government grants and fundraising and provided by employees and volunteers who work in community-based organizations. Private-for-profit organizations obtain funding through contracts with the government to provide services, or from user fees paid by people receiving services. Employees work in privately owned organizations. It is assumed that private organizations offer more choice to consumers and tend to be more efficient and responsive to demand. The sphere of Aboriginal communities, First Nations governments, and urban organizations are of growing importance in social policy and politics more generally, and are funded in large part by federal and provincial governments. In the informal sector, benefits and services are funded through personal contributions of family and friends, and delivered on an interpersonal basis. Such a variety provides social programs with some resilience, but, as we will see, the pressure placed on some of these domains by the restructuring of the government has jeopardized these same domains.

Towards a New Social Union: Changing Which Government Is Responsible

A clear example of seeking ways to remix responsibility for welfare is reflected in the intergovernmental discussions and negotiations now taking place over Canada's social union, that is, a shared political view of social purpose and citizenship.[2] The 1995 federal budget announced a 25 per cent cut in transfers to the provinces and territories for health, education, and social welfare. In response, the Provincial Ministerial Council on Social Policy Reform and Renewal prepared a report on behalf of the provincial premiers and territorial leaders setting out a framework for 'rebalancing the federation' and welfare state. The Provincial Council made recommendations about health care, post-secondary education, social services, labour market programs, and arrangements for financing the system. The provinces wish to have greater control over social programs and increased access to cash transfers and tax points. They wish to have a clearer picture of who is responsible for different parts of the welfare system. In addition, the provinces want to institute a way of limiting federal involvement in provincial program areas. At the same time, they want an agreement on how the federal government could take responsibility for all programming for Aboriginal people. Such claims reflect the changing politics of social policy and current discourse, arguing for more authority on welfare flowing to provinces.

A Social Union agreement was signed in 1999 by the federal government, nine provinces and two territories (but not Quebec). The new union is to promote equality, universality, and affordability by removing barriers to participation in post-secondary education, training, health and social services, and social assistance. The federal government is to respect the priorities of provincial and territorial governments for cost-shared or block-funded programs. It is also to consult with other governments about funding changes or social transfers one year in advance of any changes, and the federal government will not introduce changes without getting the consent of a majority of provincial governments. Provincial and territorial governments are allowed to invest program funds in ways that reflect the spirit of the new programs and will receive their share of the funding. All levels of government will review the Social Union framework after three years.

At the same time that the provinces are striving to gain more financial resources from Ottawa, they are looking for ways to share the responsibility of social welfare with municipal governments and community organizations. Peter Clutterbuck (1997:70) claims that the 'devolution of responsibility to the municipal level of government and local communities has been a driving force of public policy in the 1990s.' While the process of shifting welfare responsibilities downward moves it closer to the community, it raises important questions about how the welfare system will be financed. Municipalities and related local bodies, such as school boards and library boards, are under considerable pressure to cut services and lower existing service standards; to avoid or minimize property tax increases; and to contract out higher-cost service responsibilities to the lowest bidding commercial operators.

The political implications for the devolution of welfare programs from federal to provincial, and in turn from provincial to municipal governments, have deeply fragmenting effects. As the social policy system is devolved, it is harder to maintain standards across the country or across a province. Larger and richer jurisdictions are able to afford better and broader services. Where governments cannot provide the services, voluntary and private sector organizations are invited to participate. This opens the system up to the development of services, which some people can afford and others cannot. Clutterbuck predicts that devolution will create two-tier systems in health and education and three-tier systems in the social services. In health and education, the devolution will lead to private hospitals and charter schools for the well off and poorly funded public hospitals and schools for the rest. In the social services, there will be high-end market services responding to the ability of the well off to pay for what they need, lower-quality public services for the middle classes supported by regressive taxes, and low-end community services for the impoverished and destitute provided by voluntary agencies supported by charity.

Contracting-Out Service Provision

In addition to sharing and devolving responsibility for welfare programs, governments are remixing their social policy systems by contracting with nonprofit and private organizations to provide services. Contracting represents a transfer of property rights and obligation to a nonprofit or private organization (Hirsch 1991). The contracting process establishes the activities to be performed, the goals that should be reached, and the clients that should be served. When governments use contracting as a way of creating a mixed economy of welfare they do not relinquish responsibility for welfare but rather create partners in delivering services. As an example, instead of creating nursing homes for the elderly, hiring the staff, and offering the services, government contracts with a nonprofit or private organization to provide the services. Government continues to finance the services in full or in part, but does not directly provide them.

Contracting out provides governments with flexibility in redesigning the welfare system. Governments can enter into contracts with limited time frames, clearly identified goals and objectives, specified outcomes, and with a clearly established cost. Contracting allows a government to develop relationships with many providers offering service in local communities and meeting local needs. By calling for proposals, governments hope to create competition between potential providers. In this way, they should be able to get the best service at the lowest cost. The difficulty is that contracting may bring costs down but it does so by allowing contracting agencies to pay lower wages than government departments, and offer fewer occupational benefits and less job security. This has important implications for gender equality, since most workers in contract agencies in the health and social service fields are women.

Private providers are not limited by regulations in the same way public agencies are. As an example, when the government operates a housing program, the public agency must take into consideration the composition of the family when providing accommodations: the state must ensure for instance that there are private bedrooms for male and female children over a certain age. The private sector faces none of these regulations. It can rent housing to a family without knowing anything about its members. Similarly, when a local government provides home care it must protect staff from potential risks and clients from potential abuse. When the informal sector provides the same services, it is assumed that the conditions will be safe because they are provided by family members or friends.

Does remixing the provision of social services away from the state to other sectors constitute retrenchment? This question is too infrequently asked, but needs to be asked in the new politics of social policy. A comment by Mishra (1990b:111) offers a way to explore the issue of welfare pluralism: 'It is one thing to decentralize and privatize service delivery in such a way that entitlement is not weakened. It is quite another to privatize, that is, withdraw public services and public commitment to maintaining standards, without underwriting entitlement or ensuring that equity considerations are met.' The reallocation of service delivery clearly has implications for gender relations, the quality of employment and workplace benefits in sectors, the actual capacity of sectors to undertake the tasks, and for national or provincial standards in social programs. We consider these matters in the chapters that follow.

Maintaining the Existing System

The Nordic welfare states of Sweden, Denmark, Norway, and Finland are working hard to sustain their welfare systems. They have kept public employment high while maintaining the vast majority of their welfare programs.[3] By maintaining the status quo, governments deal with the threats to the system by making incremental modifications to programs. The system is essentially kept intact. This strategy is based on three premises. First, the strategy assumes that in order for capitalist economies to develop there must be a system of underlying supports that allow change to take place without destroying the basic social structure; the welfare system provides these important stabilizing mechanisms. The second premise is that market failures create many social problems that only social interventions can address. With the markets' tendencies to create inequality and social unrest, welfare programs must counterbalance the markets in order to maintain social integration. The third premise is that if liberal democratic governments want to keep the political support of low- and middle-income families, they must redistribute resources through their welfare systems. Without social interventions to reallocate resources, the standard of living of the majority of citizens will slowly but continually fall, leading to political turmoil.

Some writers have developed an 'irreversibility theory' of social rights (Mishra 1990b:32). The irreversibility thesis is based on the notion that welfare systems have been created on the bases of contributions from workers who then have a proprietary claim on benefits. The interlinking of contributions and income protection provided through the welfare system creates important structural supports for capitalism. Michael O'Higgins (1985) suggests that governments, even strong neoconservative ones, have difficulty abolishing existing social insurance systems. The irreversibility theory is not based on the notion that the system will remain the same as long as there are liberal democratic states. Rather, the fundamental structures of welfare – income protection, social insurance, services for meeting basic needs, and measures for preventing and relieving poverty – will remain essential ingredients of democratic societies.

The welfare system may be pushed in one direction by the neoconservatives, only to build deep resistance leading to a counter push in the other direction by the political centre-left. While the welfare system may exist in contradiction to market activities, each has a contribution to make to the well-being of the population. Many aspects of the welfare state are resilient. Welfare programs stopped many people from falling into destitution during the economic roller coaster of the 1980s and 1990s. People were protected from the worst aspect of economic change, and families were not destroyed nor entire communities decimated as they had been in the Great Depression. John Myles and Paul Pierson (1997) point out that while there have been similarities in the policy shifts between Canada and the United States, Canada has offset the rising inequalities in labour market incomes by providing social transfers. The result has been a stable level of the incidence of poverty in Canada and an increasing incidence in the United States.

The resiliency of the welfare state, or at least certain kinds of social policy, may also be due to people's suspicions about free markets. Many Canadians are inherently wary of the marketplace and 'free enterprise.' The notion of caveat emptor (buyer beware) and the thought that private enterprise exists only to make a profit at a cost to the paying public, are longtime hindrances to the dismantling of the welfare state. Relatively few people in Canada want their families to be cared for by someone who is making a profit at it, especially if the profits result in poorer services than those offered by voluntary or public sector organizations. Besides, almost everyone who understands the workings of the market believes the economy cannot and will not protect them from the risks created by a changing society. People who look back in history, before the introduction of the welfare state, see what happened to individuals and families during the dirty thirties. Social inequalities were vast; families were impoverished if the bread-winners became unemployed or fell sick; a visit to the hospital could lead to economic ruin; and the provision of relief was demeaning and coercive. Few people, if given the choice, want to return to those days.

Changes to Canadian Social Policy

Different social programs and policy areas have experienced different fates. As accounts of the changes the Mulroney and Chrétien govern-ments have made to Canadian social policy are readily available in the literature, we need only summarize these changes.[4] A substantial amount of Canadian social policy has suffered from retrenchment. With respect to paradigmatic retrenchment, we have noted the abandonment of the goal of full employment and Keynesianism as particularly significant, a topic we return to in Chapter 6. Another important example, examined in Chapter 7, is the elimination of the idea of universality as a central principle and technique in the income security system for families with children, and for seniors. Still another is the termination of the Canada Assistance Plan (CAP), representing the end of at least a forty-year commitment by the federal government to play a direct and specific role in funding social assistance in association with the provinces. All these changes illustrate in concrete terms what is meant by the weaken-ing of the social consensus underpinning social policy in Canada.

With respect to systemic retrenchment, public opinion remains sup-portive of many social programs and services, such as education, Medi-care, and equalization payments for the have-not regions of the country. The vast majority of Canadians reject calls for the privatization of the Canada Pension Plan or for the formal adoption of a two-tier health care system. In the later 1990s the general public expressed concern that governments went too far and too fast in reducing deficits, and that additional social spending is needed in critical areas such as child poverty. Public beliefs and claims are shifting, however, given the rise of new social movements and the discourse of diversity. Both the Mulroney and Chrétien governments weakened interest groups within the social policy community by cutting funding, calling into question their representativeness and expertise, and not heeding their voices and ideas in policy consultation processes such as the Social Security Review. The discourse of fiscal restraint and the claim of death-by-deficit (McQuaig 1995) seriously constrained the role and effectiveness of client and advocacy groups.

A distinctive feature of the Canadian version of retrenchment over most of the 1980s and 1990s was the extent of tax increases. Successive Conservative and Liberal federal governments did not 'defund the welfare state' (Pierson 1994) by restricting revenue flows to itself for financing programs and debt charges. Canadian governments instead sought to strengthen their fiscal capacities and stabilize their revenue sources.[5] The partial indexation of income tax brackets and numerous social benefits have allowed revenues to increase through inflation, a process dubbed social policy by stealth (Battle 1990). This process is linked closely with the centralization of power in federal decision-making structures within the Department of Finance, a topic we examine in the next chapter.

Where the federal government has defunded social policy is in sharply and unilaterally cutting back transfer payments to the provincial and territorial governments. For most of these governments, transfer payments are vital sources of revenues for financing education, health, income support, and other public services. The introduction of the Canada Health and Social Transfer (CHST) in 1996 dramatically altered the way welfare budgeting and policy making takes place. The CHST also fragments or disperses access points for welfare groups and poverty advocates across the country (Rice 1995b). The move away from CAP, a conditional cost-sharing arrangement for income assistance and social services, to the CHST, a far less conditional and smaller block fund, is a fundamental change in the systemic features of the country's social policy. To date, the federal government has resisted provincial demands, expressed through the Premiers' Council and other fora, to change the way such decisions are made; for example, how the principles and standards of Medicare as contained in the Canada Health Act are interpreted and enforced. The provinces want to develop in cooperation with Ottawa a new approach to the use of the federal spending power to avoid future acts of federal unilateralism, which inevitably generate conflict. In turn, much of the intergovernmental politics of social policy over the next decades will focus on provincial-municipal and municipal-community relations, especially in the metropolitan centres of Montreal, Toronto, and Vancouver, where one-third of all Canadians and the majority of immigrant, refugee, and visible majority populations are located.

Programmatic retrenchment – the erosion of benefits, the contraction of program designs, and the imposition of burdens – is easily seen in a range of benefits, programs, and services at all levels of government. There have been repeated and dramatic cutbacks in employment insurance and income assistance; reductions in spending on post-secondary education, Medicare, social housing, old age benefits, family benefits, and retirement and disability benefits under the Canada Pension Plan; the introduction of workfare and user fees; and public employee wage freezes. As Frank McGilly (1998:247) has written, 'such coast-to-coast, across-the-board restraint in social programs constitutes a critical juncture for social policy in Canada.' Although some of these restraint measures were negotiated and consensual in their introduction, most were imposed by governments and were highly conflictual, and a number were imposed in a stealthy or hidden manner. One measure of this restraint is shown in total program spending by the federal government as a share of the Gross Domestic Product (GDP). Federal expenditures on all programs and services has declined from about 20 per cent of GDP in the early 1990s to less than 12 per cent by the end of the decade, the lowest share since the building of the social security system began in the 1940s. Retrenchment, then, in its three forms, has been and remains a major trend in Canadian social policy.

Remixing the provision of services and programs is a secondary theme being pursued through contracting out; deinstitutionalization; devolution from one level of government to another, and the transfer of lands, funds, powers, and programs to Aboriginal governments. Remixing the welfare state also results from the restraint of public programs, such as old age benefits and pensions, putting the onus and opportunity on personal and private sector measures for retirement savings. The number of emergency shelters, food banks, and soup kitchens across Canada are consequences of the retrenchment of public programs and changes to the market economy.

Several components of the welfare state endure: universal health care, universal education at the elementary and secondary school levels; workers' compensation programs; veterans' benefits; income supplements for seniors; and provincial taxation and shelter assistance programs. The constitutional entrenchment in 1982 of the Canadian Charter of Rights and Freedoms was an important development for citizenship and politics in the midst of the crisis era. The domains of social policy based in the workplace and in the tax system are often overlooked in discussions of the welfare state, but they are important determinants of welfare, and they display continuity. Occupational welfare benefits, which are discussed in Chapter 8, have largely been maintained, and, in some cases, expanded. Furthermore, there is a multitude of tax expenditures in the personal and corporate income tax systems, as well as in the GST, which have been maintained or even enhanced. Such provisions result in foregone revenue for the public purse and therefore represent spending through the tax regime. Some occupational and fiscal provisions are for social policy purposes, others for economic interests; some are progressive, while others are regressive in their impacts on income and wealth distribution, subverting the reduction of inequalities.

Conclusions

In response to the crisis of the welfare state, governments have adopted various strategies. One approach is to dismantle social welfare systems through paradigmatic, systemic, or programmatic forms of retrenchment. A second approach has been to remix the social economy of welfare by seeking partnerships with other sectors. The third approach has sought more or less to maintain existing systems by focusing on incremental adjustments to policies and programs. Elements of all three approaches have been implemented in Canada.

The continuation of health, education, and other social programs leads some writers to conclude that, despite the efforts of neo-conservative governments, the welfare state is 'largely intact' (Mishra 1990b:14; Pierson 1994:179). Richard Gwyn (1996:83, 91) has said, 'It would be too strong to say that Canadians are entering a post-welfare state era. Medicare and unemployment insurance will be reduced, but they will always be with us ... we've gone through the "sound barrier" of the near-depression of the early 1990s with our egalitarian ideal, and a fair amount of its substance, still intact.'

It is true that some of our social programs are politically durable and have experienced less than radical changes. Many policies and programs, however, have undergone fundamental transformation, as have the paradigmatic and systemic features of the welfare state. As a guiding approach for policy makers, the Keynesian welfare consensus has declined deeply if not virtually disappeared from governmental agendas. The maintenance and expansion of the welfare state is no longer an article of faith among political parties. In the current era, all the main-stream political parties are socially conservative in their outlooks, with weak commitments to social planning, redistribution, and job creation. We would also argue that the cumulative impact of the incremental cuts and reductions over the past fifteen years have resulted in a major change. Social safety nets are now badly frayed and lower to the ground. Welfare caseloads hit record levels in the 1990s. The labour force is polarizing in terms of the availability, quality, and security of jobs. In the face of these risks and retrenchments, as well as the forces of globalization and pluralization, communities and social movements are striving for new forms of inclusion and protection.

6

Global Capitalism and the Canadian Welfare State: Impacts of Economic Integration, Fiscal Policy, and Market Liberalism on Social Policy

Classically, Canadians have viewed social programs as modifying the play of market forces, offering extra-market allocations, and protecting people inside and outside the labour force. Social welfare values were asserted over economic ones. During the building of the postwar welfare state, social policy was commonly distinguished from economic policy in terms of its goals of building identities and fostering community and integration, as well as making changes in the structures of society and the distribution of market-generated incomes. Welfare theorists (Titmuss 1968) referred to state welfare as a social market distinct in aims and standards from the economic marketplace. Under Keynesian economics, the social and economic markets were linked in a compatible manner, with social spending serving an important role in stabilizing the economy and promoting growth. Even in the debates of the 'crisis of the welfare state,' no one could dispute that the welfare state did in fact intervene in economic affairs and vary market forces. The debate was and still is over the scale of such interventions and their consequences for workers, other citizens, businesses, and the overall economy.

Things have changed. Today, more than ever in the last forty years, market forces are both defining and delimiting welfare states. In most areas of public policy it appears economic values are prevailing over community values. Within the changing politics of Canadian society, social policy and the welfare state are being pitted against economic policy and the market, heightening the tension between the two sides. Social policy is depicted as a 'drain' on economic policy rather than as a necessary partner in the capitalist enterprise. Programs that provide protection from the consequences of free markets are viewed negatively. Policies which guarantee union rights, the right to strike, or the right to collective bargaining are deemed to run counter to the essential logic of the capitalist labour market. So too are those policies that provide benefits that give people a choice between selling their labour and any other activity. And, most importantly, anti-welfare writers claim that social policies are a threat, at least theoretically, to the ongoing development of economic policy.

This tension between social and economic policy is aggravated and deepened by the globalization of the economy. Boundaries between domestic and international considerations in policy making are blurring. Canada's welfare state has become a battleground for the struggle over continental and international economic development. Given the dominance of international economies, the role, value, and techniques embodied in national social programs are called into question. Even the methods and processes used within the public policy discourse are criticized. Globalization helps force the economy to take precedent over social welfare.

Surprisingly enough, economic globalization is not fundamentally new in Canada. Ever since the early Europeans came, hoping to find silks and spices and instead finding fish and furs, Canada has had a strong dependence on exporting. Likewise, in the social welfare domain, from the colonial legacies of ideas and institutions to the policy reform experiences of other countries in the nineteenth and twentieth centuries, international debates and reforms have influenced social policy making in Canada.

What is new about globalization over the past twenty-five years or so is the increasing international flow of information and capital. More specifically, modern globalization involves the expanding geographic reach of markets, the deepening of global market relationships across a multitude of goods and services sectors and financial activities, and the elaboration of additional international institutions and agreements for promoting and regulating global trade. David Brown (1994:114) attributes this modern phase of globalization to two processes: 'a natural process of international economic integration led by market forces, and a policy-driven process composed of trade agreements and other forms of international co-operation that complement the natural process.' The so-called natural market forces Brown refers to are the growing integration of world financial markets since 1945, increasing the mobility of financial capital to search for the most advantageous places to invest; innovations in telecommunications and other technologies, most notably computers; and the newly industrializing economies of the Pacific Rim, enhancing the internationalization of production by firms. These 'natural' market forces are complemented by the rise of multinational or transnational corporations, and increases in foreign investments in many domestic economies. Policy factors that complement global market forces include international economic agreements and trading blocs on a continental, regional, and global level.

It is important, however, to see the impact of globalization beyond simply the international economy. Globalization, we believe, is best understood in broad terms. It includes not only market forces, but also cultural aspects as well as public and private power relationships. For globalization is also about the diffusion of particular cultural beliefs and the imposition of certain power relationships. To understand the breadth of the impact of globalization, we will briefly examine one facet of the cultural dimension of globalization that Andrew Cooper and Leslie Pal (1996) call the 'internationalization of human rights.'

The internationalization of human rights involves the spread of universal norms and standards. These norms are actually rooted in Western political thought and history, contained in such global reference documents as the 1948 Universal Declaration on Human Rights; the International Covenants on Civil and Political Rights, and on Economic, Social, and Cultural Rights, effective as of 1976; and, more recently, the 1989 United Nations Convention on the Rights of the Child and the 1995 Social Development Accord. The Canadian Charter of Rights and Freedoms as well as federal and provincial human rights legislation both symbolically and legally complement these global codes of moral conduct. International expressions of human rights are providing a set of standards, such as access, dignity, equality, and self-determination, against which social policy groups within Canada can assess the actions and inactions of the federal and provincial governments.

Another cultural aspect to globalization is the concern that as the economy becomes less national and more international, global trade relations and norms will diminish the willingness of Canadians to share resources across regions within the country (Simeon 1991). The split between social policy considerations and economic considerations encourages policy makers to adopt this neo-liberal financial orientation to rely more on markets and the free movement of capital. This leads to the opening up of internal markets such as health care, social services, and the cultural industries.

Given the impact of globalization on social policy, this chapter explores three questions. First, *What have been the responses by the general public and elites to globalization?* Here we outline three positions on globalism – champions, competitors, and challengers – and explore where Canadians fit. We also identify the key international economic institutions and trading agreements that are the context for decision making in contemporary social policy. Second, *What are the effects of economic globalization for the welfare state and the social union in Canada?* Here we address the issue of the sovereignty of the nation state, the balance of authority and influence within Canadian federalism, and the significance of globalism for governance. Third, and most important, *What are the implications of globalization for the politics of social policy?* This question enables us to probe more deeply than earlier chapters into the ramifications of global capitalism for the welfare state. In particular, we examine the ideas and discourse of social policy; the labour market, an institution critical to the functioning of the social security system; a range of changes in the substance of social programs, which reveal a process we call the 'marketization of social policy'; and the social policy community of clients and interest groups, many of whom are isolated and marginalized by and from the changing politics.

What Are the Responses to Economic Globalization?

Globalization often is discussed as a natural, external, and inevitable trend to which we must adapt or risk economic decline. At times, however, Canadians have hotly debated it, and international trade policies continue to be questioned by many within the social policy community. Economic globalization originates within Canada as well as outside it, and is attached to the specific interests of influential corporate actors. It is a highly political process in which more powerful states, such as the United States and Germany, impose policies on weaker states (Coleman and Porter 1996).

Three Positions on Globalism: Champions, Competitors, and Challengers

John Wiseman (1996) suggests that three types of political responses to globalization have arisen, which he characterizes as champions, competitors, and challengers. Other writers have proposed similar categorizations, which we can note where fitting. The *champions of globalization* include those who, in the words of Wiseman (1996:116), 'are fully and unashamedly committed to enhancing the global power of corporations and reducing the legal and political regulatory power of the nation state.' Canadian champions of globalism include the C.D. Howe Institute, the Fraser Institute, and the Business Council on National Issues. Brown (1994) has written of 'globalization theorists' such as Canadian economists Thomas Courchene and Richard Lipsey, who favour policies of economic integration between Canada and the rest of the world, along with social policy reforms, to complement this changing economy. 'Globalists,' as Banting (1996:36) calls those who take this position, 'also tend to believe that the effective sovereignty of the nation state is now significantly reduced and that the pressures for harmonization or at least convergence in social programs are narrowing the room for manoeuvre enjoyed by governments. In the long run, social policy that seeks to offset or delay adjustment can only lead to lower economic growth, long-term unemployment, and growing government deficits.'

The *competitors* are frequently 'sceptics of globalization' (Brown 1994), but accept the need for policies of trade liberalization. According to Wiseman (1996:116), this perspective 'focuses on maximizing the competitiveness of national and regional economies. This commonly involves policies designed to reduce costs through labour shedding [a euphemism for eliminating jobs through layoffs, early retirements, and attrition], wage reductions, [and] deregulating labour markets.' Other policies seek to improve 'productivity through technological innovation and improvements in infrastructure, training, production processes, marketing, and distribution.' Across industrial countries, trade unions and social democratic political parties have adopted variants of this position, seeking to limit the loss of jobs, to maintain employment standards and benefits, and to compensate those who are economically displaced or disadvantaged, while entering into 'free trade' agreements and promoting export competitiveness.

The *challengers* are a third type of political response to globalization. This body of opinion contests the basic assumption of economic globalism, and sets out alternative courses of action at the national and international levels.[1] As 'anti-globalists' (Banting 1996:37), challengers are strong opponents of globalization. They include the traditional political Left and newer progressive groups (environmentalists, feminists, and peace activists) who believe that policies of economic integration such as NAFTA are making things worse for the labour markets of Canada and other countries, as well as for social equality and justice (Brown 1994:117–18; Cohen 1997b). Strategies for reform proposed by challengers deal with 'the creation of alternative political, financial, and legal global institutions which can form a democratic counterweight to the power of transnational capital'; 'the enshrinement of trade union and human rights principles in international trade agreements and the creation of multilateral and bilateral social charters'; and the creation of alliances between trade unions, community organizations, and social movements 'which reaffirm and give substance to the values of sustainability, social justice, and democracy in an age of global power' (Wiseman 1996:126–7).

The dominant view in Canada towards globalization is the champion perspective, since it is the ruling elites' opinion. Canadian business executives, senior government officials, and the leadership of the Liberal, Conservative, and Reform political parties all subscribe to some form of the pro-globalist position. Trade liberalization, international competitiveness, and a restructured social policy system are core values of this prevailing ideology. Outside government and the corporate sector, groups in the social policy community tend towards the challenger or anti-globalist outlook (Banting 1996; Cohen 1997b). Different members of the general public undoubtedly hold all three viewpoints on globalization. Bruce Doern and Richard Phidd (1992:19) remark that globalization 'has made Canadians more conscious of their interdependence with the rest of the world and with the inevitability of rapid change. Canadians have also developed a greater sense of vulnerability and of being a smaller player in the world stage.' Understandably, then, Canadians tend to value social security, equality, and collective rights more highly than the elites' priority ideas of international competitiveness, individualism, and a much smaller welfare state (Reid 1997).

Community groups are encouraging the government to maintain strong social interventions. They see the high risks that are created by the globalization process and they recognize that if international corporations win in these high-risk activities, the elites will benefit at the expense of citizens. Globalization does not bring with it a commitment to jobs or the workplace. Rather it is built on the idea that jobs will come and go, and that competition and profitability are the orders of the day. Given that globalization represents a risk to citizens without much chance of providing long-term security, community groups do not want the government to give away policy space in which local social problems can be solved.

The Context for Contemporary Social Policy

If Canadians are primarily champions, then what are the key international economic institutions and trading agreements that support globalization? International trade agreements and trading blocs are not the stuff that social policy texts have traditionally been made of. Yet, as Ken Collier (1995:57) points out, events over the last decade or so 'now force attention to these topics, because social work educators, researchers and students heading for practice will find our work suffering momentous impacts from them.' There is an array of foreign and international institutions that influence domestic social policy making and budgetary decisions. The international state has grown, as has the influence of officials in the international institutions to which Canada belongs. These include international bodies such as the Organization for Economic Co-operation and Development (OECD), the General Agreement on Tariffs and Trade (GATT), the International Monetary Fund, and the World Bank, all of which were established at the end of the Second World War, and the World Trade Organization created in the early 1990s. In addition, Canada belongs to two international economic summit groups: the G-8, a group established in the mid 1970s and comprising the seven largest capitalist economies in the world, with the addition of Russia in the later 1990s; and the Asia-Pacific Economic Co-operation (APEC) group established in 1994. Canada also belongs to the continental trading bloc with Mexico and the United States under the 1993 North American Free Trade Agreement (NAFTA) which built on the 1989 Canada–United States Free Trade Agreement.

Community groups and their policy analysts are examining these global instruments and describing the implications international agreements are having on the social policy domain. They recognize that each new agreement limits the government's ability to solve social problems. They are aware that these institutions and agreements share an economic logic of free trade and economic growth through increased exports, and a neo-liberal discourse on restructuring and reducing the welfare state (Teeple 1995). They are aware that the discourse of free trade undermines the conditions of citizenship. The free trade negotiations formulate rules on global competition and promote the reduction or elimination of domestic barriers to trade; articulate mild guidelines on the ethical conduct of transnational corporations; and support economic deregulation, privatization of public enterprises, and other forms of government restraint. The negotiations affect many areas of national and provincial jurisdiction. The influence can be direct and quasi-regulatory in some instances, or they can be a subtler source of pressure through the political and professional networks they foster, for example, on government finance officials to limit program spending and reduce taxes.

The tendency for global capitalism, of course, is to advocate for less government in general, but at the same time to push often for more government in specific situations such as in loan guarantees, strategic incentives, or deferred taxation for business interests. If there is a single agreed-upon view among the international agencies as to how social policy should respond to globalization, it is that countries should pursue a mixed economy of welfare, and shift some responsibilities for the financing and provision of programs away from the public sector to other sectors.

Foreign institutions of an even more direct kind exercise power and influence over Canadian budgetary and social policy decisions. These include the United States Federal Reserve, the American central bank, whose decisions effect interest rates in Canada; and private institutions such as the New York money market bond rating houses, which assign credit ratings to provincial governments. These ratings can make significant differences in the interest rates governments must pay on their borrowing in Canada and abroad. All of these international economic institutions and trade agreements, then, constitute a substantial part of the global context for Canadian social policy.

What Are the Effects of Globalization on the Welfare State and Social Union in Canada?

For Canada, globalization significantly affects the balance between national and international policy influences as well as the roles and relations between federal and provincial governments. Both champions and challengers of globalism agree that the sovereignty of the nation state has been reduced as a result of the increased mobility of capital internationally, the creation and extension of trading agreements and blocs, and the power of huge transnational corporations. In this new world order, we are moving into the age of the post-sovereign state, according to Peter Drucker (1993), where the state ceases to be a nation state and becomes an administrative unit rather than a political entity. It is claimed that the Canadian state is losing or has already lost real control over domestic policy making is a common theme in the critical social policy literature. Diana Ralph (1994:80) conveys this belief with her statement that 'As a result of NAFTA and GATT provisions, the federal and provincial governments no longer have the power to grant even the liberal vision of a social welfare state.' Likewise, globalization significantly affects intergovernmental relations and social union. With the globalization of culture and international values, the east-west relations in Canada become fragmented and Canadian identity is eroded. Here we examine the effect of globalization on the role of the nation state and the social union of Canada.

The Role of the Nation State

Globalization has redefined the role of the nation state in the international arena. Over the past twenty-five years, the federal government has increasingly assumed the role of supporter and participator in the development of international agreements and agencies to facilitate and regulate the accumulation of capital on a global scale (Teeple 1995:69). The basic rationale of the state – the promotion of a nationally defined capitalist class – is waning, and the state's macro-economic policy has shifted from Keynesianism to a monetarist approach.

Precisely opposite to the Keynesian idea of the interrelations between social and economic policies, monetarism separates them. In monetarism the money supply is the dominant determinant of the level of economic activity. Government spending and taxation activities by themselves have little fundamental impact on macro-economic conditions. Monetarists also tend to favour minimal government intervention in the labour force and in other markets. As we have seen, this shift leads to less government involvement in the management of the economy – a more hands-off approach – and less ability for governments to use the economy to solve social problems.

In the 1980s and 1990s the monetarist-minimalist policy advocates argued that the competitive forces of markets must be strengthened in order to restore and enhance economic growth. To accomplish this, they contended that the state must withdraw from many of the areas in which it had come to play a major role over the previous several decades, because it was this very state intervention which had weakened the ability of markets to function efficiently. Keynesian-style intervention, they claimed, was ineffective. Only a monetarist policy would create the required environment for economic competitiveness.

Monetarism has in fact become the new conventional wisdom for federal governments in Canada (Lightman and Irving 1991). Monetarism has been pursued through an agenda of policies that has included free trade pacts, deficit reduction, the deregulation of certain markets, the privatization of some public services, the limitation of collective bargaining and union powers, a reduction in the number of public employees, the transformation of the tax system, the restructuring of local governance structures (municipalities, hospital authorities, and school boards), and the promotion of charities and other community groups as vehicles for meeting social needs. In short, there has been a downsizing of the state, 'the abrogation of government responsibilities for the social and economic well-being of society, [and] the redefinition of public duties by the state or the reshaping of the boundaries between civil society and the state so that intervention by the state in the affairs of the civil society are hereafter ... restricted' (Teeple 1995:101–2). The result has been the decline of social reform and the promotion of private-property rights and markets.

Likewise, Richard Simeon sees globalization constraining the sovereignty of all governments. Pressures come from corporate interests and trade agreements for tax and regulatory policies to be relaxed across all countries. For Simeon, 'globalization highlights the growing mismatch between the scope and scale of the issues with which we must cope and the reach of the political institutions through which we must deal with them. The result is that global forces increasingly escape the capacity of states to manage them' (1991:47–8).

The mismatch is readily apparent in many environmental problems, such as global warming and the fact that local and national governments are fixed in a territorial space while transnational firms and investment capital are relatively mobile and unregulated on a world-wide scale. Simeon also sees globalization creating new roles for the state to play: not only projecting national trade interests and concerns into international fora, but also mediating and cushioning the jolt of global stresses on the domestic economy and on society. The state is therefore faced with performing the contradictory functions of promoting international competitiveness and adjustment, while at the same time protecting workers, communities, and industries against the disruptions coming from global capitalism.

The Social Union of Canada

The basic rationale for the creation of a national government in Canada was the building of an east-west economy. While that original reason may have disappeared with globalization, in contrast to Teeple we see the Canadian state as continuing to serve important sociopolitical and cultural purposes. These include giving political meaning to our lives by governments granting identities, rights, and obligations; defining our sense of community under federalism; and providing an admittedly imperfect process through which we practice democracy (Simeon 1991: 46–7). The globalization of culture and international values has threatened the unity of Canada, straining east-west relations. Without the creation of connections between the east and the west, the north-south globalizing forces will dominate. If Canada wants to maintain its sovereignty it must take powerful social policy steps to reinforce the east-west connections. The present structures – the Canadian Broadcasting Corporation, Medicare, and equalization payments – are not sufficient.

Free trade on a North American basis transforms the underlying political economy of Canadian social policy. With greater continental integration of commerce producing even more of a north-south trading system, the challenge is how to maintain the political support across the country for an east-west system of transfers and equalization payments. As the Canadian economy increasingly becomes regionalized, and regions remain economically diverse, political pressure builds from at least some provinces for further decentralization and asymmetry in social programming (Courchene 1994). Labour market policy reform has been shaped by the move away from Keynesian management of the aggregate demand for labour at the national level, and the belief that Canada's economy is now a series of loosely connected regional and urban economies. An example of this regionalization of policy was the change to federal minimum-wage legislation in 1996, the first increase in the federal rate in ten years. The federal minimum wage applies to private sector industries that are interprovincial or international in scope, such as banks, telecommunications companies, and some federal Crown corporations. From being a standard rate per hour across the country, the federal rate is now adjusted to the general adult minimum-wage rates in each province and territory. Another recent example is the transfer of various federal training and employment-related activities and federal employees to interested provincial and territorial governments and Aboriginal organizations.

Globalization may well affect the assorted levels of government differently. Simeon (1991:53) suggests the federal government is especially constrained because 'it has less jurisdiction over the kinds of quality-of-life issues that are likely to become the major areas of government innovation in the future. These are largely provincial, so that in Canada – perhaps paradoxically – globalization seems to be fostering decentralization rather than centralization.' Quality-of-life issues include education, health care, healthy communities, housing, human rights, multiculturalism, race relations, sports, and recreation. Many deal with the pluralization of Canadian society and all are issues of social policy. When Simeon made his observation, the federal government was burdened with large annual deficits. By the late 1990s, however, Ottawa had eliminated the federal deficit and was running a budgetary surplus for the first time since 1970 (Prince 1998b). This turnaround in financial capacity strengthens the federal government's ability to enforce the principles of Medicare, for instance, and to initiate new national projects for social security. We examine this shift in the fiscal fortunes of governments in Canada, and its implications for the future of social policy making, in Chapter 10.

New Challenges for Social Policy

To delve further into globalism's ramifications for social policy, we canvass the ideas and discourse of social welfare, the Canadian labour market, the substance of social program changes, and the social policy community of clients and advocacy groups. We believe that the forces of globalization are restructuring the way Canadians think about social policies. The forces of globalization make difficult political choices seem to be mere matters of economic determinism. Canadian elites, as champions of globalism, are narrowing the view most people have of social policy by giving priority to economic rather than social issues. This has created a disjuncture between business and government leaders on one hand and community activists on the other. Here we look at how globalization pushes the changing politics of social policy into a fiscal debate about economic implications without adequately dealing with the new insecurity in the labour market. We look at how social policy analysts are forced into using the culture of private enterprise as the evaluating criteria in deciding which policies should be kept or cut, and the debilitating effect this new dialogue is having on advocacy groups. We explore the change of attitude towards the role of welfare (safety net versus springboard), changes in the workplace, and the fiscalization of a debate that is no longer about dreams and compassion but about dollars and cents.

From Safety Net to Springboard: The Narrowing Conception of the Welfare State

From the crisis of the welfare debates and from economic globalization have come changes in the way we think and talk about the welfare state and social provision. A new conception of welfare prevails, with a related social policy discourse that defies many of the accepted ideas of the postwar social security vision. The goals of a comprehensive social policy system and high and stable levels of employment have effectively been abandoned by Canadian governments as unattainable aims (McBride 1992; Brodie 1995).

Part of the new orthodoxy is that the Canadian network of social programs, while it may have served us well in the past, is now outdated due to the transformation of society and the globalization of the economic context. The postwar welfare state is no longer appropriate for the times we are living in, goes this line of thinking, because of the 'new realities' of fiscal constraints, global trade imperatives, and an aging population.

The new conception of the welfare state thus reframes the role of social policy as being a handmaiden to economic development and labour market adjustment. With a few exceptions, perhaps, such as cultural industries, social policy should not challenge the forces of international trade. Indeed, social policy should not even be primarily about protecting and compensating for the negative impacts of globalization on workers and their families. Instead, under the changing politics, social policy needs to be tailored to fit comfortably with the new economic order, complementing economic restructuring and international competitiveness (Brown 1994; Courchene 1994). Many of the areas concerned with quality of life are downplayed as concerns and priority is given to matters of job readiness, training, and skill redevelopment. The guiding principle for reforming social programs is that they support the work ethic and economic productivity. For many income support and social service programs this has meant a tightening of eligibility requirements and increasing work-related obligations for clients.

The way elites talk about the Canadian welfare state – the social policy discourse – has changed in the past decade. Politicians and bureaucrats consider citizens' relationship to the welfare state more as that of consumers with choices and responsibilities, than that of clients or beneficiaries with entitlements and rights. The public hears less about welfare and a national social security system, and more about workfare, 'making work pay,' and the social union. Economic change is thought of as fundamental and fast changing, a shakedown (Reid 1997), more than simply as progress or growth. The metaphor of the social safety net, with its images of security and protection, is given less emphasis than the metaphor of a social trampoline or springboard, with its 'active' programs enabling people to adjust and be catapulted back into the workforce. The discourse has also shifted away from a commitment to universality to that of selectivity. We are told that social policy can remain compassionate but that 'Canadians cannot afford to maintain their traditional level of concern over the distribution of income. Instead, they must reorient their policy mind-set towards the objective of providing meaningful work for all' (Brown 1994:124–5). Social policy, in other terms, should replace its focus on insuring against major risks, as outlined by the Marsh Report and others, with the aim of diffusing opportunities.

From Dreams to Debt Reduction: The Fiscalization of Policy Discourse

In contemporary discourse of the welfare state, the dominant theme has been the fiscalization of social policy. Other factors such as Quebec nationalism and economic globalism have also had a voice, but the paradigm of fiscal restraint and balancing the budget has been the organizing framework for social issues, programs, and policy processes. While social policies have always been made in a budgetary context of limited resources and competing claims, what is new is that financial and monetarist values have become the central guiding standard in Canadian social policy discussions and reforms. Since 1975, when the Bank of Canada adopted monetarism as formal policy and the federal cabinet adopted a budget restraint policy, 'virtually all discussion of social policy in Canada has been couched in the language of fiscal capacity' (Lightman and Irving 1991:71).

Fiscalization refers to periods when financial concerns, especially considerations of expenditure restraint and deficit reduction, dominate deliberations on setting public policy priorities and contemplating social reforms. Fiscal discourse portrays deficit reduction as an imperative, that is, as a pressing problem demanding obligatory action by governments. The necessity to reduce program spending and generally downsize the state is presented, under this perspective, as a non-ideological agenda, that is, as a common-sense response to financial problems. This is quite different from O'Connor's critical and structural analysis of the 'fiscal crisis of the state' discussed in Chapter 4. The simple arithmetic of compounding interest on the debt makes it both critical and mandatory to tackle deficit reduction. The proponents of fiscalization believe the budgetary facts speak for themselves, despite some evidence to the contrary. Social programs based on 'ideological dreams,' as opposed to the clear concept of reducing the debt, must be cut since they comprise such a large portion of federal and provincial government budgets. Social policy is placed within the context of financial responsibility, affordability, and the long-term sustainability of essential services and benefits such as health care and pensions.

Public budgeting systems in Canada and other countries largely abandoned program-planning processes by the mid 1980s, adopting instead systems built on spending limits and restraint targets. Great stress is placed on the aggregate amounts of spending on the social policy envelope of governments. Budgeting for social programs becomes a top-down process concerned more with total sums than with service priorities. Looking at totals focuses attention on the large size of social expenditures relative to other program areas. Moreover, 'in a period of ideological polarization, quantities come to stand for qualities' (Wildavsky 1988:204). Social expenditure totals serve as a crude indicator, for politicians and bureaucrats as well as for client groups and academics, of the degree of welfare or compassion or social justice in a jurisdiction.[2] To quote Edmund Burke, 'The age of chivalry is gone. That of the sophisters, economists and calculators has succeeded.'

Finance departments set the outer limits of social policy reform with arguments and analyses about fiscal imperatives. These are bolstered by pressures from business interests, the money markets, and international agencies such as the IMF and OECD. Estimates on revenues, expenditures, interest rates, and deficit reduction targets set the boundaries for social policy making. Priorities on human well-being have to be negotiated within the constraints of the assumptions and overall goals of a government's fiscal framework, which is largely controlled by central finance agencies.

A budgeting system is about making choices; it is never a neutral allocation of resources and values. The fiscalization of budgets and social policy discourse tends to promote certain ideas and objectives rather than others, favour some interests in government and in the economy over others, and some program designs and institutional arrangements over others. Consider, for example, the following consequences:

1. *Fiscal discourse erodes the legitimacy of the social security system.* Government deficits and growing debts are attributed, in large part, to social programs and the rising costs of welfare. Social spending is seen as spending borrowed money, money we do not have, thereby

placing a burden on future generations. We must cut social programs in order to save them and to be fair to our children and grand-children.

2. *Public and media attention are diverted away from other critical issues that need to be on governments' agendas* – issues such as the consequences of monetary policy, the effectiveness of industrial grants, and who benefits from social and business tax expenditures. Likewise, major social policy reform exercises in Canada have been based on a nar-row conception of public sector social welfare precluding other pro-grams, options, and possible future directions. At the same time, the fiscal debate encourages welfare pluralism – the meeting of social needs through the efforts of other sectors and charitable giving by individuals.

3. *Within federal and provincial governments, fiscalization has concentrated power in Finance portfolios while weakening the influence of social policy departments and their clientele, as well as that of social advocacy groups.* Finance officials have essentially determined the development, dead-lock, and decline of social policy making in Canada over the last two decades. Consequently, groups wanting to affect the social policy process have had to target more of their efforts at officials in eco-nomic and finance departments and treasury boards. Through the 1990s the political right has enjoyed considerable support and influ-ence.

4. *In an age of government austerity, fiscalization changes policy discussions from ones with a socially redistributional outlook to ones with an inward-looking reallocation of resources.* Through the 1980s and 1990s deficit reduction was the governing objective of social programs, overshad-owing the goals of anti-poverty and social integration. Among other effects, it intensifies competition among social programs, between governments, and among community groups desperate for funding.

5. *The emphasis on spending cuts in aid of deficit reduction has constrained and at times divided as well as co-opted segments of the social policy community.* Many human service organizations and workers have more or less accepted the fiscal discourse and have tacitly supported governments' restraint agendas. Gordon Ternowetsky (1987:386) has written of social policy groups: 'we have been asked to participate in

the process of consulting on ways and means of further rationalizing expenditures on social programs.' The 1994–95 Social Security Review of the Chrétien federal government is a striking example of this sort of structured and hurried process. At other times, reforms have been introduced with little or no public consultation. Either way, in the face of strong neo-liberal reforms, progressive social policy advocates have found themselves in the awkward position of defending status quo programs, many of which advocates had long criticized.

6. *Community development and social policy planning are subservient to economic management.* Strategic planning and resource allocation are oriented to controlling costs and finding new revenue opportunities rather than assessing needs and addressing public issues. At its extreme, the fiscalization of social policy ignores the substantive aspects of programs, disregarding questions of their impacts and results, and concentrates on the degree to which a program's budget is growing or not and thereby contributing to deficit and debt reduction.

From Giants to Gerbils: Canada's Labour Market

Economic globalization has serious implications for domestic labour markets. As Canadian economist Harvey Lazar (1991:149) states, 'global market forces have come to play a growing role in determining the supply of and demand for different kinds of labor.' This growing role of globalism has repercussions for the quantity and quality of paid work available, the distribution of income in society, and the overall performance of the economy. It also raises questions of the proper function of social policy, especially human resource development programs, in view of several disturbing trends in Canada's labour market.

Workplace downsizing is occurring throughout North America, due to corporate mergers, plant closures and the 're-engineering' of firms, causing unemployment and involuntary retirements, dashing career plans, and changing the skills required for jobs remaining. A report by the former Economic Council of Canada, entitled *Good Jobs, Bad Jobs* (1990), drew national attention to a widening disparity in the quality and security of jobs available for many Canadians in the middle and working classes. More and more work is becoming what the council called 'nonstandard employment,' that is, more workers have temporary part-time jobs, are self-employed, or are multiple-job holders. Ralph

(1994:75–6) describes 'bad jobs' as low-paid, dangerous, insecure work with few rights or services for employees. As industrial and technological sectors require higher-skilled workers, 'the availability of relatively low-skilled jobs in Canada is being reduced,' according to Brown (1994:111), but he admits, 'demand for less-skilled work will continue, although at lower wages.'

A federal government discussion paper on reforming social security (Canada 1994:9) frankly notes that since about 1980 'our society increasingly has begun to be polarized between well-educated, highly-skilled Canadians in demand by employers – today's economic elite – and less educated people without specialized, up-to-date job skills, who have been losing ground.' Other studies have examined the bifurcation of Canada into economically secure and insecure classes. Research by Rene Morissette, John Myles and Garnett Picot (1995), on earnings polarization in Canada over the 1969–91 period, found that earnings and wage inequalities are partly a structural feature of the economy and not simply a cyclical phenomenon associated with recessions. They conclude (1995:24) that this trend is 'being driven by growing inequality in the distribution of working time. More workers are working part-time, but, more importantly, more are also working longer than the usual thirty-five to forty-hour work week.' Other alarming trends are the growth in underemployment, long-term structural unemployment, and economic disparities (Broad 1995; Lazar 1991).

For far more people than in earlier decades of the postwar welfare state, unemployment is a prolonged interruption of earning capacity. The visionaries of Canada's social security system saw family needs arising from the gap between a family's income, even at reasonable levels, and the large number of children they might have. Today, the need arises from an inadequate or unstable income even with just one or two children in the family. Today, the risks of the labour market, in Leonard Marsh's (1943:21) words, 'are constantly making their appearance as realities.'

Trends and risks of economic globalism have a direct bearing on social policy because several benefits, in terms of their access and value, are based on paid employment and occupational status. Examples include benefits regarding pensions, unemployment, disability and workplace injury, dental care, extended health care, and maternity and family leaves. The availability and adequacy of these occupation-related social programs vary by sectors of the economy, size of workplaces, and whether workers are full-time or part-time, unionized or non-unionized, self-employed, an employee, or an owner. For instance, a person working full time in a unionized setting in either the public sector or a large firm in the private sector is far more likely to have an employer sponsored pension plan. When we reflect on the fact that governments and large corporations have been downsizing, and that most new jobs over the past twenty years in Canada have been in small, typically non-unionized service businesses, then potentially large social problems appear concerning retirement income security in the near future.

In response to these global forces, Canada has entered into social security agreements with over thirty countries in recent decades.[3] An example of the internationalization of public policy programs under the federal government's jurisdiction are explicitly linked to like policies in other welfare states. The purpose of these agreements, from the perspective of Canada, is to coordinate the operation of old age benefits and the Canada Pension Plan with comparable programs in other nations that provide pensions for retirement, old age, disability, and survivorship. The intent is that Canadians working abroad would have the same rights under the social security laws of another country as the citizens of that country, and that citizens from another country now living in Canada would not face restrictions here upon receiving payment of the other country's pension.

From Volunteer to Vulture: The Marketization of Social Programs

The marketization of social programs is a process routinely overlooked in analyses of welfare state politics. Customary themes of restructuring concern the contraction of the public sector (or 'rolling back' of the state), the expansion of the private sector, the expectation that the voluntary sector can and should do more, and, in feminist analyses, the regulation and imposition of additional burdens on the domestic realm (Brodie 1995; Teeple 1995). Explorations of Canadian social policy still employ the concepts of residualism and institutionalism. The former, residualism, holds that most government social services should come into play only when the family and/or market breaks down. The latter, institutionalism, asserts that the welfare state is just as integral an institution in modern life as the economy and family (Guest 1997; Prince 1996b). These mini-ideologies imply a sharper conceptual division between the market economy and the state than exists in practice.

The politics of retrenchment is usually evaluated in terms of whether welfare state benefits and services are taken away from clients, and whether social budgets are slashed or at least significantly reduced. In a detailed examination of welfare politics in Britain and the United States, Paul Pierson (1994) concludes that there have been substantial continuities in social policies in both countries while under strong conservative administrations, with few radical changes. A limitation of this approach is that regardless of the welfare state's size or the apparent stability of policies, fundamental changes can take place within existing social programs and budgets. Indeed, major reforms of a residualist nature can and do occur even when the welfare state is expanding.

At a macro-level, marketization is one of the basic processes for mediating the relation between our capitalist economy and liberal democracy.[4] It involves the blending of the logic of the market (private property, competition, and profit) with the logic of the state (ultimate authority, public interest, and citizenship). This is what democratic capitalism and the mixed economy, in part, are about. It is also what welfare pluralism is partly about. A traditional portrayal of the Keynesian welfare state, as we noted at the outset of this chapter, is that it politicizes economics and modifies the market, substituting public values and activities for private sector ones. The market, however, also modifies the welfare state. It always has. The marketization of social programs is the phrase we use to highlight this phenomenon. External to the state, marketization entails the influence of economic values on social policy; conditioning the goals and means of benefits and services; and shaping public attitudes as to which groups and needs are deserving and worthy of support, and which are undeserving and the object of exclusion or stigma. Internal to the state, marketization involves the culture of capitalism moving into public sector activities. It is the injection and expansion of private sector principles into social programs, ideas, structures, and processes. It also includes the injection of 'sound business principles' into social welfare systems and public administration more generally.[5]

While marketization of welfare is quite an old process, what is new is the intensification of designing social programs on the ethic of the economic market. Economic conditions and market values are more influential today in determining social policy developments than in earlier periods of the welfare state (Spivey 1985). The death of the universal income programs, Old Age Security and Family Allowances, in the 1990s dramatically symbolizes the decline of communal social principles and the subordination of welfare values to market norms. Eligibility for child benefits and senior benefits now rests entirely on income testing. In our view, several factors are behind the increasing importance of economic criteria in policy making. These include globalization, of course, and the prominence placed on international competitiveness; related concerns about declining productivity and continuing high unemployment; the fiscal discourse of crisis and government restraint; and the narrowing conception of what social policy can and should be about.

Consider the following vignettes that illustrate versions of marketization in a range of social policy domains. The first example is the Employment Insurance (EI) Program. A longstanding debate over this program is how much of it is insurance (a market concept) and how much is social welfare (a public policy concept). Amendments to the program by the Mulroney and Chrétien federal governments have pushed the program closer to market ideas. Financial contributions to the program directly from the public purse have been eliminated, placing the onus for full funding on employees and employers. Both the amount and duration of benefits have been decreased numerous times. Eligibility requirements have been tightened, penalties toughened, and disqualification provisions expanded. Such changes are motivated by business complaints and government concerns that EI has a negative impact on employee and employer incentives, the unemployment level, and the mobility of workers. The general thrust of these reforms has been to strengthen the EI program's contribution to labour market policy goals, while weakening the program's traditional income protection and macro-economic stabilization functions. The proportion of unemployed workers covered by EI, and therefore potentially protected, has dropped from over 90 per cent to about 40 per cent of the labour force. This is the narrowest scope of coverage since the original legislation of the early 1940s.

Arts and cultural policy is a second example of marketization. Thelma McCormack (1984) describes the turn in Canadian cultural policy away from a nationalist model towards a market model. Under the nationalist model, art is regarded as a central part of our heritage, the objective of policy is to foster national awareness and identity, and the role of the audience is in part to be patriots. At times this approach has been joined by what McCormack calls a welfare model in which art is viewed as a public resource belonging to everyone as a social right. The focus is on public art, not private collections, and the role of the audience is as citizens. Under the market model, which has gained ground in governmental circles, art is a commodity to be bought and sold at auctions and showings. The laws of supply and demand set the value of art and culture. The largely public and nonprofit art systems of the nationalist and welfare models are replaced by a profit-oriented approach. The role of the audience here is as consumer and investor. The ascendancy of a market approach in the arts and culture field, which McCormack and others (Woodcock 1985) observed in the 1980s, continues.

Still other examples of the marketization of social policies can be sketched, as follows:

- The working conditions for many in the public services are effectively being adjusted downward to match those in the private sector. Driven by the politics of deficits and debt, public sector labour relations in Canada have deteriorated over the last two decades. Federal and provincial governments have imposed pay freezes and wage rollbacks; restricted what may be negotiated and even suspended collective bargaining; and introduced back-to-work legislation. This may be the beginning of the end of public sector collective bargaining in Canada (Swimmer and Thompson 1995).

- In Canadian educational policy, the new agenda for curriculum reform and the role of schools is 'technological liberalism' (Manzer 1994). The job of public education in the global economy is to prepare a highly skilled and competitive labour force. There is considerable interest in measuring performance, ranking schools, and seeking corporate donations and sponsorships for school activities and facilities (Barlow and Robertson 1994).

- Canada's recent immigration policy has emphasized an economic orientation by both policy makers and the public. There is deep interest with, and many misgivings about, the impact of immigrants on job creation, social programs such as welfare, and other public services. A prominent theme is to think of immigrants as human capital, either at the low- or high-skill level (DeVoretz 1995). Like some other industrialized countries, Canada has a business immigrant policy for securing foreign capital and stimulating economic growth domestically. Trevor Harrison (1996:9) argues that such programs 'reflect a growing commodification of immigration policy and of the notion of citizenship.'

- Since the mid-1980s, a strong importance has been given to trade interests and export promotion in Canadian foreign policy and international assistance, particularly bilateral aid and even food aid (Freeman 1985; Charlton 1992; Pratt 1994). Development aid is often a means to pursue economic policy goals and advance domestic commercial and bureaucratic interests.

• Provincial welfare reforms of the 1990s and related 'work incentive' policies are based on a 'market-oriented economic perspective' (Low 1996:189). The focus is on financial rewards at the margin and individual choices, with little attention given to social costs and structural factors. The discourse of welfare reform speaks of breaking dependency on welfare, making work pay, and encouraging self-reliance. More stringent work obligations are directed at single, able-bodied applicants and clients. In some provinces, single mothers with young children have been redefined as employable with the expectation that they will enrol in training courses (Evans et al. 1995). For nonparticipation in work-for-welfare programs, benefits are commonly reduced by a significant amount. As Eric Shragge (1997:17) states, 'Workfare represents a departure from the postwar welfare state, and is leading us in the direction of a punitive system in which welfare will no longer be a right but instead will become contingent on a type of work that is "paid" at a rate far below the social norm.'

These market-centred approaches to social issues do not signal the resurrection of 'economic man' in Canadian social policy, since market principles were never dead in the welfare state. Instead, what we see is the reassertion of these principles in a number of program and service areas. The market ethos is alive and flourishing in the public sector as well as in the private sector. With the marketization of social policy currently in vogue, we have market capitalism and market welfarism in concert. State intervention does not necessarily mean there is a corresponding decline in market systems or values. The infusion of some market principles into the state and politics compromises the notion of absolute authority or absolute good (Offe 1984:183), yet contributes to the preservation of capitalist institutions.

Marketization should prompt us to always ask 'how social is social policy?' 'In principle,' writes Charles Lindblom (1977:44), 'governments can redistribute income and wealth and repeat the redistribution as frequently as wished. Their disinclination to do so requires a political explanation rather than reference to market forces.' This analysis is flawed, in our view, as it draws too sharp a dichotomy between state and economy. As well as an established institution, the market is an ideological phenomenon. Part of the political explanation for limited redistribution, we believe, rests on market interests embodied within state structures and activities. Income redistribution is frustrated by the prevalent use of market beliefs in taxation and expenditure policies and services. The wage-based inequalities of the economy are reproduced, for example, in tax assistance for retirement savings plans and in the Canada and Quebec Pension Plans.

The traditional arguments used to justify social services and transfers relate to meeting needs, providing compensation for certain losses, and offering insurance against specific risks. In recent years, the principal reasons advanced to justify social spending and intervention refer to investments in human resources, economic growth, and competitiveness. While traditional concerns such as assistance to the disadvantaged are still important, they have been overshadowed in the past fifteen years by initiatives more acceptable to the requirements of a globalizing economy. The policy environment and social objectives are described increasingly in terms of ability to respond to labour market trends, human capital development, and the imperatives of international trade. This has altered the composition of many social programs as well as changed somewhat the meaning of human well-being and social development.

The degree to which social policies have become more reliant on an economic rationale has important ramifications for program design and delivery. The marketization of social policy can affect eligibility criteria for program benefits, the level and duration of benefits, disqualification provisions, program financing, and other uses of programs – as the case of EI shows. Moreover, the level of public understanding and support for programs can be affected. For social agencies, cloaking budget requests in economic terms can provoke heated internal debates as to the desirability and utility of such a strategy. Some staff may see it as selling out, while others regard it as an essential tactic for survival in these times.

From Empowerment to Impotence: Political Impacts on
Social Policy Advocacy and Client Groups

For many social policy clients and interest groups, economic globalization and the companion processes of fiscalization and marketization are debilitating. For them, the changing politics of Canadian social policy is a politics of isolation, resignation, and marginalization. Globalization has contributed to the isolation of the social policy community. Part of this is due to fiscal constraints, the limited resources of advocacy groups, and the complex diversity of the community itself, which poses challenges in building alliances and speaking on issues with a strong united voice. More importantly, though, is the increasingly global context of social policy. Globalism has reinforced the central place of the Finance Department in defining the social agenda and determining policy decisions. Canadian social policy groups, according to Banting (1996), have lagged in their response to global issues, and their participation in international realms has generally been limited. Social advocacy groups are politically isolated because most are, in John Wiseman's terminology, challengers to globalization. For these groups, taking part in policy reviews means fighting the discourse and concrete reforms proposed by the government and business elites who strongly favour a social policy agenda motivated by globalism. 'In a world of tightened international constraints, there is a danger that public consultations will heighten, not reduce, the cynicism about the responsiveness of our political institutions' (Banting 1996:45).

Others, too, report a growing sense, not only of cynicism, but also of resignation and political impotence (Teeple 1995; Reid 1997). Many Canadians are distrustful of politicians and governments and are disenchanted about the outcomes of reforms and cuts to services. Clients of social services often feel disempowered, treated as passive recipients. Such experiences and sentiments translate into a politics of resignation. Social movements such as those representing labour, the poor, and women, along with the traditional Left, have been placed on the defensive, seeking to protect universal programs, national standards, and other valued aspects of the postwar Canadian welfare state. Considerable time and energy have been devoted to guarding social programs against cutbacks, resources that might otherwise have been directed to developing a new agenda of progressive change.

New and old social movements alike have been the targets of marginalization by business and political elites. Anna Yeatman (1990:131) points out that elites minimize the status and import of social movements by 'denying their universal significance and making them appear vehicles of particular sectoral interests.' Elites portray them instead as disaffected and disadvantaged groups, lying outside the mainstream, 'for whom special provision [if any] is to be made.' This politics of marginalization is readily apparent in Canada. With respect to the Canadian women's movement, Janine Brodie (1995) identifies several other methods used to attack social advocates. These include funding cuts to community groups and their associations, restricting or closing their access to government decision makers, and questioning the groups' knowledge or expertise on issues such as trade policy or the deficit and the debt. Other strategies involve weakening employment equity and related affirmative action measures; excluding particular groups, such as gays or visible minorities, from social policy reports and narratives; and emphasizing selective and targeted programs. The consequence is that services are aimed at the 'truly needy' and 'high-risk' groups. 'Instead of exposing the structural links among race, gender, sexuality, poverty, and violence, targeting serves to pathologize and individualize differences, as well as to place the designated groups under increased state surveillance and administrative control' (Brodie 1995:74).

Conclusions

At the advent of the twenty-first century, Canadian social policy is more deferential and exposed to market forces than in the heyday of the welfare state. The concept of marketization indicates that government need not deinstitutionalize or privatize a service in order to extend the market system. Some elements of the welfare state have been dismantled and others sharply cut, but much of what has been and still is happening to social policy is a realigning in aid of domestic and global capital. A central goal of social reform, in this context, is changing benefits and programs so as to promote a more mobile labour force and to order a more work-ready group of welfare clients for low-wage employment. In this chapter we have examined the globalization of economies, the fiscalization of public discourse and priority setting, the marketization of social programs, and the marginalization of public interest groups and social advocates. These processes all tend to constrain and challenge the welfare state. They all illustrate the complexity of change in both the context and content of social policy formation. All are engaged in shifting boundaries among the state, market, community, and family.

Under continental trading blocs and international commercial regimes, and in the face of transnational corporations, Canada's sovereignty to regulate and restrict capital has declined. Yet sovereignty is not an all-or-nothing affair. The state continues to exercise authority in regulating workers, welfare recipients, and women, among others in the social, moral, and domestic realms. The decline of sovereignty is just that, a comparative decrease and not a complete disappearance. Sovereignty is a relational condition set in a given place and time. Externally, colonial, continental, and capital interests have always limited Canadian autonomy. Internally, Canadian sovereignty is constitutionally divided between the federal and provincial governments; between the courts and the legislatures; and, under the Charter of Rights, between governments and citizens as individuals and or as members of certain groups. Jurisdiction and authority is also divided, and will become more so through treaty negotiations and self-government legislation between public governments and Aboriginal governments.

While economic globalization has shifted the social policy debate, we believe national governments still have a role to play. Harmonization of welfare states is neither inevitable nor likely under globalization (Watson 1998). We share Drucker's (1993:11) belief that 'It may remain the most powerful political organ around for a long time to come, but it will no longer be the indispensable one. Increasingly, it will share power with other organs, other institutions, other policy makers.' Even as a semi-sovereign state, Canadian governments still make laws and implement them; still enforce a national criminal code; still preserve a military and maintain federal, provincial, and local police forces; still make tax and expenditures policy choices; and still uphold an independent judiciary. Issues of social cohesion and protection remain pressing issues. Social policy advocates, analysts, or academics should therefore not ignore the state at all levels as sites for political action and policy development.

7

Diversity and Equality in a Pluralist Welfare Community

In a thoughtful examination of justice and the politics of difference, Iris Marion Young (1990:168) says, 'Integration into the full life of the society should not have to imply assimilation to dominant norms and abandonment of group affiliation and culture.' This statement captures a main aim of social movements advancing the claims of women, Aboriginal people, seniors, persons with disabilities, gays and lesbians, and ethnocultural groups. Among other activities, these social movements develop and promote positive self-definitions, and endeavour to make group identities a matter for public policy. They seek the affirmation and recognition of group differences, the elimination of oppression and discrimination, mutual respect of different experiences and perspectives, and the social equality of individuals and groups (Young 1990). We begin this chapter by looking at some of the critical analysis of the welfare system and move on to look in detail at the universality-selectivity debate. Williams (1992:209) observes that 'Diversity carries with it a very different meaning to that of selectivity or targeting. The latter are associated with a top-down objective assessment: the selecting or targeting of need is defined by the administrator. Diversity, on the other hand, suggests a more subjective and self-determined approach to need. Diversity reveals itself in the demands or experiences of people's own actions.'

Our purpose here is to examine how the state uses social policies to manage and regulate the way people meet their needs, and to highlight the tension that many community groups feel. The welfare state, while providing important benefits and creating social cohesion, has a darker side. It is a form of social control that is often used to regulate people's lives and to shape the way they connect with others in society. Critics from the community point out that there is no such thing as a unified category of citizen or client or carer; that programs and services relate differently to different groups; that policy makers cannot assume unitary interests and needs even within groups; and that various groups have been oppressed by the market economy and the welfare state while being excluded from a full range of civil, political, and social rights. The changing politics of social policy questions the principles of universalism, standardization, and uniformity, and moves more towards particularism, fragmentation, and diversity. It emphasizes subjectivity and difference as opposed to universal and homogeneous kinds of experience, needs, or forms of provision. Pluralist critiques of the welfare state deconstruct universal categories and hegemonic constructions of the world.

In this politics of difference and diversity, where do welfare programs fit in general, and universality in particular? We argue that the changing politics of social policy will force governments to create policies that protect groups of citizens from the damaging impact of social change. Community groups redefine work so that greater support is provided to women who provide care in the non-paid labour force. The personal becomes political. Gay and lesbian communities lobby to have the fundamental basis of the criminal code amended so that sexual orientation will be normalized. Aboriginal people gather strength to rebuild the core of their nation so that their historical ways of solving social problems will begin to dominate. Community activists seek ways to ensure that income is redistributed from those benefiting from international economic development to those who work and live in the context of local economic initiatives. The self-correcting mechanism of Polanyi's 'double movement' is already being felt in many areas. Jane Ursel (1997:177) points out, for example, that the number of services for wife-abuse victims grew tenfold between 1982 and 1990, and that government expenditures rose even more dramatically during a decade of fiscal constraint, to demonstrate that women (those who were battered and those who are at risk) are better off today as a result of state involvement. There are other examples. In Cape Breton, community economic development initiatives have restored some small commodity capitalism to local levels of control through worker co-ops.

The struggle to have governments support community initiatives is challenging. There are a number of views about how the process should unfold. At the heart of all of them is the question of whether social policies will be divisive in the way they are created or if policy makers can find universal themes that cross groups and therefore foster social cohesion. Peter Taylor-Gooby (1994:387) suggests, with some concern, that 'a universal and ameliorative social policy conflicts with the postmodern emphasis on diversity and pluralism in views of what is desirable.' He worries that the postmodernist themes of difference, decentralization, and choice may pay insufficient attention to trends of growing inequality, stricter regulation of the poor, and privatization of health and social services. He fears that postmodernism is a great leap backwards for social policy. Martin Hewitt (1994:44) is more optimistic about the fit between diversity and universality in light of the role of the new social movements: 'These movements challenge the failure of government to apply traditional universal ethics, such as justice, need and citizenship, appropriately in identifying the needs of specific groups. Indeed it can be argued that social movements are motivated towards a new order of particular *and* universal values.' In this context, Fiona Williams (1992:206) concludes that 'fragmentation of class politics and the development of identity politics implies that demands upon welfare will be about meeting the specific needs of particular groups, rather than about pressing for universal provision to cover the needs of all.'

Patrick Kerans (1994:129) makes the point that 'citizenship in Canada is changing from that which accrues universally and uniformly to each individual Canadian, towards a still vaguely defined sense of the equal respect which should be accorded to groups, as groups.' The prevailing policy discourse of the Canadian government speaks of promoting diversity and advancing equality, while, aside from Medicare and the Canada Health Act,[1] universality is rarely mentioned. Major federal policies related to the theme of diversity include the Aboriginal agenda for self-determination, the Canadian Human Rights Act and Commission, immigration and refugee policy, multiculturalism policy and programs, and support to persons with disabilities. Major federal policies related to advancing equality include the Canadian Charter of Rights and Freedoms, the Court Challenges Program which finances groups seeking to establish or confirm their legal and constitutional rights under the Charter, the Canadian Race Relations Foundation Act, and the Employment Equity Act.

Two important examples of linking universal policy values with diverse needs and differential capacities were added to the Canadian Constitution in the 1980s. Section 15 (1) of the Charter of Rights deals with equality rights, and states that every individual is equal before and under the law and has the right to the equal protection and equal benefit of the law without discrimination. Subsection (2) adds, however, that 'Subsection (1) does not preclude any law, program, or activity that has as its object the amelioration of conditions of disadvantaged individuals or groups including those that are disadvantaged because of race, national or ethnic origin, colour, religion, sex, age, or mental or physical disability.' Thus the first subsection provides for the universal application of every law, while the second subsection immediately qualifies that by validating affirmative action and equity programs, what the social policy literature has called 'positive discrimination' on behalf of or by the underprivileged.

Under Section 36 of the Constitution Act of 1982, which lies outside of the Charter of Rights, the federal government and the provincial governments are committed to (a) promoting equal opportunities for the well-being of Canadians, (b) furthering economic development to reduce disparity in opportunities, and (c) providing essential public services of reasonable quality to all Canadians. Furthermore, the section states that the federal government and Parliament are committed to the principle of making equalization payments to ensure that provincial governments have sufficient revenues to provide reasonably comparable levels of public services at reasonably comparable levels of taxation. This constitutional guarantee of equalization codifies a practice in intergovernmental financial arrangements that dates from the late 1950s. Each year the federal government makes equalization payments to most of the provinces totalling several billions of dollars. The federal payments help ensure that provinces with tax-raising capacities below a defined national average do not need to have substantially lower levels of public services or far higher levels of taxes than residents in wealthier provinces. Constitutional expert Peter Hogg (1985:119) has said of the equalization section: 'This obligation is probably too vague, and too political, to be justiciable [that, is, subject to the jurisdiction of the judiciary and enforceable by the courts], but it suggests that equalization payments will continue into the foreseeable future.'

The Dark Side of Welfare: The Use of Social Programs to Exert Control

In Chapter 4 we described the general criticisms that community groups have about the welfare state. Here we go a little deeper into these criticisms so that a fuller debate about the role of universal programs can emerge. Feminist writers describe the way social policies construct interventions that control the private and domestic sphere of life (Pascall 1986). They suggest that social policies have been used by the state to maintain a specific form of the family in which men, women, and children have specific roles. Elizabeth Wilson (1977:9) believes that social welfare policies amount to no less than the state organization of domestic life. Aboriginal people claim that social policies are used against them to control many aspects of their lives. The most powerful example is how education policy was used as a reason to remove children from Aboriginal families; place them in residential schools; and strip them of their language, culture, and heritage. The Indian Act was used to isolate and control Aboriginal people in such a way that it removed them from their homelands, suppressed their identities, and created an ongoing feeling of colonialization. The gay and lesbian community was outlawed through the process of social policies and people who were not heterosexual were made to live deviant lives. Even when legislation removed the criminal label from private sexual preferences, the stigma was maintained in many other social policies.

When governments use social policies to constrain and control individuals and families, they are constraining the development of civic society. Social policies then become instruments that shape the way communities are organized and the way people interact within these communities. The government's primary concern is to control the public's moral and social conduct and to define a particular type of citizenship with certain rights and benefits. All levels of government play a part in creating policies that modify the statuses and roles of people within the community. Government uses four types of civic regulations that have direct implications for community groups: human rights, justice and public order, moral sexual regulations, and welfare programs and social union. This line of analysis suggests a trend towards the greater use of rules in managing social policies.

Human Rights

Social policies dealing with human rights shape the terms and conditions on which people become citizens of a country. They create what T.H. Marshall (1963) called the right to the social dimension of citizenship and through it access to social benefits such as education, social security, and health care. As such they determine the basic eligibility criteria for all social benefits. The concept of citizenship was introduced in 1947 legislation and expanded in the 1960 Canadian Bill of Rights and the 1977 Canada Human Rights Act. Citizenship was finally entrenched in the Constitution by the Charter of Rights and Freedoms in 1982. Group rights have been expanded in the Charter to include Aboriginal people, women, gays and lesbians, and people with disabilities. The naming of these groups implies they will be treated equally within the context of the regulatory process and insured of their entitlements to fair consideration in the allocation of benefits.

The darker side of being identified as a category in the context of citizenship is that it carries with it a subtle form of stigmatization. There is an underlying suspicion, held by those who are not named, that preference will be given to those who are. This was manifest recently in the case of young white males, who historically have been favoured when it came to being hired for police or fire departments. Now that there is consideration given to others, they feel left out of the process and claim to be unfairly treated.

Social Order

Civil regulations concerned with social order reflect the essential functions of government as lawmaker, umpire, and enforcer. The primary institutions concerned with justice and public order are the courts, police, law offices, prisons, and parole boards. There has been ongoing tension between community groups and these regulatory institutions of the state.

For the most part, Aboriginal people, people of colour, gays, and lesbians have felt harassed by the justice system. The Charter has provided some increased protection against unreasonable search or seizure, but people of colour still feel a certain threat in communities such as Montreal, Toronto, and Vancouver. The gay community has also felt under attack for a long time. Even though Canada in 1969 decriminalized gross indecency between consenting adults in private, there was an ongoing struggle between the police and the gay community. In 1981 the Toronto Police raided four gay steam baths and arrested more than 300 men. As George Smith (1990:259) points out, the scope and violence of these raids made them a *cause célèbre*. The gay community was both angered and perplexed by the viciousness of the raids, and sought to understand the nature of the attacks and how to make sense of the behaviour of the police.

Although the law allows homosexuals to have sex in private, it does not allow them to create a 'public' space in which they can come together to meet, develop relations, and create liaisons for the purpose of having sex. This means the police, as an expression of the authority of the state, treat the gay community differently than they treat the heterosexual community. Smith, in his research, wanted to determine how the regulations contained within the Criminal Code affected police behaviour in relationship to the gay community. He traced the three-step process of investigation-raid-arrest to determine the roots of harassment. The regulations allowing the police to behave in this way are deeply entrenched in the Criminal Code, and Smith believes it will take enormous energy and a long time before substantial changes are made. At a broader level a number of challenges to the Charter have expanded the protection afforded members of groups, although critics claim it is only a modest shift in the balance of powers from police to citizen (McLeod and Schneiderman 1994).

Morality and Sexuality

The third dimension of civil regulation concerns morality and sexuality within the social policy domain. This area has also been criticized by community groups. Janine Brodie (1996:359) and the contributors to her book are critical of the relationship between the state and non-state actors involved in developing and reproducing codes of morality. She claims that 'Moral regulation is the privileging of certain forms of expression that results in the subordination of other forms of self-identification and social recognition. Sexual regulation forms a crucial part of the larger project of the production of moral subjects. The legal regulation of sexual representation through obscenity laws and pornography policy is a key example of moral regulation.'

Regulating morality represents one of the ways in which the government seeks to create an environment of control over the way people think about certain issues and the way community members construct their relationships with each other. Moral regulations deal with abortion, contraception, divorce, drug use, euthanasia, family law, marriage, pornography, prostitution, reproductive technologies, and sexual orientation. All of these areas are highly contentious. Different community groups have different positions on each of the areas, and governments find it difficult and politically dangerous to venture too far from existing legislation (Campbell and Pal 1989:150). The pluralization of the community means that there is a growing array of interests and claims, which limits the government's willingness to create new policy.

It is difficult for governments to move incrementally on issues or to bargain with stakeholder groups because cutting deals are viewed by many as ethically unacceptable.

Welfare Programs and Social Union

This brings us to the final area of civic regulation. Here we are concerned with the restrictive practices of the welfare state. Community groups are particularly concerned with the way welfare regulations control the behaviour of individuals and families. As Margaret Biggs (1996:1) points out, welfare programs create a 'web of rights and obligations between Canadian citizens and governments that give effect and meaning to our shared sense of social purpose and citizenship.' All welfare programs have rules that control entitlement, regulate the flow of benefits, create conditions for withdrawal of support, and establish power and dependency relationships. As we have seen, in the last five years there has been a general tightening of rules and regulations governing almost all welfare programs. While governments have made claims about fraud (with little evidence to support such claims), it appears that the underlying motive is to make work more attractive relative to social benefits.

The growth in civic regulation has been one of the consequences of the creation of the welfare state. Those who view these regulations as new forms of social cohesion holding a fragmenting society together may see much of this growth in positive terms. On the other hand, those who see this as a way of extending social control and control of the forces of patriarchy, capitalism, and racism will see much of it in negative terms.

Divisive Debate: Universality versus Selectivity within the Welfare State

There is a natural tension between the concept of universality and the increasing pluralization of the community. The fundamental question is, can there be a universal welfare program when the community has become so diverse. The fate of universal income programs in Canada is reflected in the various editions of *Social Welfare in Canada*, by Andrew Armitage, a standard text in the social welfare field for over twenty years. The first edition, subtitled *Ideals and Realities*, was published in

1975 at the end of the expansionist period of social policy in Canada. In it, Armitage examined the advantages and disadvantages of selective versus universal transfer mechanisms. The second edition, released in 1988, near the end of the crisis period and was subtitled *Ideals, Realities, and Future Paths*, again covered the debate and similarly concluded that both universality and selectivity were needed in the income security system. The third edition, in 1996, subtitled *Facing Up to the Future*, noted that the universal Family Allowance and Old Age Security transfers no longer existed in their original form. 'Thus for all practical purposes this once intense debate is over' (Armitage 1996:42). Other writers also have expressed pessimism about the likelihood of universality reappearing on the federal income security policy agenda.

The decline of universality is among the most striking changes to social policy in Canada in modern times. With the universal family and old age benefits replaced by selective income-tested benefits, two of the pillars of the universalist welfare state in Canada have fallen. 'Universal health care remains standing, but there are strong pressures to allow the growth of a two-tier system which would permit Canadians to purchase some health services if they have the desire and – more to the point – the means to do so; ... some provinces have created *dé facto* user fees by reducing the range of insured services' (Battle 1997:38).

Williams (1992) suggests that fragmentation, change and uncertainty, and contradiction distinguish recent welfare policy and provision. On the changing politics of social policy, Williams (1992:202) observes, 'whilst many of the universalistic policies and assumptions of the post-war period have been eroded, they have not been replaced by an overarching commitment to individualism, family, self-help and the market. The situation is more fluid, more complex, and more contradictory.' Williams's comments pertain to Britain but also apply, we believe, to Canada. The question of universality or selectivity may appear to be decided for now in the income security system, but the question in that field as well as in education and health care and possibly other fields is never completely closed. This uncertainty and continuing controversy is rooted in the presence of contending views of social policy, the role of the state, and a just society. 'In this sense,' Alan Pratt (1997b:213) notes, 'the universality-selectivity debate can also be seen as one dimension of a perennial, profound fault line in western political thought: the relationship between state and civil society, between the market and the state.'

Universality in Health Care and Child Care

The principle of universality remains at the core of the politics and provision of education and health care in Canada, and is evident in recent reform proposals and initiatives. As described in Chapter 3, the five federal principles associated with the public health care system, also called Medicare, were set out in the Canada Health Act of 1984. These are the principles of accessibility (there will be no financial barriers to insured health care), comprehensiveness (all services provided by hospitals and physicians deemed to be medically necessary must be covered), portability (all Canadians are entitled to coverage wherever they are in the country), public administration (health insurance plans must be administered on a nonprofit basis by a public authority), and universality (all legal residents of a Canadian province or territory must be eligible after a residency period of no more than three months). Note that it is the principle of accessibility that most closely fits with the notion of universality in income support programs, whereas the principle of universality under the Canada Health Act addresses the scope of coverage of the population. This subtlety in the different meanings of universality is not commonly recognized and may add to the confusion of what universality means in social policy.

The National Forum on Health, a panel of experts established by the Chrétien government, recommended in 1996 that a universal home care program be developed for the frail elderly. Given the aging of the population, reductions in institutional care and the limitations of time and the skills of family caregivers, the case for universal home care is to ensure equality of care, to assist informal caregivers, and to reinforce Medicare. This proposal relates to issues, discussed in Chapters 4 and 8, of overloading volunteers with community care responsibilities and expecting family members, which usually means women, to provide essential services.

Recent federal budgets have increased tax relief for people who care for infirm dependants, largely elderly relatives, at home. Such tax relief has been fairly selective in impact, however, as many caregivers are ineligible because the senior relatives they care for receive the federal elderly income benefits (the Old Age Security and Guaranteed Income Supplement), which put them above the threshold for relief. The Liberals' 1997 election platform committed them to work with the provinces and territories in establishing a national pharmacare program, building on the assistance programs these governments currently offer to seniors to help defray the cost of prescription drugs. In seeking to ensure people have access to medically necessary drugs in the public health care system, such a program has universalist elements. To date, neither the provinces nor the general public seem very interested in the idea of a national pharmacare program, indicating provincial mistrust of federal intrusion into their jurisdiction and past unilateral cuts to joint programs, and the public's wariness of embarking on new, potentially large expenditure programs just as the federal deficit has been eliminated.

The continued relevance and attractiveness of universality is illustrated by the Quebec government's implementation of a universal system of day care over the 1997 to 2000 period (Philp 1997). Building on the province's own universal Family Allowance program and related tax credits, Quebec is providing subsidies to families with young children regardless of their incomes. Parents will pay a flat $5 daily fee for child care in daycare centres and home-based settings, though parents receiving social assistance will pay a $2 daily fee. This major policy initiative is expected to help reduce poverty, encourage people to move off social assistance and seek employment, and assist parents in balancing the responsibilities of family and paid work.

The Canadian Council on Social Development (CCSD), a national organization dedicated to promoting social and economic security, has urged the federal government to develop a comprehensive strategy to support *all* families with children, not only low-income families. The CCSD specifically commends Quebec's family policy as such a strategy, with universal income support, through the tax system, to all families with children; universally accessible and affordable child care being introduced; and, within this universalist infrastructure, service supports and income supplements for low-income families with children. In addition, the CCSD (1997a:6) notes that 'Canada stands apart from most other advanced industrial countries that already recognize the societal value and personal costs associated with raising children through their tax structures.' From the discussion earlier in the chapter, we can see that the CCSD is seeking to restore the horizontal equity objective in the tax/transfer system so that families with children, at all income levels, receive tax relief on grounds of international practice, tax fairness, and the collective benefits and responsibilities of raising children. In our view, these are compelling arguments for reform.

Which Social Programs Qualify for the Term 'Universal'?

Differences of opinion are apparent in the media and in academic literature concerning which social programs in Canada are universal and which are selective. There is general agreement on four main social programs to which universality applies: Medicare, public education, and, until their recent demise, Family Allowance and Old Age Security. Even on this list, education is frequently forgotten in discussions and writings on social policy, as are the Veterans' and Civilians' Disability Pensions.[2] Beyond this, there are various other programs thought to be universal, such as the Canada and Quebec Pension Plans, Employment Insurance, and Workers' Compensation. In fact, these are all social insurance programs. Even further afield, municipal services such as snow removal and garbage collection, transportation services, public utilities, and the services of Canada Post have been identified as universal programs (Findlay 1983). In the mass media, one can read or hear of selective programs such as tax credits, social housing, or even welfare mistakenly called universal.

Traditionally, universal income programs in Canada, also called 'demogrants' in federal parlance, provided benefits to persons who met certain demographic conditions regardless of their financial situation. As an instrument of allocating public resources, the central characteristic of universality is that benefits or services are provided according to criteria other than individual or family income. Access to universal programs is not to be determined by a test of means, need, or work.

Social insurance programs, by contrast, pay benefits to defined groups of workers with benefit levels usually tied to previous employment income levels. No doubt a large part of the tendency to equate social insurance programs with universality is that, like universal programs, they commonly provide comprehensive coverage to a client group, offer benefits as a right rather than as a charity or by means testing, and promote the goal of social security. Social insurance programs are not universal programs, however, because a person's eligibility and their benefits are dependent on an attachment to the labour force. Social insurance benefits are not based on citizenship alone, with a flat-rate benefit paid to everyone in a broad category. Rather, eligibility is based on previous contributions in the form of premiums or payroll deductions, earnings, and the ability to work.

The meaning of universality within the income security system has changed over the past several decades as the design and impact of programs have been adjusted. In the 1940s and 1950s, when universal family allowances and old age pensions were introduced in Canada, universality involved paying an equal pre-tax dollar benefit to everyone in these designated demographic groups. The interaction between the benefit transfer and the income tax system was not taken into account by the federal government, nor were benefits indexed to compensate for inflation, which in any case was low during these years. The important design feature at the time was the absence of a means test. From the 1960s into the 1980s, family allowances and old age benefits became taxable income, yet were also indexed. Universality shifted to mean a variable, after-tax benefit, yet with everyone keeping a substantial portion. In effect, the net benefit was now income tested. This feature permitted defenders of universality to argue that redistribution to the poor could be achieved within universal programs by taxing back some of the benefits of higher income people.

Over the 1989–91 period, a surtax or clawback was applied to family allowance and old age benefits so that while all families with children and all seniors over age sixty-five continued to receive the benefit, some families and seniors would retain little or no benefits (Rice and Prince 1993). The Mulroney government insisted that universality was still alive in these programs as everyone in the client categories still received a monthly payment in the mail. This perspective conveniently disregarded, though, the size and incidence of the net after-tax benefit as an important element to universalism. However, most social policy commentators, and we concur, declared the death of universality in family and elderly benefits as a result of the special surtaxes. Any doubt of this was removed in subsequent policy developments. The Family Allowance program was abolished at the end of 1992 and replaced by the income tested Child Tax Benefit. Old Age Security benefits became income tested at the front end as of July 1996; benefits are now reduced *before* they are sent out rather than being taxed *after* seniors have received their cheques. Old age pensions are now, every dollar of them, a selective program (Prince 1997). Thus today, only Medicare and public education qualify as major universal programs.

The Political Theory of Universality

The concept of universality has been an important policy instrument in the development of the welfare state. Based on the notion of citizenship, it has conferred benefits to everyone in the same category. But with the pluralization of the community, the relevance of universal programs has come into question. Critics have wanted to know, for example, why a banker's spouse should receive the same family allowance as women in low-income families. The fiscalization of social policy dictated that for economic reasons the banker's spouse should not get the benefits. But the changing politics has raised the question of social cohesion in a new way, and universality appears to be a policy instrument able to meet the fragmented demands of a diverse population. While no complete theoretical framework of universality exists in social policy analysis or practice, the main elements of such a theory can be found grounded in the literature, dispersed throughout many works. The following discussion is adapted from Prince (1991).

The theoretical case for universality does not exist as a well-codified set of hypotheses; instead, it is expressed in narrative form containing key ideas, arguments, and predicted relations among certain factors. What makes the narrative a theory is the effort to explain and predict events and policy outcomes. What makes the narrative a *political* theory are the beliefs and assertions that universality promotes social integration, fosters wide public support for maintaining universal programs, and indeed their improvement over time; ensures political protection against cutbacks; and creates public sympathy among the better off for adequate and quality programs for the poor. Universality is seen therefore as a powerful policy instrument for building relations between social groups and across classes, enhancing social cohesion and tackling inequalities on the basis of a solid public consensus. Universal programs are seen to be built upon the notion of citizenship, with eligibility based simply upon membership in the community.

The theoretical core of universality consists of five propositions. Each can be found, in one form or another, in the literature. Each is based on the history and politics of social policy and welfare states, especially in Canada, Britain, and the United States. The five propositions are examined here.

1. *Without a universalist policy framework, selective programs for the needy will tend to be punitive and of poor quality.* This first proposition contends that stigmatization of recipients, low standards of service, lower take-up rates of benefits, and greater social divisions are associated with stand-alone, selective social programs. When social benefits are targeted for those most in need, tensions and prejudices emerge. Selective social programs, the Canadian Council of Catholic

Bishops has said in public statements, inevitably serve to create divisions between those 'who pay' and those 'who receive,' further stigmatizing the poorer members of society. Peter Findlay (1983:19–20) has outlined theoretically what can happen when selective programs are aimed at clearly identifiable groups such as women, Aboriginal peoples, recent immigrants, and the poor: 'pressures will arise to define the group more precisely, to lower benefits, and to build a large bureaucracy which will regulate and police more rigorously as people adjust their behaviour to ensure they fall within the policy's parameter.' Thus without a universalist policy framework, the needy will be served by second-rate selective programs that punish them.

2. *Universal programs in cash or in kind services fulfil various functions: social recognition, investment, economic stabilization, prevention, social integration, and stigma avoidance.* The second proposition is that universal programs serve many roles, in both the economy and the rest of society, with the vertical redistribution of income often only a secondary objective. One such role is the fostering of societal recognition of the contributions made by groups such as families with children, seniors, and veterans with particular reference to the costs they incur and the contributions they make to society. This role relates to what is called horizontal equity: providing financial or service support to a broad category of people with some shared characteristics, irrespective of their income differences.

A second role of universality is encouraging investment in the health, morale, and education of children, family stability, and social development. Closely related is the idea of prevention of disease and sickness through public health measures and regular medical examinations. A third role is fostering economic stabilization by maintaining the flow of consumer purchasing power through the provision of monthly payments to families and seniors. The latter two roles were notable themes in the Marsh Report and in the Keynesian paradigm of government policy discussed in Chapters 3 and 5.

Finally, it has been argued that universality serves the purpose of social integration and stigma avoidance by providing a general system of benefits and services, by avoiding punitive eligibility tests, by treating all clients more or less alike, and by establishing spheres of common interest and experience. Universal income programs at the federal level of government may also foster national unity. The relative weight given to these roles will depend on the prevailing values and interests in a given country. Thus there are many different functions that universal programs fulfil that are not based simply on economic redistribution. Universal programs enjoy broad public support, which serves to maintain service levels as well as provide the political base for further social policy reforms.

3. *By including the middle class as clients, universal programs enjoy mass public support, and also provide a political context for other progressive social reforms.* The third proposition has two parts. The first holds that universal programs are widely supported by the public, which helps to maintain and improve them; for example, the middle classes have a direct sense of personal stake in the education and health care systems, and in income security programs. Inclusion in these programs, as actual or potential clients, makes middle-income Canadians a supportive and strong political constituency. Findlay (1983:21–2) elaborates: 'Benefits or services will be kept at decent levels because influential groups will insist on it ... and service providers will be more accountable and less heavy-handed because they will be dealing with influential and assertive groups in the population.' Furthermore, the participation of the middle classes in National Health Services in Great Britain with 'articulate demands for improvements, have been an important factor in a general rise in standards of service' (Titmuss 1968:196).

The second part of this proposition suggests that universal programs, with mass public inclusion and support, provide a favourable political climate for progressive reforms on other social programs such as welfare or child care. In Canada, the National Council of Welfare (1983:26) has argued that 'Rightly or wrongly, many middle-income Canadians feel that they bear more than their fair share of the tax burden relative to what they get from government in return. Universal programs such as Family Allowance and Old Age Security are among the few benefits that most taxpayers receive from the social security system. The middle-class majority's willingness to finance improvements in selective social programs directed to low-income persons, or even to maintain such spending at its present level, could well decline if universal measures such as family allowances were dismantled.' Thus through maintaining universal programs, broad public support is gained both for maintaining present programs and for introducing new ones.

4. *Universal programs, because of their broad base of public support, are less susceptible to cutbacks than selective programs, especially those for the poor.* On the one hand, selective social programs are viewed as serving small, politically weak constituencies, so that service reductions and benefit cuts would not generate mainstream public criticism and dissent. On the other hand, universal programs such as the old age pension, with a large and growing clientele, could generate a much louder response and greater political impact. The essence of the argument is that universal programs enjoy broader public support and better protection against cutbacks in an era of fiscal retrenchment, than do programs affecting the poor, because of their core middle-class constituency.

5. *Universalism is a necessary prerequisite for promoting social integration, but requires complementary selective programs for tackling inequalities and implementing affirmative action policies.* Finally, the fifth proposition represents an acknowledgement of the linkage between universal social programs and quality selective programs. Universalism is a necessary but not sufficient condition in 'reducing and removing formal barriers of social and economic discrimination,' but by itself, not enough to create greater social equality in education, medical care, or income security (Titmuss 1968:196–7). Recognizing that selective programs alone are undesirable (the first proposition) and that universal programs alone are insufficient, the issue becomes one of determining what relationship between selectivity and universality would be most effective in promoting social inclusion and reducing social inequality. Quality (non-stigmatizing, accessible, effective) selective social programs are only possible, according to this perspective, within a framework of universal programs which provide the general values and opportunity bases for specific groups and regions.

Perspectives on Universality

The principle and practice of universality face a paradox; as a social value and policy instrument it is not universally agreed upon by Canadians. Three dominant perspectives are evident: those of the anti-universalists, the administrative universalists, and the active universalists. For anti-universalists' the rallying cry is to 'slaughter the sacred cow of universality,' arguing that 'wealthy bankers' wives shouldn't get family benefits' (McQuaig 1993), or that 'private funding and user fees are necessary to preserve public education and keep Medicare alive.' Business lobby groups, certain economists and editorialists, conservative think-tanks, and many individuals do not agree with paying social benefits to better-off Canadians. The universality of income support programs is regarded from this perspective as a huge waste of money, unfair to the poor, and irresponsible in a fiscal context of high public deficits and accumulating debt. Anti-universalists would make income or needs tested benefits the primary instrument of the income security system rather than universality or even social insurance. It is often unclear whether anti-universalists want to use the 'savings' generated from de-universalizing programs to reduce the deficit or debt, enrich selective social programs, or finance economic initiatives.

Most anti-universalists in Canada focus their opposition to universality on the federal income support programs, while favouring universality in the health insurance and education fields. Undoubtedly some hard-core anti-universalists are also anti-government, that is, people generally against the state having a role in the social policy field, and who call for privatizing sections of the health care system or introducing voucher schemes in the school system.

The position of administrative universalists can be summed up in a quintessential Canadian way as 'universality if affordable, but not necessarily universality.' People and groups holding this viewpoint support universality in principle but believe the nation can no longer afford to pay family or elderly benefits to middle- and upper-income households. Some administrative universalists support the idea of a surtax on higher income recipients, perhaps on a family rather than individual basis, while others called for the replacement of the universal Family Allowance and Old Age Security. The universal distribution of benefits, for administrative universalists, is more a convenient technique than a cherished principle; no intrinsic normative superiority is assumed either for universality or selectivity. The choice is a pragmatic one, based on what seems to work in a given policy setting.

Active universalists are vigorous defenders of universality in the Canadian welfare state. They call for retaining and improving existing universal programs as well as possibly introducing new ones. Proponents of this viewpoint include seniors' groups, church groups, most social policy organizations, organized labour, social democrats, some liberals, many child care advocates, most womens' groups, and health care, education, and social work professionals. For these groups, universality is not simply about common accessibility and non-financial eligibility; it is also about a system of social relations, community values, and political forces. With regard to income security, active universalists believe that all parents with children and all seniors should receive a family benefit or elderly benefit from the Canadian government in recognition of their contributions to Canadian society; they are also energetic defenders of national health insurance and public education. Active universalists contend that there are far better ways than abandoning universality for 'taking from the rich to help the poor.' They favour eliminating regressive tax breaks and introducing a wealth tax, inheritance tax, and other reforms to establish a more equitable system of taxes and transfers.

The coexistence of these three orientations to universality suggests a continuing controversy in the politics and formation of social policy. Indeed, public-opinion trends over the past twenty years show that Canadian public attitudes towards universality are well formed and significantly divided. Through the 1980s and into the 1990s, for example, about 60 per cent of the population was of the view that only those persons who have financial need should be eligible for government benefits such as family allowances, while about 40 per cent of Canadians believed that everyone should receive such benefits (Prince 1991). What is less certain, however, is whether universality is the dominant value in various social policies. While universality is a major value undergirding health care and education policy, the contributory principle of social insurance and the selectivity principle are also significant precepts in pensions, disability benefits, unemployment benefits, social housing, and welfare benefits. Strong public support for the notion of targeting is also apparent in public and governmental preferences regarding daycare policy. While most Canadians agree that daycare services should be available to anyone who needs them, there is relatively little support for the principle of a universal national child care system for all families. Most Canadians and their governments favour a targeted approach to spending on child care based in part on the ability to pay of the parent or parents (Phillips 1989; Bach and Phillips 1997). Even on the Left in Canada, there are differing views on how best to develop child care (Rosenblum and Findlay 1991).

The Dismantling of Universal Income Security Programs

The forces of globalization have undermined the economic reasons for universal programs. Here we examine how the two major universal programs came to an end, as well as the economic argument put forward at the time. Events of recent years have severely tested all kinds of income security programs and other social policies in Canada. A series of cuts to the Unemployment Insurance program in the 1980s and 1990s culminated in its transformation to the Employment Insurance program in 1996, with yet further cuts in the level and duration of benefits. The formation of the Canada Health and Social Transfer in 1996 involved a substantial cut in federal transfer payments to other governments for health care, postsecondary education, social services, and welfare. The income support program of last resort, welfare, now has but one federal condition attached to it, and the provinces and territories are not under any obligation to spend the transfer payment on welfare (Rice 1995b). As of 1998 the Canada Pension Plan's contributions were to rise faster than previously planned while retirement and disability benefits for future retirees were to be cut back (Prince 1997).

Contrary to the political theory of universality, universal income programs have not been untouchable or irreversible in the face of neoconservatism and government retrenchment.[3] In particular, the Old Age Security and Family Allowance programs were not endowed with superior protection against restraint. Neither of these universal programs' basic benefit rate was raised after 1973, at the end of the expansion era of the welfare state in Canada. In 1979 a cutback in Family Allowance benefits was used to help fund a new, selective Refundable Child Tax Credit. Both the Family Allowance and OAS programs had their indexation provisions capped in 1983 and 1984 by the Trudeau Liberal government, thereby limiting their guard against inflation. Family Allowance was partially de-indexed as of 1986 and both programs became subject to a clawback of benefits, phased in over the 1989–91 period, implemented by the Mulroney Conservative government. The Conservatives then terminated Family Allowance in 1992, replacing it and two other family related benefits with the selective, income-tested Child Tax Benefit (Battle 1993). The Chrétien Liberal government introduced income testing of Old Age Security payments in 1996, marking the formal end of the universality of this elderly benefit.

The one exception to dismantling universal income programs is veterans' financial benefits. Both the universal Veterans' and Civilians' Disability Pension and the income tested War Veterans' and Civilian War Allowances have been improved over the last fifteen years. This experience may reflect the impact of a universalist framework in this benefit system, but the child and elderly systems had similar frameworks. The special treatment of Veterans' Disability Pensions more likely reflects the positive ranking of veterans as meritorious by the general public and politicians. Military service-related disabilities – a specified risk resulting from a contribution – have long been regarded as highly deserving needs to be met as forms of compensation and appreciation by the state. In fact, the Pensions Act of 1919, offering disability pensions for soldiers, was 'the first significant and continuing [federal] intervention in the social welfare field' in Canada (Bryden 1974:8). The 1943 Marsh Report noted that social security provisions for the armed forces and their dependants were more advanced in scope and in benefits than those for Canadians in ordinary civilian life. It is the status of veterans and the nature of their needs, more than universality itself, which makes their program enduring and politically resistant to restructuring.[4]

After being an important feature of Canadian social policy for close to fifty years, recent Conservative and Liberal federal governments successfully eliminated universality as a central principle of income support for families and seniors. The income security system is once again a residual sector of the welfare state in Canada. Why did this happen and how was it accomplished?

In an analysis of social policy retrenchment in Britain and the United States during the administrations of Margaret Thatcher and Ronald Reagan, Paul Pierson found that some selective programs were vulnerable to cuts while others were not, and the same was true for universal programs. The belief that universal programs are more durable than selective programs does not hold. Pierson gives two reasons why governments have gone after universal programs:

> An ideologically committed and consistent conservative government would object most strongly to governmental provisions for the middle class. It is universal programs rather than targeted programs that compete with viable private-sector alternatives. If conservatives could design their ideal welfare state, it would consist of nothing but means-tested programs. Furthermore, conservatives are very concerned with reducing spending, and it is hard to squeeze much spending out of marginal, means-tested programs. The largest potential targets are bound to be those that include the middle class; budget cutters will find their attention drawn to universal programs. (1994: 101–2)

In an examination of the administration of Brian Mulroney, Ken Battle and Sherri Torjman (1995) echo these factors in suggesting that Conservative social policy reform was motivated equally by deficit reduction and anti-welfare state ideology. It defied common sense and fiscal prudence, Conservatives argued, that Family Allowance benefits should go to middle- and upper-income households (McQuaig 1993). The political vulnerability of the Old Age Security pensions was linked to the aging of the Canadian population and the slower growth of the labour force, with an anticipated budgetary crunch associated with the greying of the 'baby boomers,' who were having to be supported by the smaller 'baby bust' generation. As the largest transfer program to individuals and families in Canada, the OAS was a big target for cutbacks. The discourse of federal policy makers justifies targeting old age pensions to those who need public assistance, making the program affordable and thus sustainable for future generations (Prince 1997).

Universal programs live in a selective policy world and a stratified market economy and society. These are other factors that limit the political potency of universality. Of the more than 100 programs in the Canadian income security system, only a few are based on universal principles. Income support programs such as social assistance, tax expenditures, or social insurance with defined contributors and recipients, reflect and reproduce societal divisions. Within the framework of the child benefit and elderly benefit systems, selective programs grew over the past three decades both in absolute terms and in relation to Family Allowance and OAS, thus de-emphasizing the universal nature of these benefit regimes. Though universality may generate a clientele attached to the program, it is uncertain that such programs create a strong sense of solidarity across groups and classes in society. According to Canadian pollster Angus Reid (1997:276), 'Government safety nets may be more important than ever during tough times, but a sizeable percentage of the population is determined to cut some of those nets adrift before too many more Canadians start depending on them.' Public opinion surveys by the Angus Reid Group and other polling firms show that most Canadians believe there is abuse of the welfare system, and that a majority of middle-class and wealthy Canadians accept or enthusiastically support social program cutbacks. The part universal programs play in our everyday worlds, therefore, is partial, not total; it is inconsistent or in partial tension with other practices and beliefs; and it is subordinate to more dominant interests in our liberal democracy and capitalist economy.

Another reason for the political vulnerability of universal income programs was the old argument, which became increasingly persuasive during the rising government deficits and debt of the 1980s and early 1990s, that large universal spending programs could not effectively pursue a redistributive vertical equity role at the same time as they attempted to serve a horizontal equity purpose. If income support programs were to more vigorously tackle poverty, the argument went, then something had to give; namely, universality had to be eliminated and funds redirected to those in need. Contrary to the theory of universality, the very demise of universal Family Allowance and Old Age Security, rather than their continuance, was viewed as an opportunity for social policy reform. As Ken Battle (1993:421) observed of the child benefits system, 'With existing resources, it is simply not possible to increase substantially the benefits for low-income families and maintain the same level of benefits for middle- and high-income families.'

Battle's own thinking on universality for income programs reflects the shift away from universality towards a new orthodoxy on selectivity in the 1990s. Once a strong supporter of universality in the social security system, Battle is now what we would term a progressive selectivist with respect to income security, though he remains an active universalist for health care and education. A former director of the National Council of Welfare and currently president of the Caledon Institute of Social Policy, an independent think-tank, Battle does not mourn the loss of the Family Allowance and Old Age Security programs 'because they were replaced by fairer and more sustainable income-tested programs' (1996:17). Far more damaging than the abolition of universal child and elderly benefits, Battle believes, has been the cuts in federal transfers to the provinces and territories, the partial indexation of the tax system and certain benefits, and the changes to unemployment insurance.

Conclusions

The death of universal income programs came not with a crash but with a clawback. Family allowances and old age pensions fell victim to the artful practice of social policy reform by stealth (Battle 1993; Rice and Prince 1993), effectively executed by the Mulroney Conservatives as well as the Chrétien Liberals. As Battle (1993:439) points out, 'The main reason the Conservatives got away with their cuts to social programs ... is that most Canadians have no idea what has happened to them because the policy changes are so arcane and technical. This also makes the public more susceptible to government propaganda, which has become more bold and blatant in recent years.' The partial de-indexation of the Family Allowance program and the clawback imposed on both Family Allowance and Old Age Security benefits was done through federal budgets by the Department of Finance with no prior consultation, little media attention, and minimal public debate. Thus stealth as a policy instrument and process of covert change assisted the government in de-universalizing these two programs and cutting federal social spending with little political harm at the time.

Key institutional features of the Canadian political system have also enabled governments to retrench universal programs. Under federalism, cuts in intergovernmental financing for universal health care and education, either from the federal government to the provinces and territories or from the provinces to school boards, municipalities, and hospital boards, have allowed one level of government to offload costs and shift the burdens of restraint onto other levels, often with little political harm to the higher level. Under our parliamentary cabinet system of governance, the political executive is dominant and a majority government usually prevails in making policy changes, a tendency reinforced when those changes are developed under the shroud of budget secrecy and the pre-eminence of the Finance Department.

Social policy groups and women's organizations active in defending universality and challenging the Conservatives' changes to universal child and elderly benefits had a marginal impact on the government's agenda. Social sector groups lacked sufficient political organization and the mobilization of a strong mass constituency to counter the moves to selectivity (Moscovitch 1990). Meanwhile the Conservatives appealed to their own constituency of anti-universalists and administrative universalists, using the discourse of deficit reduction and the necessity to reduce social expenditures to justify targeting limited resources to those in greatest need.

The politics of universality has gone through several stages: from the creation of universal benefits and services from the 1940s to the 1970s; the attacks on and defence of them in the 1970s and 1980s; and the tactic of stealth in ending universal income benefits in the late 1980s and early 1990s; to a new orthodoxy of selectivity over who should be targeted for financial assistance and on what terms and basis. In addition, the postmodern politics of identity and difference and the new social movements pose challenges and opportunities for universal values and policies. The extinction of the universal Family Allowance and Old Age

Security programs are pivotal social policy changes and political events of the 1990s. The death of these universal programs is not only the demise of a social transfer mechanism, it is also a serious challenge to the political theory of universality outlined in this chapter. The universality-selectivity debate may be over for income security for now, at least at the federal level, yet it remains a passionate issue in health care and in public education. In other fields, equality rights are a prominent item on policy agendas, and, in relation to postmodernist politics, the terms of the debate may be shifting towards reconciling universal policies and practices with the realities of diversity and group differences.

8

Gender and Social Policy: His and Her States of Welfare

Feminist writers conceptualize and theorize about the globalization and pluralization of the welfare state. They provide important models and concepts for understanding what is happening in the community and the family. They have a penetrating analysis of the labour market and the way changing market conditions affect women. Most feminist writers organize their material around gender, but an analysis of it also takes us deeply into community. Our purpose here is to examine the gender dimension of the Canadian welfare state, including differences in the roles, rights, and duties of men and women in relation to families and caring, jobs and workplaces, and the political and governmental systems. We discuss both feminist perspectives on social policy and the contemporary processes of restructuring and retrenching the state.

The welfare state is, and always has been, highly gendered, that is, men and women have distinctive sets of relationships to the social security system. Women, for example, experience a different welfare state and social world than do men. These life experiences include having the greatest responsibility for the family, child care, and elder care; being victims of male violence; and generally being poorer. There also are differences in the causes and experiences of death. Since men marry younger women, who tend to live longer, over half of Canadian women will be widows, whereas only 20 per cent of Canadian men will be widowers. With respect to family formations, women head over 80 per cent of all single parent families in Canada. Women now constitute almost 60 per cent of the seniors population, and 70 per cent of all persons aged eighty-five and older. Differences in work experiences include continued occupational segregation for women in many sectors of the labour force and lower rates of earnings, benefits, and pensions. In the world of politics and governing, women remain significantly under-represented in legislatures, cabinets, the courts, and in senior levels of public bureaucracies and business corporations. In social programs, there are gender inequalities regarding access to many services and rights, benefit levels, and redistributive outcomes. Women also experience disproportionately the adverse consequences of social service cutbacks and other policy reforms. Here we examine the feminist perspectives on social policy, the gendered division of work, women's roles in the welfare state, and women's experiences with social programs.

Feminist Perspectives on Social Policy

In her presidential address to the Canadian Political Science Association, Caroline Andrew (1984:667) contended that to adequately understand the welfare state, 'it is necessary to examine the question of gender, the relations of women and the welfare state.' She described the overall relations between women and the welfare state as ambiguous and contradictory, yet also vital to women's well-being. And as Lois Bryson (1992:159), among several other feminist writers, has demonstrated, 'The conventional literature has been malestream and the provisions of the welfare state were developed by men from within the dominant male perspective, to solve problems as men perceived them. The significant point is that this is rarely acknowledged.' Despite Andrew's call over fifteen years ago for more feminist thought concerning the welfare state, gender analysis has not permeated mainstream texts in Canadian public administration, public policy, or political science in any significant way (Brooks 1993; Doern and Phidd 1992; Howlett and Ramesh 1995; Pal 1997). In other words, such texts contain little on gender, women, and the women's movement; and none treats feminism as a distinct analytic approach to studying and explaining policies and programs. The social policy and social work literatures are relatively more informed by feminist perspectives and critiques (Armitage 1996; Mullaly 1997; Pulkingham and Ternowetsky 1996; Tester, McNiven, and Case 1996). Some works are especially so (Baines, Evans, and Neysmith 1991; Brodie 1995) while others have decidedly little or no gender analysis (Banting and Battle 1994; Courchene 1994; Mishra 1990b; Teeple 1995). It seems Andrews's challenge has been ignored. Feminist analysis has remained primarily a women's perspective.

Mainstream Literature and Feminist Thinking

To highlight the critiques and the contributions of feminist thinking we will briefly consider the mainstream literature on social policy. Here the major models of social policy are the residual and institutional conceptions, first articulated forty years ago (Wilensky and Lebeaux 1958) and still applied and widely discussed (Guest 1997). Variations on and additions to these models include industrial achievement (Titmuss 1974) and social development (Callahan, Armitage, Prince, and Wharf 1990). The models all focus on government–market relations and the degree of state intervention and responsibility for meeting needs. Perhaps the best known typology of welfare states today is in Gosta Esping-Andersen's *The Three Worlds of Welfare Capitalism* (1990), wherein the three regimes are defined along a continuum of scope of coverage and level of generosity of benefits. The continuum moves from the least extensive liberal welfare states (including Canada, Britain, and the United States), to conservative welfare states (including Austria, Germany, and France), and ultimately to social-democratic welfare states (including Sweden and the other Scandinavian countries).[1]

The ideologies of social welfare commonly examined in the mainstream literature reflect the focus of these typologies and models on state intervention and matters of political economy. These ideologies are those of the the anti-collectivists (social Darwinists, neoconservatives, the new Right), the reluctant collectivists (liberals, modified individualists), social democrats (the old and the new Left), and the Marxists (George and Wilding 1976, 1985; Djao 1983; Mishra 1984). These ideologies of welfare range along a traditional Right to Left political spectrum, yet they all feature a male breadwinner and dependent-family model.

Feminist Alternatives

The feminist literature identifies a number of limitations inherent in these models, typologies, and ideologies. As Diane Sainsbury (1996:40) notes, 'feminists have underlined the importance of ideology in shaping welfare policies but they have cast light on a completely different set of values than the residual and institutional models. Rather than ideologies of state intervention or distribution, feminists have made familial and gender ideologies pivotal to the analysis of the welfare state.'

In this vein, feminist writers have named and proposed several alternative models of social policy to replace the male breadwinner model: the universal breadwinner model, which encompasses women as well as men; the female caregiver model, a parity model whereby caring is recognized and given remuneration; the male pauper model, which points out that amidst the feminization of poverty across societies, a portion of the male population also experiences destitution; and, finally, is the individual model, in which family roles are shared, and employment, wage taxes, and social policies are aimed at individuals rather than at heads of families or households (Baines, Evans, and Neysmith 1991; Sainsbury 1996). Some of these models are more fully developed conceptually and theoretically than others, but all offer new ways of thinking about the gendered division of social programs and social rights. With respect to ideology, women writers have added liberal, radical, socialist, and Marxist streams of feminist analysis to the traditional ideologies. Other ideological perspectives include Black feminism, disability feminism, and lesbian feminism, as well as neo-maternalism and pro-natalism. Feminist writers and advocates have also surfaced, shattering ideologies that have long remained hidden or taken for granted in society, such as the public-private divide or the ideology of separate spheres (Boyd 1997). The ideology holds that there is a clear separation between the private sphere of family, home, and unpaid work of women on the one hand, and the public sphere of paid work, the market, and the state on the other.

Familism

Another ideology of great importance to social welfare and gender equality is familism, which Neysmith (1991:285) describes as 'the idealization of what we think a family should embody: a conflict-free domain where emotional and physical needs are tended to.' Within this haven, family care is seen as natural and positive and therefore intrinsically superior to most kinds of care offered by other sources in the public or private sectors. The belief that families (that is, women) are the fitting venue for the care of young children, elderly relatives, and other dependent members is widespread in social policies across Canada. Underlying this family ethic is the assumption that women will be available and responsive to others, including volunteering for work outside the home, and being undemanding for themselves (Aronson 1991; Williams 1989). The welfare state built from the mid-1940s to the

1970s was based on a particular notion of the family. 'It presumed a stable working-/middle-class nuclear family supported by a male bread-winner, a dependent wife and children, and the unpaid domestic labour of women' (Brodie 1995:39). A characteristic of the changing politics of social policy is that ideas of marriage, family, and what represents 'normal' family life are under intense debate and shifting in different directions. The feminist literature describes how important the family, community, and social relations are to the maintenance of social cohesion, but also emphasizes that these social relations need to be constructed in ways that promote an inclusive civil society which is respectful of the role of women.

Feminist writers have framed new conceptions of the welfare state that challenge traditional notions of citizenship, universality, and the boundaries of social policy. Carole Pateman's (1988) notion of the 'patriarchal welfare state' draws attention to male privileges reflected in family-state-market interactions. Pateman was among the first feminist writers to challenge the idea that social citizenship, as a bundle of rights and duties based on membership in the community, was politically neutral and universally available to all groups. Thelma McCormack (1991) notes several essential differences in the way men and women envision the welfare state. McCormack suggests that for most men 'welfare state' means government-supported health and social services and assorted social insurance programs, as well as public investment and countercyclical budgeting for stabilizing the economy. Men also see the welfare state as a limited set of administrative and economic measures, a number of which are temporary arrangements set up to respond to economic crises.

In contrast, McCormack claims that for women, 'the welfare state includes social insurance for the vulnerable groups – the unemployed, the sick, and the aged – but goes beyond these to include education, the arts, and cultural life. This viewpoint reflects women's experience as cradle-to-grave caregivers, doing unpaid or underpaid work outside the competitive, profit-driven economy' (1991:3). This women's concept is a welfare society model with an emphasis on culture, society, and demographic trends, including 'groups that fall outside the definitions of the workforce: the aged, children, the disabled, victims of sexual abuse, immigrant groups – rather than economic ones' [groups inside the paid workforce] (McCormack 1991:39). In addition to social insurance and other income support programs, this perspective also features services, laws, and regulations. Though the two models overlap somewhat in terms of concerns and policy instruments, what we have in Canada is a retrenched but still existing welfare state, not a welfare society, within a mixed economy and a patriarchal social structure.[2]

The Dual Welfare Thesis

Feminists point to a gendered division of social provisions embodied in welfare states, a line of analysis called the dual welfare thesis. It is also referred to in the literature as the two-channel welfare state, two-tier welfare, and double-standard welfare.[3] Whatever the name, the common idea is that the welfare system is divided with reference to men and women. From this perspective, welfare states are complex systems of differentiation and stratification. The dual welfare model has a more critical and a less critical line of this argument, and a narrow and wider scope of application. The less critical version of the model is that women as welfare state clients and beneficiaries predominate in certain services and benefit programs, while men are the primary claimants in other social programs. The more critical version asserts that men's and women's basis for entitlement to benefits, and the nature of the benefits themselves, are sharply segregated: 'Women and men are channeled into separate programs, resulting in a system of dual welfare. Men's maintenance by the state is through social insurance schemes based on claims as earners, while women make their claims on the basis of domestic work and rely more heavily on public assistance programs' (Sainsbury 1996:129). This dualism is rooted in a second division: the traditional division of work between men as earners in the pubic sphere and women as unpaid caregivers in the private sphere.

In the narrow version of the dual welfare model, the analysis focuses on selective income support programs provided by the state. Programs for men tend to be based on labour force attachment, such as unemployment insurance, workers' compensation, and other social insurance programs. Programs for women tend to be means- and income-tested programs based on weak conceptions of need, such as public assistance, mothers' pensions, and survivors benefits. A wider approach to welfare dualism goes beyond public income programs to encompass occupational welfare in the workplace and fiscal welfare provided through the tax system. The dualism here is between public and private provisions.

As we now show, differences in the labour market status of men and women are changing, but slowly, with the result that occupational and fiscal welfare still favour men. The retrenchment of the welfare state in recent decades, traced in Chapters 4, 5, 6, and 7, has different consequences for women and men. As the dual welfare model underscores, such cutbacks have intensified the gendered dualism of social entitlements and reinforced many inequities and disadvantages facing women.

Gendered Division of Work and Positions of Power

The struggle lead by feminists to influence the way governments create and implement social policies has been only partially successful. A sexual division of roles and resources is still evident in the activities of informal caring and work in the home, paid work in the labour market, and holding public offices within the Canadian state.

Caring and Working for the Family

In the private or domestic sphere, most informal care for children, relatives with disabilities, and the elderly is still provided by women, regardless of the women's participation in the labour force. A gradually growing number of men, yet a small proportion, are the primary caregivers, but it is still the exception to the general pattern of women caring for the needs of their families (Baines, Evans, and Neysmith 1991). This duty to care continues throughout a women's lifespan. Adult daughters, for example, are expected to be the natural caregivers for aging parents. Public programs and social services have always depended on the care provided by women in families, and this reliance is growing under the guise of community care and deinstitutionalization. Traditional gender roles and imbalances also persist in the division of work in and around the house. In addition to child care, where applicable, women still have principal responsibility for meal preparation and cleanup, cleaning, laundry, and shopping, while men have responsibility for house repairs, maintenance, and yardwork.

Little has changed over the past twenty years. A 1990 survey found that of dual-earning couples working full time with dependent children, only 10 per cent shared the responsibility for housework equally. For 80 per cent of these couples, women had all or most of the responsibility for household chores (Marshall 1993). A 1992 study revealed that employed women with a spouse and at least one child under age five spent 5.3 hours a day on household and child care activities; about two hours more each day than their male partners (Statistics Canada 1995b:9). 'Without a more equal division for housework, women will have to continue to juggle employment, household chores and family time' (Marshall 1993:14). Many women consequently work a 'double shift' each day, one shift at home, the other in paid work, resulting in serious 'time crunch' problems which in turn lead to stress, poor health, absenteeism, and guilt about their parenting.[4] Women are far more likely than men to lose outside work time due to family responsibilities. In 1994, female workers missed six days of work on average because of family duties compared to less than one day for men, with subsequent collective effects circling back on women's careers and on their labour force participation. The equal allotment of housework remains remote in most Canadian families.

The Canadian Labour Market

It is in the area of women's labour market involvement that feminists have had the greatest impact. Canada has introduced employment equity and pay equity programs. In 1986 the federal government introduced employment equity, a law meant to overcome discrimination in the workplace by encouraging employers to hire people from four designated groups: women, people with disabilities, Aboriginal peoples, and members of visible minorities. The law requires that any employer in the federal domain with 100 employees or more must create and file with the federal government a statistical profile of the population, indicating the proportion of the designated groups in their community. They must then submit a plan for hiring people so their workforce reflects the general population. Pay equity, on the other hand, was meant to provide a process of revaluing the compensation paid for work and removing from such evaluation the sex stereotypes that are built into job descriptions. While the steps are complex, they are meant to have employers, in consultation with employees (and unions), work out a way to revalue jobs based on skill, effort, responsibility, and working conditions.

This legislation was introduced during a period in which there was a dramatic increase in the participation of women in the paid labour force, a growing unionization of women workers, and an expanding share of nonstandard forms of employment. Concurrently, men's labour force participation and unionization rates have gradually declined in recent decades. In 1994 52 per cent of all women aged 15 and over were in the labour force, representing 45 per cent of all paid workers, up from 37 per cent in 1976.[5] Since the mid-1980s, a *majority* of single women, married women, and separated and divorced women have been employed in the Canadian labour force. Only a small proportion of widowed women are employed, and this number has been gradually declining over the past few decades. The reasons for women's increasing participation rate is due to their wish for a decent job and good family care, or to financial necessity, especially if the man is unemployed or the woman is separated, divorced, or unmarried with children. Along with these economic and social reasons, general public expectations today are that women can and should work, and the welfare reforms by many provincial governments seek to cajole and coerce single mothers on social assistance into obtaining work.

For many years now, approximately 70 per cent of all part-time jobs in Canada have been held by women. In 1994, 26 per cent of employed women worked part-time, that is, less than thirty hours a week, in comparison to only 9 per cent of employed men. A 1992 survey of alternate working arrangements of all paid workers found that similar percentages of working men and women had compressed workweeks (working extended hours some days or fewer days in a week), did shift work, and worked some regular paid hours at home. Men are more likely than women to be self-employed and to enjoy flex-time arrangements at work (Fast and Frederick 1996). Significant growth in part-time employment has taken place in accommodation and food services, personal services such as cleaning, and in retail trade. Many men and women 'choose' to work part-time for family reasons or other considerations, but a sizeable minority, one in three, do so involuntarily because they cannot secure full-time employment. Working part-time can help to juggle family responsibilities and work demands, but the trade-off often is lower earnings, weaker job security, and fewer occupational benefits.

From the Kitchen Table to the Boardroom Table (Lochhead 1997) is a useful examination of the costs of raising and caring for children, and of the pressures on families to manage the often competing demands of home and paid work. The report's title, however, inadvertently suggests that women have left the home and housework (the kitchen table) and entered the upper echelons of corporations and government agencies (the boardroom table). As we have seen, however, comparatively few women are in executive positions in either the business or public sectors. Significant occupational segregation endures in the economy, with substantial wage gaps between men's and women's work.

Table 8.1
Women's Average Annual Earnings as a Percentage of Men's
Average Annual Earnings, Selected Years, 1967–1995

Year	Full-Time, Full-Year Workers	All Earners
1967	58	46
1971	60	47
1981	64	54
1991	70	62
1995	73	65

Source: Statistics Canada, cat. no. 13-217 (1995b).

At the end of the 1990s, most employed women are still in occupations that historically have been female jobs. 86 per cent of employed women and 63 per cent of employed men work in the service sector of the economy. In 1994 70 per cent of all employed women, compared to just 31 per cent of employed men, were employed in secretarial, clerical, or sales positions, or in teaching, nursing, and related health occupations such as physiotherapy. Far more women than men work as dental hygienists, nutritionists, social workers, elementary and secondary school teachers, and child and youth care workers. Men predominate as dentists, engineers, physicians, community college instructors, university professors, senior executives, judges, and cabinet ministers. Several other traditionally male-concentrated sectors remain so: construction, manufacturing, mining, forestry, fisheries, and politics. Some fields are changing, such as law, medicine, and accounting; others, such as sales and personal services, are more or less balanced between men and women. This pattern of employment segregation has ramifications for earning levels, poverty, and occupational benefits.

For years, statistics have shown that the average earnings of women working in the paid labour force are significantly lower than those of men. As Table 8.1 shows, the wage gap has been narrowing over the past thirty years, but progress is slow. The persistence of this earnings disparity is evident at all levels of educational attainment. A number of factors influence the gap, and among them sexual discrimination is certainly an important element (MacIvor 1996). In 1995 women employed on a full-time, full-year basis earned 73 per cent of the earnings of their male counterparts. This progress hides the fact that, on average, men's earnings have not been keeping up with the cost of living in recent years.

Women generally have lower incomes than men because of occupational segregation, the wage gap, and the unpaid nature of providing care to family members. In 1993 the average annual pre-tax income of women from all sources was $16,500, or 58 per cent of the $28,600 for men. Women comprise over half (56 per cent in 1993) of all persons living below Statistics Canada's low-income cut-off measures, which are commonly referred to as poverty lines by the mass media and the social policy community. These lines refer to people who are substantially worse off than people with average incomes. Women also have a higher incidence of low income than men do. In 1995 the poverty rate for women was 18.2 per cent of the female population compared to 14.3 per cent for men. The incidence is even higher among certain groups of women: 57.2 per cent of single mothers, 43.4 per cent of elderly women living on their own, and 38.7 per cent for unattached women under age sixty-five (National Council of Welfare 1997:85). The 'feminization of poverty' is not a new social problem. Unfortunately, it has been a systemic feature of the society, the economy, and the welfare state in Canada. What perhaps is new is the increased attention to women's poverty by feminists (Evans 1991), though currently the dominant discourse on poverty puts the greatest emphasis on children.

Occupational Welfare

Workplace benefits such as dental, medical, and paid leave are a frequently overlooked and unexamined part of social policy. Yet occupational welfare – the provision by employers of a range of services and benefits to employees – is a significant feature of the Canadian social security system, coexisting with public provisions. Although they are often regarded as private transactions between a union and management or employer and group of employees, occupational benefits represent an important source of support and financial assistance. These benefits supplement public programs or are substitutes for the lack of public programs. 'The value of occupational welfare is magnified by the fact that it generally avoids [or minimizes] the level of taxation that is levied on ordinary earnings' (Bryson 1992:132).

The status of a person's employment is a pivotal determinant of whether they receive occupational benefits. There are major differences between full-time and part-time workers in receiving dental, medical, or pension plans, or paid sick leave, among other benefits. Full-time workers are far better provided for than part-time workers are. Between two to four times as many full-time workers as part-timers in the

Canadian labour force have these benefits. In this sense, there is a dual system of occupational welfare. Even among full-time workers, from 30 to 40 per cent do not have one or more of these benefits. The availability of such benefits varies between the public and private sectors, types of industries, size of organizations, and whether or not the workers are unionized.

For full-time workers, there is not a high degree of gender differentiation in entitlement to these four kinds of benefits. Of course, this information says nothing about the level of benefits actually provided to male and female employees. In view of the wage gap and occupational segregation, earnings-related benefits result in lower benefit amounts received by women. In short, inequalities in wages are reproduced in workplace pension plans. As successive federal governments have cut back and restrained public pensions such as Old Age Security, greater reliance is placed upon occupational pension plans. This, in turn, contributes to benefit disparities between men and women. Among the retired population in 1993, 92 per cent of men were claiming Canada or Quebec Pension Plan benefits compared to 73 per cent of women, and 58 per cent of retired men had income from a registered pension plan compared to just 37 per cent of women.

For part-time workers gender differentiation is detectable. Less than 10 per cent of male part-time workers and about 21 per cent of female part-time workers receive these occupational benefits. At first glance it appears that women are, relatively, far better off than men are. Recall, however, that 70 per cent of all part-time workers are women. This means that the proportion of female part-time workers covered by the benefits (33 per cent) is lower than the proportion of male part-time workers covered (38 per cent). About three-quarters of all part-time workers remain in services, clerical, sales, and blue-collar jobs. For the most part, these jobs have low wage rates, little security, and few workplace benefits. A study by the Canadian Council on Social Development on the nature of part-time work reports that 'in 1995, nearly half of all part-time workers earned less than $7.50 per hour, compared to less than one-tenth of all full-time workers. Only 10 per cent of part-time workers earned $20 or more per hour, compared to nearly 30 per cent of full-time workers' (Schellenberg 1996:10–11).

Politics and Government

A gender dualism also exists in Canadian politics and government.

Political scientist Heather MacIvor (1996:227) observes that 'Women participate equally with men at the mass level of politics, but they are dramatically under-represented at the elite level of politics.' Women and men are both as apt to vote, attend political meetings, or work for a party and candidate. Men are more likely to take part in the governance of political parties, participate in trade unions and institutionalized pressure groups, and run for and hold public office. Within the main-stream political party structures, 'men make policy, women make cof-fee' (1996:253). Women engage more than men in alternative and grass roots political organizations such as protest actions, neighbourhood and community groups, and social movements.

Polling data over the years indicate a divergence in beliefs between men and women on a range of topics and policy issues. Women are generally more supportive than men of social policy initiatives (McCormack 1991). In the late 1990s public opinion surveys reveal significant differences by gender as to what the federal government should do with any budgetary surpluses (Prince 1998b). While a similar proportion of men and women support cutting taxes, more women think the Goods and Services Tax should be cut first, while more men think cuts should be made to personal income taxes. Men are far more likely than women to call for debt reduction. Conversely, more women believe Ottawa should spend more on government programs, particu-larly for education, health care, child care, and alleviating poverty. Further, more women consider that the federal government went too far in cutting benefits and services. These instances of a gender gap in public opinion no doubt are linked to women's greater reliance on public services, fiscal transfers, and social protection, and thus their greater vulnerability to cutbacks. 'Women's greater dependency on the state,' Jill Vickers (1994:137) has noted, 'is not an essential or inevitable relationship. Rather it reflects women's current unequal social, politi-cal, and economic situation.'

MacIvor (1996:245) indicts Canada's political system as 'sexist, exclusionary, and geared towards people without constant and press-ing family responsibilities.' Canadian federalism is also a hindrance to efforts by the women's movement to achieve equity and equality: 'For women's groups the costs in human and other resources to be effective at all three levels [of government] is extremely demanding given wom-en's greater family responsibilities and smaller economic resources' (Vickers 1994:142). As a constitutional form of governing, federalism recognizes and structurally empowers territorial-based interests and issues over others such as gender or social class. The intricate system of intergovernmental fiscal arrangements operative in Canadian federalism obscures which level is responsible for what issues and policies, making it harder for groups to advocate constructively for reforms. Executive federalism – the arena of usually closed conferences and meetings between cabinet ministers and senior officials across the levels of government – substantially omits women, despite the fact that executive federalism depends on women to maintain the homes and communities of the men who sit in the conferences.

Over the last twenty-five years, women have made noteworthy progress in increasing their representation in government institutions. Up to and including the 1980 federal election, women comprised no more than 5 per cent of Members of Parliament. Since then, the proportion of women MPs has grown steadily: 9.6 per cent in the 1984 election; 13.5 per cent in 1988; 18.3 per cent in 1993; and 20.3 per cent in 1997. The current share is less than women's representation in the national legislatures of the Nordic countries, but more than in Australia, Britain, France, and the United States, among other nations. As a share of the federal cabinet, women comprise about 22 per cent and about 27 per cent of the Canadian senate. Over the 1976–94 period, women's share of provincial legislators in the ten provinces went from less than 3.6 per cent to 18 per cent, and their representation in provincial cabinet positions went from 3.8 per cent to 21 per cent over the same interval (Studlar and Moncrief 1997). Women no longer have token spots in a cabinet, but rather a tangible share of portfolios. In the New Democratic Party (NDP) Government of Ontario from 1990 to 1995, 42 per cent of the cabinet was women, double the previous high. (It subsequently dropped to 19 per cent in the 1995–9 Progressive Conservative Government.) In a case study of this NDP cabinet, based on interviews and documentary research, Lesley Hyland Byrne (1997:601) found that this historically high share of women in power did make a difference to institutional reforms and policy outcomes in the Ontario government. Byrne also found, however, 'that those transformations were not as dramatic as the feminist progressive components might project nor as extensive as the women's movement had hoped.' Overall, Byrne concluded that the impact of these female cabinet ministers on deconstructing 'hierarchical gender-based-power' was 'extremely limited' (1997:611).

Women cabinet ministers in Canada are concentrated in social policy departments, in what may be considered 'feminine portfolios.' Typically, women head departments of health, welfare, education, family, culture, and recreation. They infrequently oversee 'masculine portfolios' such as agriculture, industry, finance, natural resources, and transportation. A similar pattern appears in the membership of parliamentary committees (MacIvor 1996:280–4). At the municipal level of politics, women are also substantially under-represented. A study of Quebec urban governments, for example, found that women had made some gains, increasing their presence on municipal councils from 11 per cent of all councillors in 1985 to 21 per cent in 1995 (Gidengil and Vengrof 1997). The study also found that many municipal councils had no women members at all. Another study reports that in 1996 women held 25 per cent of council seats in the eight major cities in Canada, that is, Halifax, Montreal, Ottawa, Toronto, Winnipeg, Edmonton, Calgary, and Vancouver (Graham, Phillips, and Maslove 1998). There is a distance to go if federal, provincial, and local political institutions are to fully reflect the Canadian electorate.

Women, Men, and the Canadian Welfare State

In a comparative analysis of gender relations and welfare states, Ann Shola Orloff (1993) concludes that social provisions offered by the state not only affect women's material circumstances, but also shape gender relationships, contribute to the mobilization of identities, and may offer political resources to women. In a feminist perspective on the caring work done by women, Carol Baines, Patricia Evans, and Sheila Neysmith (1991:26) have observed that 'Women's relationship to the welfare state is an ambivalent one. It is the source of both protection and control.' Women's relationship to the welfare state is a constellation of roles and interests: women are citizens, activists and advocates, workers, clients and consumers, non-clients, taxpayers, informal caregivers, formal volunteers, and grassroots service providers.

Citizens

Over the twentieth century, Canadian women fought hard for and eventually obtained a cluster of political, civil, and social rights of citizenship. For much of the century, women were excluded from full citizenship, illustrating that it has not been a gender-neutral ideal. Today, women have the right to vote and seek office, to receive equal treatment before and under the law, and to have access to a range of economic and social security programs. At the dawn of the twenty-first century, in the face of the restructuring of the economy and state, the Canadian women's movement is defending existing rights of social citizenship and seeking to develop new rights dealing with matters such as multiculturalism, reproductive technologies, and the rights of same-sex couples. Feminist writers are also rethinking the concept of citizenship to see if and how it might be squared with the diversity and equality discourse examined in Chapter 7.

Activists and Advocates

In groups outside the state structures and in occupational groups within them, women have long advocated social policy measures. Women's activism and their organizations were crucial to the development of social programs and welfare agencies in the reform era from 1880 to the 1920s: 'Child Care, Mothers' Pensions, the Kindergarten Associations, the Home and School Associations, reforms for juvenile delinquents and, of course, temperance campaigns – all can be seen, at least in part, as women's issues. They were women's issues because women were seen as particularly affected by the problems but also because women had been involved in the solutions. Furthermore, it was women that were pressing for change' (Andrew 1984:673). In modern politics, women's groups form coalitions, appear before parliamentary committees and cabinet ministers, interact with bureaucrats and the media, and intervene before tribunals and the courts on Charter of Rights and Freedoms cases. In addition to participating in political parties and unions, women are heavily active in community groups and other local agencies.

Workers in the Welfare State

For women, the welfare state has been an important source of employment, unionization, and relatively good benefits. On women as state employees, Andrew (1984:678) points out that 'Women play a very major role as workers in the welfare state but their power is limited. They provide many of the front-line direct services but they do not determine the form of these services. They care for the clients of the welfare state but they have little influence on the direction of the welfare state.' While on one level we agree with Andrew's observation, on another it narrowly conceptualizes the welfare state as its policies, failing to treat seriously its practices. We believe that what gets done is often determined by what women continue to do despite budget cuts to welfare programs; that as welfare state employees and as volunteers and informal carers, women do influence the direction of the welfare state.

Clients and Consumers of the Welfare State

For many social programs and services, women are the primary clients. Prominent examples include anti-stalking laws, social assistance, old age pensions, maintenance enforcement programs, daycare subsidies, and social housing. As consumers of welfare, as Linda Gordon (1990:15) has written, 'women continue to do the work of consuming welfare, always vastly underestimated – waiting in lines, making phone calls, processing applications, scrimping when checks are late, begging help and favours when checks are inadequate, etc.' Under the male bread-winner model of social policy, women have been defined as clients in a dependent relationship to a man in their role as mother, wife, widow, victim of male violence, and so forth. As women have entered the labour market in greater numbers over the last twenty-five years, they have become eligible as clients of Employment Insurance (EI), Workers' Compensation, and other benefits on the basis of being paid workers.

Non-clients

Inaction and non-decision making by governments and state agencies are critical in defining the scope and quality of women's relationships to the welfare state. When governments choose not to intervene, not to extend a right or enforce a law, or not to grant a benefit or provide a service, they produce non-clients. 'The absence of policy has also threat-ened women's interests, the clearest example being the refusal of police authorities to intervene in cases of wife battering' (MacIvor 1996:311). Such inactions reinforce existing institutional rules, practices, and values. They also thwart the efforts of individuals and groups to make claims, improve their lives, and promote social change.

Taxpayers

With increasing numbers working in the labour force, more and more women are paying personal income taxes and payroll taxes for EI and the Canada or Quebec Pension Plans (C/QPP). If they are running a business, as more women are, they pay corporate income taxes and federal and provincial retail sales taxes. As major clients of public services, women also pay user fees or charges. Until recently, divorced parents receiving child support payments and alimony, overwhelmingly women, were required to declare them as taxable income.[6] Over 60 per cent of two-parent families today are dual-earner households. Women's income is critical for paying the bills and taxes, including property and school taxes. Despite what many Canadians may assume, women in poverty pay taxes, whether they are on welfare and/or are working.

Informal Volunteers

Women are the principal caregivers within families and other networks of personal relationships, which entails both caring for and caring about the emotional, physical, mental, and spiritual needs of others. Baines, Evans, and Neysmith (1991:13) state that 'the welfare state has served as a powerful reinforcer of women's caring' by stressing, through a familial ideology, the importance of women's providing care to children, the sick, and the elderly.

Formal Volunteers

Women's activities as volunteers and charity workers have a long history in Canadian health and social services. The voluntary sector is closely linked to the modern social security system. As volunteers, women offer supports to people who need assistance, extend companionship, and offer a voice for their cause. They also raise funds for local agencies and projects which help to strengthen communities (Rice 1995a). As the state withdraws from providing support through social policies, it shifts additional burdens of caring for others onto women. While women are only slightly more likely than men to volunteer, as we discuss in Chapter 9, a gendered division of roles and responsibilities appears to prevail within the voluntary sector.

Grassroots Service Providers

Outside the welfare state and the conventional voluntary sector, many women are engaged in providing services, consciousness-raising, and mutual aid through collectives, women's shelters, rape crisis centres, alternative bookstores, and cafés. 'Many grassroots groups do not choose to engage directly with the state; they do not believe that a patriarchal state can really help women, or reject the hierarchy and bureaucracy that characterizes state organization' (MacIvor 1996:332). For feminists, politics is far more than government and public administration.

In general, the mainstream literature's discussion of the relation of women to the welfare state in their capacities as clients, caregivers, and volunteers has tended to portray women as relatively powerless dependents. Women as policy advocates, taxpayers, citizens, and state employees have often been downplayed or ignored. These roles represent women as active agents of change with some independent command over economic resources. Various roles contain different kinds of claims and issues, and all are worth noting to appreciate the ambivalent association between women and the welfare state.

Women's and Men's Experiences with Social Programs

In determining the extent to which women and men have distinctive connections with the welfare state, we examine five social policy areas: health care, education, income support, the criminal justice and legal systems, and the tax system.

Health Care

The front-line provision of health care in Canada is that provided by women in the so-called private domain of everyday family life. With respect to the formal health care system, women are slightly more likely than men to be in contact with the system at least once in a year. Women are more likely to visit a physician, and more frequently, than men, as well as to consult with a wider range of other conventional and alternative health care providers. Women again are more likely to be hospitalized, in large part because of pregnancies, childbirth, and care needs in later life. Women are diagnosed more frequently with mental disorders (and with different mental illnesses than men) and hospitalized in psychiatric institutions. The two leading causes of death for both men and women are cancer and heart disease, though for men lung cancer is more common, while for women it is breast cancer. Women are much more prone to suffer lasting adverse health effects from sexually transmitted diseases such as gonorrhea and syphilis. In contrast, men ac-

Table 8.2
Full-time Teachers in Canada by Sex and Level 1995

Level	% Women	% Men
Elementary and secondary	61	39
Community college	40	60
University	22	78
Total	56	44

Source: Statistics Canada, cat. no. 81–229 (1995a).

count for about 95 per cent of the AIDS (Acquired Immune Deficiency Syndrome) cases in Canada (Statistics Canada 1995a).

Education

In the 1990s women make up the majority of full-time and part-time students in Canadian community colleges and universities, and across most faculties. Women outnumber men two to one in education and health-related programs. The percentage of women and men with university degrees has gone from 3 and 7 per cent, respectively, in 1971, to 10 and 13 per cent in 1991. As of 1993 approximately 205,000 women and 165,000 men worked full time as teachers, instructors, or professors in the education system. As Table 8.2 shows, at the elementary and secondary-school levels, teaching remains a female-dominated profession. School administration at the principal and vice-principal ranks, however, is not (Cusson 1990). At the community college level, and especially at the university level, men prevail, particularly at the higher levels.

Income Support

The Canadian income security system is a network of federal, provincial/territorial, First Nation and municipal programs that provides direct financial benefits to individuals and families. Major programs include seniors' benefits, public pensions, EI, Workers' Compensation, veterans' benefits, social assistance, and various tax credits. To this list can be added labour market policies dealing with minimum wages, equal pay, and employment equity. Compared to men, women receive a larger part of their total income from income security programs. For men aged fifteen to sixty-four, 8 per cent of their total incomes in 1993 were from government income programs, while for women it was 13 per cent. For men aged sixty-five and over, 47 per cent of their income was from government benefits, and for senior women it was 62 per cent. The differences are even more striking by family types. For two-parent families with children, 9 per cent of their income came from government income benefits in 1993, compared to 19 per cent for single-father families and 37 per cent of the income of single-mother families.

Women rely on certain income security programs more than men do, especially social assistance, the provincial/territorial and municipal welfare programs of last resort. Societal stigma, benefit inadequacy, and the administrative control of clients mark these programs. There are many reasons why women are overrepresented in poverty and welfare programs. Women receive low wages and lower earnings in the paid labour force. They are employed in nonstandard jobs and underemployed in part-time work. Quality child care is expensive or unavailable. The work and caring provided by women in the family and community is unpaid. Moreover, low-paid workers, both men and women, receive little if anything from the more lucrative and stigma-free workplace benefits and tax advantages.

Senior women are less likely than senior men to have income from private pension plans, Registered Retirement Savings Plans, or the C/QPP. When they do, women receive smaller average amounts than men because of lower labour force participation, lower earnings, and lower coverage by workplace plans. The C/QPP illustrate how assumptions about women as dependents are embodied in the social security system. For the first decade or so they were in effect (1966–77), neither public pension plan allowed pension credits earned during a marriage to be split in the event of a divorce or annulment of marriage. Not until 1980 was employment of a spouse in an unincorporated family business considered pensionable employment. The QPP in 1984 and the CPP in 1987 removed a provision that survivors' benefits ceased upon remarriage. In addition, in 1987 the CPP, and two years later the QPP, extended the pension-splitting provision to include common-law spouses and separated partners.

Under EI women are almost exclusively the recipients of maternity/parental benefits, and are the main users of the sickness benefits. By contrast, women obtain 40 per cent or less of training, job creation, and self-employment assistance benefits under EI. The most common benefit for men and women who receive EI is the regular benefit. As a proportion of total EI beneficiaries, women have fluctuated between 40 and 45 per cent. Over the past twenty years, from the welfare state crisis period to the present restructuring era, women have more often than not had slightly higher levels of unemployment than men. Specific groups – Aboriginal women, women with disabilities, and visible minority women – still consistently have significantly higher levels of unemployment than men or women on average (Statistics Canada 1995a).

Criminal Justice

Women and men have different experiences as well with the criminal justice system, legal aid, and the administration of law and order in Canada. In general, these are considered 'masculine' areas of the state. In 1993 men accounted for 89 per cent of violent offenders, 83 per cent of people charged with criminal offences, and 76 per cent of adults charged with property crimes. Most drug offenders and young offenders are male. Most charges (80 per cent) against women are for minor offences. Men represent 97 per cent of all federal prisoners and 92 per cent of provincial prisoners. On the law enforcement side, a similar gendered pattern is evident: men account for about 90 per cent of police officers, 80 per cent of judges and magistrates, and 65 per cent of lawyers in Canada. However, women's share of occupations in all three of these fields is continuing to grow.

While men and women are about equally likely to be victims of crime, four times as many women as men (42 per cent versus 10 per cent) worry about their personal safety. Fewer women than men are victims of homicide, but women are far more likely to be the victims of a sexual assault, and more likely by a man they know than by a stranger. Men tend to be assaulted by strangers (Statistics Canada 1995a). The National Council of Welfare (1995:10) has pointed out that, 'the vast majority of criminal legal aid clients are men, while most of the beneficiaries of civil legal aid are women.' Women resort to legal aid for advice on family law, welfare rights and wrongs, and landlord-tenant issues. 'Single-parent mothers, and some women who still live with their husbands, need legal assistance for family matters such as separation and divorce, division of matrimonial property, child custody, and access and support payments. Some also have legal questions related to their roles as mothers, such as problems with child welfare authorities or the need to have a child's paternity legally recognized' (National

Council of Welfare 1995:12). With respect to court decisions on the custody of children involved in a divorce, in about three-quarters of cases mothers get sole custody. Over the last generation, the number of joint custodies has increased and the number of sole custodies by women and men has declined. However, 'Although women are usually awarded custody, few are given adequate financial resources to look after their children' (MacIvor 1996:131).

The Tax System

In a detailed review of the 1985 tax year, Kathleen Lahey reports that 'Women in Canada are overtaxed, relative to men' (cited in Cassin 1993:108). Lahey found that women paid 46 per cent of their income as taxes, while men paid only 30 per cent. Furthermore, while women had 32 per cent of all pre-tax incomes, they received only 27 per cent of all after-tax income. The overall system of taxation actually diminished women's income and increased men's total share of incomes. In their analysis of how to design a more equitable tax system, the Ontario Fair Tax Commission (1993:28) concluded that 'The impact of the tax system on women is different from its impact on men. This differential impact is not the result of any explicit discrimination against women in the Income Tax Act. Nothing in the letter of the law singles out either men or women for special treatment. The income tax has differential impacts on women because of the way provisions interact with differences in the economic position of women and men in society.' The commission noted that women have lower earnings and lower incomes than men do, and are thus more likely to be poor. From these facts, the commission noted two effects: 'women are less able to take advantage of subsidies delivered through the tax system. Moreover, even when they are able to take advantage of these provisions, women derive less benefit from them. Second, because women on average earn less than men, elements of the income tax that affect the economic relationships between people, and that are technically gender neutral, are not neutral in their outcomes' (1993:28).

Since women have less wealth than men, Lisa Phillips writes, 'income as a proxy for ability to pay therefore obscures the full nature and extent of gender bias in the tax system' (cited in Bakker 1996:41). With women constituting a majority of the poor, consumption taxes such as sales taxes, property taxes, user fees, and even lottery revenues are regressive forms of taxation which take disproportionately more from people with low incomes than from people with middle and higher incomes. The absence of an estate or inheritance tax in Canada gives preferential treatment to the accumulation of wealth and its inter-generational transfer. The lack of a wealth tax also means that govern-ments must rely heavily on personal income taxes and sales taxes as revenue sources. From a gender-sensitive perspective, not having a wealth tax in the tax policy mix favours men and promotes the idea that families are a private domain separate from the public sphere.

Conclusions

In her presidential address to the Canadian Political Science Associa-tion, Caroline Andrew (1984:683) predicted that gender would become an increasingly explicit part of welfare state politics. The subsequent years in Canadian social policy certainly support Andrew's forecast and her characterization of the welfare state as a mixed blessing for women. On the one hand, the welfare state offers women benefits, jobs, and some supportive laws and services; on the other, it imposes controls, perpetuates stereotypes, and reinforces dependencies. Some notable progress has been made in gaining access to the political pro-cess, yet women remain a small portion of legislators and cabinet ministers. The welfare state does offer women, and men, resources and places for meeting needs and engaging in acts of politics and citizen-ship. Many, if not most, feminists still regard the public domain, despite its contradictions and gendered features, as the sector with the most potential for women to achieve equality, equity, and diversity.

At the conference Women and the Canadian State held at the Univer-sity of Ottawa in 1990, a number of academics and community activists celebrated twenty years of accomplishments since the report of the Royal Commission on the Status of Women. Reflecting on the achieve-ments and shortcomings of the women's movement, it was clear that many things had been accomplished. There was now major legislation regarding human rights, employment equity, and pay equity; growth in the number of women's shelters; legislation concerning sexual harass-ment; and changes to the criminal code dealing with sexual offences. Unfinished business included the question of violence against women and the issue of women's participation in political power.

For the Canadian women's movement, the changing politics mean continuing to struggle for gender equality, responding to a backlash against feminism, and defending imperfect social programs and rights against the restructuring of the welfare state. As we have argued at various point in this book, restructuring goes well beyond restraint. Restructuring is altering gender relations and the political landscape. Brodie (1995:10) has argued that rolling back the state is 'eroding the very political identities and public spaces that empowered postwar Canadian feminism.' In light of women's roles as caregivers, volunteers, welfare state employees, and clients, cutbacks to public sector services and programs fall disproportionately on women (McCormack 1991; Bryson 1992). Even before the present era of restructuring, Elizabeth Wilson (1977:171) noted the effect of cutbacks on women in the private sphere: 'Hospital patients prematurely returned home to convalesce, elderly patients denied meals on wheels or home helps, children on half-time schooling, unemployed husbands for that matter, all require more attention from Mother.' In the public sphere, downsizing and contracting out of work, now threaten the education, health, and social service fields that have advanced women's earnings and their access to occupational and tax benefits. As women are the majority of those on welfare in Canada, cuts to social assistance are cuts to women. In the community sphere, as we noted in Chapter 4, when governments talk of home care as an alternative to institutional care, they really mean more work by women. Likewise, when governments speak of community care and moving heretofore institutionalized residents into the community, it effectively means that additional burdens of care are placed on women. There is no such thing as gender neutral restructuring.

9

Civil Society and Community Capacity: Links between Social Policy and Social Capital

The changing politics of social policy are turning attention back towards the community as a resource in solving social problems. Academics, policy makers, and practitioners are trying to determine how to design social policies that encourage communities to use local abilities and resources to solve local problems. While there is not an untapped reservoir of resources in the community, and many communities are fragile because they face difficult problems and have limited resources, there is room for optimism. Many people help contribute to the community by volunteering in nonprofit organizations. They provide leadership to hospitals, universities, and arts councils. They operate local homes for the elderly, and group homes or social housing for those in need of support. As either formal volunteers or informal helpers, Canadians are taking care of the sick, shopping for people who cannot get out of the house, mowing lawns, babysitting, or looking after other people's pets. Some volunteers are organizing political rallies, unions, or protest groups. Others are cleaning up the environment, debating where a road or a dump should be located, or fighting for social justice and human rights. The more volunteers give, the more social capital they produce, and the more civil the community becomes.

This chapter makes the case that social policies can and must be used to encourage people in the community to come together to identify common problems, develop local solutions, allocate resources to address problems, and open the process so it includes a diverse group of participants in the community-development process. We begin with a discussion of the important concepts in the literature and go on to discuss the need for the state to create a supportive context if communities are going to develop the capacity to solve some of their problems.

We then examine the local conditions within communities that affect the development of community capacity. Here we argue that the beliefs members of the community hold about community involvement, the structure of the community, and the resources in the community shape the ability for members to solve problems. We also touch on the darker side of community: how communities can exclude some people and provide benefits that do not meet the needs of all. We next turn our attention to steps community organizers can take to develop local capacity, including locality development, social planning, and social reform. Finally, we look at community-capacity in action by examining the volunteer activities of women, men, and the elderly.

Taking Stock of Key Concepts

While all the concepts in the community-capacity literature stress the role of the locality in the development of community capacity, they share a vagueness that needs clarification. In current discourse, however, these concepts remain somewhat ambiguous because they are emergent and contested ideas. The social science literature in general and the social policy literature in particular use four concepts to describe and analyze the nature of community capacity: civil society, civic engagement, social capital, and community capacity.[1]

Civil Society

As Table 9.1 shows, different types of definitions of civil society are evident in the literature: those based on normative views of the goals of civil society; those based on an institutional and organizational analysis; and writings that use a behavioural interpretation of the concept. The normative view is evident in Sherri Torjman's (1997b:2) writing, in which she describes the goals and objectives of civil society – it sustains and enhances the capacity of all its members to build a caring and mutually responsible society. The underlying ideas in this definition expose its normative base. By 'capacity' Torjman means the ability, resources, and willingness of people to become involved with all of their neighbours. From this perspective, civil society is made up of inclusive relationships based on the notion of mutual responsibility in which people find ways to express their caring for each other. This definition goes beyond the entitlements and rights contained in welfare state policies to create a sense of reciprocity between citizens.

Table 9.1
Three Concepts of Civil Society

Concept	Emphasis
Normative	Societal values and goals
Institutional	Voluntary sector and other institutions
Behavioural	Civic actions and relations of cooperation and reciprocity

An institutional definition of civil society draws our attention to the organizations and structures that make up society. A narrow institutional view focuses on the voluntary sector. Civil society assumes the existence of voluntary and civic organizations that provide help and assistance to members of the community. Organizations such as the Red Cross, United Way, and service clubs would be considered essential parts of a civil society. Wider institutional definitions include informal helping, families and kinship networks, religious institutions, political parties, and unions as parts of a civil society. These definitions usually exclude the state and the private sector.

Robert Putnam suggests a more behavioural definition of civil society. For him an active, public-spirited citizenry that is involved in community activities marks a civil society. People are connected in ways that create egalitarian political relations and enhance community members' trust and cooperation. Putnam claims a civil society is bound together by horizontal relations of reciprocity and cooperation, not by vertical relations of authority and dependency (1993:88). A more conservative behavioral definition views civil society as a social arrangement in which morally and economically autonomous individuals, seeking their own self-interest, come together with other individuals seeking their self-interest. The interactions of such self-regarding individuals form the basis of the civil society (Seligman 1992:119).

Our own theoretical approach, presented in the introductory chapter, inclines us to view civil society as encompassing all three dimensions: goals, institutions, and actions. A full understanding of the activities and potential of the civic sphere requires a careful consideration of the actual values, organizational arrangements, and methods of interrelating which are taking place. We regard civil society, both historically and in the current age, as serving important roles in human and social development, but we do not wish to romanticize and exaggerate either its caring capacities or level of social inclusiveness. We also perceive civil society in Canada as an organizational sector not detached from the state, but closely interconnected as well with public sector agencies and other institutional domains.

Civic Engagement

Most writers agree that civic engagement takes place when people become involved in self-governing community associations made up of members who understand how to organize and run these organizations (Lee 1992). Members of these associations learn how to cooperate, manage mutual tasks, come to some agreement about goals and objectives, be respectful to each other, and maintain loyalty. Self-governing association have an effect on the community because they encourage people to take positions, debate issues, support causes, and become involved in community activities. These forms of engagement foster the pursuit of the public good at the expense of purely individual and private ends (Putnam 1993:173–6). Civic engagement encourages an understanding of broader public needs, an appreciation of the interests of others and an acceptance of obligations for others. Hence, the concept is closely related to the ideas of active citizenship, community involvement or voluntary action, and political participation. Measures of civic engagement can include the turnout in elections, the number of people who join self-governing organizations, the number of neighbourhood associations, and the levels of volunteering in the community. These activities are often based on the principle of equality between the participants, and they assume that group members can meet their common interest through social interaction. People who belong to community associations display more political sophistication, social trust, and political participation than non-members (Almond and Verba 1963).

Social Capital and Cohesion

The concepts of social capital and social cohesion are the most abstract of this cluster of ideas. Putnam, following James Coleman's (1990) lead, defines social capital as trust that flows through social networks. Thousands of small, everyday acts contribute to the social capital of a community. When someone helps another person cross the street, gives them directions, or helps them fix a flat tire, they create social capital. Putnam suggests the existence of social capital and social cohesion is strongly correlated. Citizens build social cohesion out of the interactions of sharing, caring, and giving. These small acts build into networks of social engagement and norms of reciprocity, each contributing to the fabric of the community. As people interact, each deed adds to the trust and respect community members have for each other, which produces interlocking relationships and social solidarity. Jane Jenson (1998:38) concludes from a literature review that 'The distinguishing characteristics of the concept of social cohesion is the theoretical proposition that shared values must underpin processes of social ordering.'

Community Capacity

Like the concept of social capital, community capacity is the existence of individuals, local groups, and associations who are prepared to voluntarily provide assistance, time, or resources to others in the community. This entails people providing care for others, helping others find needed services, solving common problems, and sharing information. Community capacity includes being a good neighbour, but goes beyond it to include informal and formal volunteering. Informal volunteering takes place when a neighbour shovels the snow off another person's walk because he or she is ill or too old to go out. They may help with shopping, put their neighbour's groceries away, help clean the local skating rink, or prepare the field for a game of baseball. Formal volunteering takes place when people give freely of their time, energy, skills, or knowledge through the auspices of an organization.

Creating the Policy Context for Community Capacity

Creating, expanding, and relying on community capacity has become a renewed objective in social policy thinking and development in Canada. It offers a strategy for bringing community members together to form community-based organizations which can be used to address local issues, and assumes that there is a solid economic base upon which community activities can take place. Torjman (1996:8) points out that while most Canadians derive their economic security from paid employment, governments play an essential role in ensuring a stable social environment through social policies. These conditions allow community groups to become involved in activities that create community capacity to solve social problems. This policy context includes building and strengthening caring communities, promoting economic security, and promoting social investment in the development of people. Groups and organizations trying to encourage civil society believe that communities must build upon the existing government welfare system by encouraging the creation of partnerships and collaborative working arrangements to insure the creation of civil society (Torjman 1997b:3). These partnerships should include governments, business, labour, education, foundations, and social agencies.

Prime Minister Jean Chrétien, in a speech to the 15th Biennial World Volunteer Conference of the International Association for Volunteer Effort, stated, 'As a country, we have always honoured and admired the work of the volunteer sector. But, to be honest, we have not known how to harness your energy and creativity. Governments have looked upon your sector as – first and foremost – a preserve of high ideals and noble intentions. Not as a valuable source of insight and experience. In my judgment this has been a mistake. A mistake our government is working to correct' (Chrétien 1998:1–2). To begin the sharing of ideas and plans for working together, a Voluntary Sector Roundtable was convened by the federal government in 1996. New tax measures to encourage charitable giving have been introduced in recent years and new models for overseeing and registering charities are actively under consideration. The federal government also committed $15 million over the 1998–2001 period to create VolNet, a dedicated network charged with linking 10,000 voluntary arts, faith groups, and health and social service organizations to each other and to the Internet.[2]

Governments at all levels in Canada are pursuing new ways for promoting the formation of greater community capacity. Human Resources Development Canada, the leading social policy department in the federal government, is forging partnerships with voluntary organizations and community groups in order to remain relevant to citizens in their communities; it is also building the capacity of communities and groups that represent Canadians with special needs, such as seniors, Aboriginal peoples, persons with disabilities, and children and youth at risk. The department is transforming its local offices into resource centres that support more equitable access to the full range of programs and services. In British Columbia, in 1998, the provincial minister of Human Resources was also appointed minister responsible for Volunteers and the Community Services sector. The British Columbia provincial government, like others, is working more actively and collaboratively with the voluntary sector in developing priorities and policies. In Canada's cities, too, urban governments support community capacity by recognizing cultural diversity and encouraging social sustainability. This support takes the form of crosscultural training of staff, employment equity within municipal governments, community-needs surveys and focus groups, ethnocultural and race relations committees attached to city councils or school boards, community-based delivery of services such as policing, and partnerships with self-help groups and voluntary agencies (Graham, Phillips, and Maslove 1998).

John McKnight (1992) believes the development of civic society rests on the creation and maintenance of self-defining associations. Such association are groups of people who come together to try to solve mutual problems, provide resources to local communities, and stimulate debate about local issues. Community organizations can creatively address social problems by developing new methods for providing goods and services. To achieve this, McKnight argues that governments must shift their welfare expenditures from a maintenance orientation to an investment capital orientation. Governments must find new ways of financing nonprofit organizations while not undermining the economic security of members of the community. Governments can contribute to the development of community organizations by providing start-up funds, training sessions, and access to private capital through bank guarantees or tax incentives for investors.

Torjman (1997b:4) cautions that a danger in promoting more active citizenship is that it inadvertently can encourage governments to abrogate their responsibility for economic, social, and environmental well-being. When this happens community groups often feel like the government is dumping problems onto them without the resources to deal with them. There was a strong reaction in Ontario when the provincial government sharply cut social assistance benefits in the mid-1990s: community-based food banks were crushed under the demands for support. The government had unloaded its cost onto the community without providing the support that the community groups required to address the problem.

For community capacity to be developed by local people, governments must not undermine the feelings of trust in the community. Many people, if they think that their voluntary work or charitable giving will weaken or remove public responsibility for pressing social issues, will be reluctant to help. Similarly, if the problems are too large and overwhelming, and community groups do not have the resources to solve them, agencies and volunteers can end up feeling like failures. Governments can help prevent this from happening by promoting citizens' well-being through adequate economic and social policies. Once this basic condition is met, community groups can work to solve some of their local problems.

Local Conditions for Community Capacity

Communities are made up of people linked together through kinship, locality, shared ideals, or common beliefs. Whatever the size or complexity of communities, Wharf (1992:16) says the essential common denominators of a community are a pattern of relationships among people and the existence of needs shared by these individuals. Wharf analyses the conditions within communities that affect their members' ability to come together and solve local problems. In summing up his findings – these include a range of examples, from First Nations communities that developed locally controlled child welfare services through to women's groups who fought for women's rights in the abortion issue – Wharf states that 'most social reform organizations do not have the power to put into place the reforms they see as desirable. Neither do they have the funds to devote to expensive public relation campaigns or to hire equally expensive lobbyists to act on their behalf. To add to their woes, social reform organizations are not usually well connected to policy makers, and their reforms represent causes that, if not downright unpopular, are at best of marginal interest to policy makers' (Wharf 1992:187).

To overcome these limitations and develop the abilities to solve problems, community organizations must develop new capacities that allow them to rely more on their own abilities and less on the government. Developing these capacities depends upon three factors: the beliefs community members have about the nature of cooperation, the nature of connections between community members, and the level of resources that exist within the community.

Beliefs about Cooperating

Community members have different views about whether they should cooperate with each other. If members believe there is a shared sense of community, and they feel a mutual obligation, then the capacity of the community will be nurtured. If, on the other hand, members believe that the community is made up of relationships between self-interested individuals, then it will be difficult to create and use internal capacities.

Amitai Etzioni takes the first view and offers a *communitarian* definition of community: 'A community is a group of people who share affective bonds and a culture. It is defined by two characteristics: Communities require a web of affect-laden relations among a group of individuals (rather than merely one-on-one relations or chains of individual relations), relations that often crisscross and reinforce one another. And being a community entails having a measure of commitment to a set of shared values, norms and meanings' (Etzioni 1995:14). This definition highlights the relationship between community members as they share resources and create a sense of connection and feelings of mutual commitment. This sense of community reflects the preindustrial communities that Polanyi described in Chapter 1.

A dramatically different view of community is provided from the *neo-liberal* perspective. From this perspective, individuals have no moral sentiments towards other members and the only grounds for sharing resources is self-serving: 'I will help you if you will help me.' There are no affect-laden relations or measure of commitments from this perspective. Philip Selznick (1995:34) argues that in the liberal imagination, people are fundamentally separate, unencumbered by obligations they did not choose; they are responsible for their own fates, authors of their own opinions, makers of their own worlds; and group membership is voluntary, and a contract based on mutual consent is the preferred principle of social organization.

Selznick has criticized the liberal tradition as being excessively individualistic in both theory and practice. The image of people who are autonomous and self-distancing is radically incomplete as a convincing or attractive portrayal of what participation in a moral community should entail (Selznick 1995:34). If communities are to liberate their internal capacities, they must find ways to go beyond absolutist notions of self-interest and encourage participation and cooperation based on notions of collective survival. Communities must find a balance between the individual and the collective, between liberty and equality.

Etzioni (1993:x) claims that to maintain a balance between the abstract rights of the individual and the social entitlement created by the mutual-welfare community, members must imagine the course of a community as akin to that of a bicycle, forever teetering in one direction or another, that is, either towards the anarchy of extreme individualism and the denial of the common good or towards the collectivism that views itself as morally superior to its individual members. Like Polanyi,

Etzioni believes there is a tense relationship between the centripetal forces of community and the centrifugal forces of autonomy, that these forces must be kept in balance if the social system is to operate successfully. Neither the individual nor the community must dominate the other.

Community Connections

A second factor affecting the ability of communities to come together and share resources is the nature of the connection between members in the community. Community members can be tightly bound and highly interdependent or they can be loosely bound and primarily independent. The tighter the ties that bind people together and the greater the interdependence between members, the stronger the social cohesion within the group and the deeper the sense of community. One need only think of the members of a religious order or motorcycle gang to imagine the structure of a tightly bound community. In both exists a high level of interdependence and strong social cohesion.

There are also communities that are loosely bound. In such communities, members share relatively weak connections with other members. They often belong to more than one community and their loyalty is spread across a number of groups. A person may belong to a tennis club, a home and school association, a union, a community association, and a religious group, as well as to a service club and a political party. These overlapping connections create a rich network of relationships which reflect civic engagement and represent an example of social capital.

Differences between the tightly bound and the loosely bound community are important to the development of community capacity. A motorcycle gang is a closed community with a tightly knit social network and a strict code that controls membership and access to resources. Members often share resources with each other but seldom outside the group. The new members to the club must make an unflinching commitment based on the very fundamental perception of a shared common fate, and this extraordinary commitment is based on the universal, generic, social processes of networking and bonding which themselves are the cornerstones of any genuine community (Wolf 1994:321). When membership becomes as closed as it does with this type of community, then entries and exits are difficult and loyalty to the club and to one another is paramount. The community can develop considerable capacity, but it flows inward rather than outward.

In contrast are community associations that invite members to join freely. Service clubs provide an example: members share many of the common feelings of friendship but the bonding is much less formal, the membership is much more open, and the focus is as much outward as it is inward. While these associations may have more difficulty in developing community capacity, when they do it flows both within the community and to members outside of the community. Most communities are loosely tied together through informal connections. People can come and go as they please, there are few formal arrangements that force people to interact, and there are no binding regulations for membership. Communities have the remarkable feature of being nourished by many layers of connections – families, groups, institutions – which characteristically claim respect and protection. Selznick believes people prize open communities, ones in which members do not seek unity of any sort at any price but unity that preserves the integrity of the parts (Selznick 1995:34). The ability of people to use community resources to help others, therefore, depends upon the balance between being both inward- and outward-focused.

Over the past twenty years or so, the pluralization of the community has turned many people inward, looking to each other for help and support. The feminist movement asks women to turn to each other for recognition and support. Some women's groups want young girls to have the right to go to all-girls' public schools and be taught by women. Ethnic groups are demanding social services in their language, with services provided by people from their culture. While such demands may be reasonable and fair, they turn communities inward. The Deaf community has gone the furthest perhaps in seeking to close its ranks and formalize the nature of its community: for many in the Deaf community, being Deaf is a source of pride, and an increasing number of people have said they would not choose to be hearing. Andrew Solomon (1994) claims that for some Deaf people the term 'Deaf' denotes culture, as distinct from 'deaf,' which is used to describe a pathology. People who are Deaf now often wear Deaf Pride t-shirts or buttons (one woman claimed she wanted her children to be born Deaf so they could be part of her culture) (1994:44). This turning inward by community groups strengthens the internal social cohesion and increases the ability of communities to deal with internal problems. At the same time, however, it can splinter the larger collective and limit the ability of communities to solve common problems.

Community Resources

Another factor affecting the ability of the community to develop internal capacity is the level of resources within the community. McKnight (1992:6) believes it is important to stop looking at the 'pathological needs' or deficits of a community and to focus instead on the positive aspects. He believes the first step in community development is for members to carry out a serious inventory of the community's current resources, skills, and capacities. Resources include financial, natural, and human assets that exist within a community; skills include the talents and expertise of individuals and organizations that can be brought together to address problems; and capacity is the ability to join the resources and skills together in a way that allows the community to address its own problems. The Aspen Institute Rural Economic Policy Program (1996) has identified eight outcome measures which examine the level of resources in a community. These include asking the following questions:

• Does the community foster expanding, diverse, and inclusive citizen participation?
• Does it have an expanding leadership base?
• Does the community offer ways of developing and strengthening individual skills?
• Do community members share a common vision of the community?
• Do community organizations share a common strategic community agenda?
• Does the community get things done?
• Are community organizations well organized?
• Are resources balanced between self-sufficiency and the use of outside resources?

Everyone in a community has abilities, skills, and productive motives that are powerful attributes that must be identified and used if the community is going to develop the capacity to solve local problems. Equally important, from McKnight's perspective, is the recognition of locally controlled associations. The basic power of associations is their problem-solving capacity. They are tools, unlike systems and agencies, that command local loyalty because they are self-governing (McKnight 1992:8). The regeneration of associational capacities and authority is essential if productive neighbourhoods are to re-emerge. This regeneration of community associations is one step in the development of a civil society able to draw upon the local community to help address local problems.

The Darker Side of Communities

As we have stated earlier, communities also have a dark side: they can be authoritarian, discriminatory, traditional, and conservative. A collection of studies on community organizing effort in Canada concludes that 'community activities are not always progressive and do not always serve the interest of all community members' (Ng, Walker, and Muller 1990:309). Likewise, state policies, programs, and procedures can be oppressive and coercive for community groups. In some cases, government funding, regulations, employment programs, administrative and managerial processes, 'further fragment the already marginalized groups (women, immigrants, and native people), creating new divisions and contradictions within these groups' (Ng, Walker, and Muller 1990:314). Government policies on contracting for community-based services can produce unhealthy competition rather than cooperation among agencies, resulting in 'agency turfism' that adversely effects clients and the community. Even within groups with shared experiences and identities, such as HIV/AIDS groups or ethnic communities, there are power differentials and dynamics which may well reproduce larger forms of patriarchy or other types of discrimination within the local group. However, marginalized groups as well as mainstream communities can influence and affect social programs and the administrative practices of government officials (Lee 1992; Wharf 1992; Wharf and Clague 1997).

This darker side has important implications for the way community capacity will be used. For community members to be willing to share resources, they must believe the person receiving the assistance deserves to be helped. This often means the recipient must be from the local community, be of sound moral character, and have no other visible means of support. Local communities will be unwilling to help strangers or others they believe can help themselves. The darker side of community takes social policy back to the fundamental question of legitimacy and the right recipients have to receive help from the community.

The movement back to the community weakens the universal rights implied in national social programs. Social rights are replaced with the bare minimum of social assistance provided, and are based on needs rather than entitlement. Local initiatives are also more expensive than national ones. While it is possible to reduce the benefit levels so they fit with local conditions, a community can only go so far before it impoverishes some of its members. Local programs often require duplication of administration; they are difficult to administer, given size considerations, and they are labour intensive. Thus administration often falls into the hands of people such as those in Charles Dickens's *Oliver Twist*, who are rewarded for keeping the costs of programs low, making them wardens of the poor and undermining the very democratic notions of equality that are the foundations of the modern state.

While the state in Canada can be properly thought of as deeply embedded in society (Cairns 1986), the state is not a homogeneous entity. Further, the state is not equally connected to all communities and groups in Canadian society, nor has it similar relationships with all groups and communities. As community activists, policy analysts, and some administrators and politicians well know, relationships between community organizations and government agencies can be primarily cooperative or conflictual, stable or highly fluid, restrictive or supportive. Some of the recent literature on civil society and civic community, which speaks of social partnerships and mutual responsibility, tends to ignore inequalities in the distribution of power and thus tends to simplify these complex and contradictory relationships between locally based groups and active or inactive governments. State support of community organizations can be a mechanism of social control and social change.

Wharf (1992:21) describes a paradox in that, while responsibility for social policy has largely been passed to senior levels of government, social problems are experienced and played out in local communities. This means there is often incongruence between the type and form of intervention developed within the federal or provincial bureaucracies and the needs of the local community. This asymmetry has led many social policy analysts to believe that it would be more effective if the services designed to address these issues were embedded in the local community (Davies and Shragge 1990). But governments often have little idea about how local communities will be able to solve difficult social problems. Governmental plans to simply cut things and let the chips fall where they may is extremely dangerous (Rice 1995a). At every point in every policy decision there is the choice between two paths, one encouraging respect and trust and the other discouraging it. When governments or other institutions make decisions which discourage the development of respect and trust they push the community down a destructive path.

Developing Community Capacity

In developing community capacity, there are three types of activities used by community workers: locality development, social planning, and social action (Rothman 1974). Locality development, the process of assisting individuals and groups to identify and meet local needs, is based on the notion that community members have the capacity to solve their own problems. Community workers identify potential people in the community who have some latent skills, and they encourage these people to draw others together to begin to develop a capacity to identify problems. The community workers provide training and support to the natural leader so they can form a group to work cooperatively in solving local problems. Social planning, on the other hand, is a rational, technocratic approach in which the community worker uses research skills to identify and study social problems. This process assumes that community members can develop the skills necessary to influence the larger social system. The community workers use the information from the planning process to provide evidence why steps should be taken to solve the local problems. Finally, the community workers encourage people from the local community to become involved in the social action process, which assumes that society is governed by an elite few who rule in their own interests (Wharf 1992:17). Community workers encourage community members to confront the elites about the existence of the problems and then force them to take steps to solve the problems.

One way for community members to encourage community capacity is to facilitate the creation of new organizational partnerships willing to address local problems. The Caledon Institute of Social Policy, in cooperation with a number of foundations, is testing the ability of these new partnerships to address social issues. The partnerships most often involve a business organization with a nonprofit group. One way for the partnerships to work together is for the businesses to agree to promote a social cause as part of their own marketing strategy. A positive image is created for the business and the social concern is highlighted, as is the community organization trying to solve social problems. Torjman (1997b:12) describes the partnering of the Canadian Women's Foundation with Tambrands Canada Inc. Tambrands promotes the Canadian Women's Foundation and makes an annual commitment of $100,000 over three years. In return the Women's Foundation developed a granting process for shelters for assaulted women on behalf of Tambrands. Another example is Chevron Canada Resources, which allows employees to volunteer eight hours a year on company time. Most formal volunteers in Canada, 65 per cent according to a recent national survey (Statistics Canada 1998), are employed, and one in four takes time off from work, with the support of their employer, to volunteer.

The nonprofit sector can offer businesses a number of resources (Pante 1996:28). Nonprofit organizations can provide the businesses with knowledge about the community and consumer's interests, access to community members, credibility in a local community, enhanced public image, an opportunity to act in a socially responsible fashion, the vitality of working with people who believe their work can contribute positively to the community, the skills of volunteers, and insight into different management styles. The private sector can offer nonprofit organizations skills and expertise, financial resources, public relations and accounting skills, the use of equipment, access to business community members, influential voices with particular audiences, improved image or credibility through association, and insight into different management styles.

Community partnerships can range from the traditional financial arrangements where a business provides resources to the community group, through to partnerships which try to create fundamental social change. While the first type is based on the donation of money, the second partnerships may focus on alleviating poverty, creating social housing, providing access to capital, or advocating for major social intervention. Traditionally, as we have seen in earlier chapters, governments have played the major role in combating poverty, dealing with low-income housing, and developing major social service interventions. Programs designed to deal with these issues have been made available to large segments of the population and have not been focused at the community level. The development of new partnerships is changing this widespread approach.

Community development, as a social policy tool, deals with the alleviation of problems as part of the larger process of creating community-based economic, social, and democratic development. The process integrates economic and social goals by combining job training and placement, job creation and retention, and self-employment. As well as helping people obtain more skills, the community-development process tries to create long-term assets in the community, such as a stock of low-income housing, child care centres, health clinics, services for elderly people, and physical assets such as parks and sports facilities.

While community interventions are perhaps best focused on local problems, there are examples of using community capacity to deal with large problems such as poverty.[3] Torjman (1998) describes four essential strategies for community-based poverty reduction: meeting basic needs, removing barriers, building skills, and promoting economic development. Before skills development can begin people must be able to meet their basic needs for food, housing, clothing, clean water, and sanitation. These basic issues can be met through government supported programs such as social assistance benefits, employment benefits, child benefits, or old age security. Community programs such as food banks, used clothing outlets, community gardens, community health clinics, and community-based social housing can support public social programs.

Once the basic needs have been met, community organizations can think about removing barriers which stop people from obtaining employment. These could include offering literacy programs, child care, support for transportation, work clothing, and other supports that facilitate people who are looking for employment. They could also include community groups' helping to remove attitudinal barriers that limit or prohibit access to people who are disabled; and accreditation barriers, so that people who have learned their skills outside of Canada are not hindered from finding employment (Torjman 1998:12). Removing as many barriers as possible greatly assists community organizations to focus on building skills ranging from life-skills training through to particular employment skills, including the proficiency necessary in the search for a job. In Nova Scotia, for instance, the provincial government has partnered with the federal government to create community resources dedicated to connecting people with the workplace. They created a position called a 'job developer,' whose role is to act as a broker, linking people looking for work with companies looking for employees.

Another aspect of community-based poverty reduction involves the promotion of economic development. This includes job creation and retention, self-employment, access to capital, and technical assistance. Each step is meant to create capacity within the community to create conditions supportive of job generation. Partnerships between businesses and community organizations, however, are no substitute for a solid public sector. Partnerships that are collaborative both complement and supplement the public sector. They can and should never be expected to replace the role of government in redistributing income, making essential social investments, and building caring communities through the promotion of citizenship (Torjman 1997b:14–15).

In addition to creating the capacity for solving social problems, being a member of an association has intrinsic rewards for the individual and the community. To be a member of an association is to participate in public life and to have a public identity outside of oneself. This public identity makes a statement about how a person cares about his or her community. When people join together to form a community group they create a sense of equality, part of the implied metaphysical equality that is assumed to exist between people in modern democratic states. Membership, like citizenship, carries with it rights and responsibilities (Lee 1992), and the manifestation of individual rights and responsibilities are part of a person's public persona and part of the fibre of community capacity.

Community Capacity in Action

Community capacity is the ability of people to help each other meet the demands of daily living and seize opportunities to realize their hopes and goals. This capacity includes people helping each other provide care, find resources, solve problems, and share information. Community capacity includes being a good neighbour, but goes beyond it to include informal and formal volunteering, joining community associations, and otherwise contributing to society. This helping capacity often lies dormant until events encourage people to come forward or demand that they do. The Red River flood of 1997 and the ice storm of 1998 were just such events.

During the 1997 flood in Manitoba, thousands of people helped their neighbours by filling sandbags, cooking food, and taking care of people who were forced out of their homes. Others from across the country donated money, food, and supplies to help people in need. Jim Silver (1997:87) points out that the flood epitomized Canada itself – an often harsh environment supporting a people who have learned the merits of responding to its demands with collective action in the interests of the community.

The same pattern repeated itself during the ice storm of 1998. The storm went on for several days, causing a power failure that eventually affected more than three million people from Kingston, Ontario, to the Annapolis Valley in Nova Scotia. Municipal water systems failed, hospitals lost their primary power, there were no streetlights or subway systems, banks closed, and the Canadian Forces were asked to provide assistance as communities claimed states of emergency. While workers from official organizations such as the police, fire departments, and hydro companies maintained order and repaired the hydro system, the public responded with both informal and formal help. Neighbours invited each other into their homes, volunteers staffed community centres and provided food and accommodations, and strangers pitched in and helped cut firewood for home heating in rural communities. Helplines were inundated with calls offering to take people into their homes, and people from across the country donated material, generators, and money.

At the simplest level, community capacity takes place when neighbours look out for each other. Jane Jacobs, in her 1961 classic, *The Death and Life of Great American Cities*, described this aspect of community capacity. For her, one of the central ingredients of community life was the 'eyes on the street': neighbourhood people, usually elderly ladies peeking out from behind front window curtains, keeping an eye on everything that takes place within their view. This 'neighbourhood watch' was not organized by some outside agency, nor was there any external reward for looking out for the neighbourhood. However, Jacobs credited 'eyes on the street' with keeping many dense urban neighbourhoods safe.

Jacobs's analysis of community involvement directs our attention towards invisible or underlying forces that become manifest as community capacity. These forces are organized through the development of community connections, informal self-help groups, community associations, and nonprofit organizations. People come together and form organizations that perform every type of task, from providing child care to counselling recent immigrants. These organizations have become interlocking networks that have political, economic, and social significance (Baum 1996).

As it is put to use, community capacity expands. It is, in other words, a renewable resource. Two neighbours decide to organize a holiday celebration of fireworks for their street. They purchase firecrackers, make popcorn, and advertise the event by having their children drop notices off at neighbours' houses. The two organizers hold the event on the street in front of their homes. Neighbours of all ages come with their lawn chairs and watch the fireworks. Families contribute a little money towards the cost of the fireworks, so it is cheaper than if each parent bought their own. By the second year, other parents take responsibility for safety by keeping the children organized and away from the fire-works' site. Still others obtain barriers to block the street from traffic, organize the popcorn and other refreshments, and one parent offers to make up a flier on her computer and have her children advertise the event. By the fifth year there are two hundred people attending the fireworks display. Sparkler parades, singsongs, and a seniors' viewing area on one of the neighbour's front verandas are all established. The result is an event that remains informal, draws upon the abilities of many people, and provides a wonderful evening for the immediate community.

In a 1987 National Survey on Volunteer Activity, two thirds of the adult population in Canada reported they were involved in informal volunteering. These spontaneous activities included visiting the sick or elderly (57 per cent), shopping for or driving others (49 per cent), babysitting (47 per cent) writing letters or helping solve problems (39 per cent), helping with outside work, and a whole variety of other activities (Rice 1990). While two-thirds of Canadians volunteer infor-mally, 27 per cent volunteer formally. A similar survey done in 1997 found that 33 per cent of the adult population formally volunteered. Formal volunteers work under the auspices of a group or organization, are involved on a regular or planned basis, and make long-term com-mitments to community organizations. In 1997 approximately 7.5 mil-lion Canadians volunteered their services to the more than 80,000 nonprofit organizations that make up the formal voluntary sector (Sta-tistics Canada 1998). These organizations use the services of volunteers to provide a wide variety of activities such as counselling, teaching, coaching, preparing food, performing, and fundraising.

Gender and the Voluntary Sector

Within the Canadian voluntary sector exists a gendered division of par-ticipation, labour, and structures similar in some respects to that operat-ing in the economic, domestic, and state domains. Gender lines are easily identifiable among the largest voluntary organization in the coun-try: Big Brothers and Big Sisters, the Kinsmen and Kinettes, the Guides

and Scouts, the Young Men's Christian Association (YMCA) and Young
Women's Christian Association (YWCA), the Lions Club, and the Wom-
en's Institute. The 1987 and 1997 national surveys of volunteer activity
found that women are slightly more apt than men to volunteer: some
55 per cent of all volunteers are women compared to 45 per cent of men.
Among seniors who volunteer, 61 per cent are women, here the rate of
participation was also slightly higher for women – 29 per cent of all
adult women volunteered, compared to 25 per cent of men. This proportion of female volunteers is lower than the classic stereotype: married,
older, well-to-do women, who are not in the work force and are regularly engaged in charities. In the modern context, another way to look at
this is to recognize that despite a substantial increase in labour market
participation, women are still the main source of informal and formal
volunteers. To be sure, paid employment may well influence when
women can volunteer, why they do, and how many hours they can give,
but it has not resulted in a dramatic decline in women's volunteering.
Feminist writers speak of the double shift; in actuality, for many women
it is a triple day consisting of paid work, housework and family caring,
and volunteer work (Catano and Christiansen-Ruffman 1989:4).

Women predominate as volunteers in several service areas and for
certain client groups. Women outnumber men two to one or more as
formal volunteers in the fields of health care, international agencies,
and education and youth development, as well as in religious organizations. More women than men participate in formal mutual-aid/self-
help groups. As well, women form the majority of volunteers in the arts
and culture, in law and justice organizations, and in informal helping.
Men predominate as volunteers in the fields of the environment and
wildlife management; fire services; leisure, recreation and sports; and
economic and employment interest groups such as chambers of commerce, industrial associations, and trade unions.

Much of the work that women do in the labour market,' notes Patricia
Evans (1991:178), 'mirrors their work in the household and incorpo-
rates a significant component of personal service.' Likewise, a great
deal of the voluntary work women do, reflects caring and household
chores. Comparing men's and women's formal and informal volunteer
activities reveals a number of traditional sex role differences. As formal
volunteers, women are more likely than men to prepare and serve food,
provide care and companionship, collect or distribute food and other
goods, and make and sell items for raising funds. As informal volunteers freely offer help to people outside their own families, women are

more active in helping with cooking and cleaning, shopping, or driving someone to appointments or stores, babysitting, and visiting the sick or elderly. Both women and men are active in organizing events, teaching or educating, collecting information, and writing letters for neighbours.

As formal volunteers, men are more likely than women to coach, referee, or judge events; repair, build, or maintain facilities; provide advice; and do public speaking. As informal volunteers, men are most likely to help by doing outside work or assisting with the operation of a business. The 1987 national survey found that 33 per cent of men volunteers sat as board members, compared to only 21 per cent of women; and 41 per cent of men volunteers said they helped run the organization, compared to 31 per cent of women. Within the health care part of the voluntary sector, women comprised 77 per cent of volunteers, but more than two-thirds of the board members were men (Kent 1989). Kelly Thompson (1989:2) has suggested that men prefer voluntary positions with a visible power base. Perhaps men thus make themselves more available to be elected and hold influential or prestigious volunteer positions. The result, whatever the motives, is a specific form of patriarchy, the under representation of women in the policy and decision-making positions of voluntary organizations.

The Volunteer Sector's Contribution to Community

Governments have identified the voluntary sector as one of the prime sources in the community for providing additional social care and volunteers as an untapped sources of community support. In the 1994 federal budget, Minister of Finance Paul Martin (1994:9) noted that charities play an essential and increasingly important role in Canadian society at a time when governments are being forced to withdraw from some activities. In a 1998 speech, Prime Minister Chrétien remarked that 'the days in Canada when the volunteer sector is overlooked and underrated are over – for good. Working together we can accomplish so much more then working apart' (Chrétien 1998:4). Canadian policy makers are seriously considering how to encourage volunteers to help provide additional social supports to others in the community. Increasingly questions are being asked about the ability of nonprofit organizations to take on more responsibility for delivering social programs. In trying to assess how community capacity could be increased, Judith Maxwell (1995), a prominent policy adviser, has posed the question: If more of the elderly population is healthy but inactive, are there ways to tap that energy to provide social and community services needed by families and the elderly?

The analysis of elderly people as a potential source of community capacity provides a useful way of determining whether there is a large pool of untapped resources in the community or whether the vast majority of those resources is already being used (Prince and Chappell 1997). As noted earlier, the national surveys on volunteer activity found that 27 per cent of Canadians in 1987 and 33 per cent in 1997 volunteered formally. When we turn our attention to the elderly, people over sixty-five, we see that almost 60 per cent volunteered formally, a much larger percentage than that of the general population. Senior volunteers spend much of their time visiting the sick and elderly. More seniors than non-seniors are involved in activities related to providing care, companionship, and friendly visiting, as well as activities related to the preparation or serving of food, while younger volunteers are more involved than seniors in teaching, coaching, and refereeing. Elderly women are the most likely group to be involved in service delivery; this is consistent with the wealth of caregiving literature which demonstrates that women provide more hands-on care than do men.

For the most part the elderly provide direct care for other elderly people, they are less interested in providing management services for nonprofit organizations, and have little interest in providing programs and services to young adults. They are involved in the arts and culture groups, health organizations, international activities, and religious organizations, and so these areas provide the greatest potential for future development.

Both an opportunity and a challenge exist in drawing senior volunteers deeper into providing services to community members. Those who did give time, spent approximately two hours a week on average volunteering for an organization. When asked if they would give more volunteer service, the vast majority of elderly people said they would be willing to give more time (81 per cent). This should not be surprising: those who volunteer report higher levels of satisfaction with their life than do their non-volunteering peers. Thus it appears there is some potential for even greater voluntary action by seniors in Canada.

Conclusions

The emergence of apparently new concepts such as 'civil society,' 'social capital,' and 'community capacity' are part of the changing politics of social policy. Definitions, though, are never politically neutral. We must always ask not just what these terms mean, but what they exclude, who is doing the defining, for what purpose, and who benefits and who does not from a given discourse. Community activists, volunteers, and human service workers are becoming increasingly aware of and interested in policy. Reasons include government moves to devolve services to municipalities and local groups, initiatives on healthy and safer communities, and the rhetoric of community care which arose out of the crisis politics of the welfare state in the 1980s and early 1990s.

The creation of community capacity comes through the existence and development of mediating institutions. These include self-help groups, nonprofit organizations, religious congregations, professional associations, and other local organizations where people come together to meet their needs. Through these institutions, community members develop leadership skills, improve their problem-solving abilities, develop ideas and strategies for solving local problems, and draw together the resources needed to achieve community objectives. Underlying these practical skills is the development of community trust and cooperation. The development of mediating institutions brings together people with different skills, values, and ideas about how to solve problems.

Both the welfare system and the voluntary sector address social problems and provide protection to vulnerable Canadians. Both offer services and support to people who need assistance, and both share many of the same goals. There are many overlaps between the two systems, and in many ways they have become mutually dependent. When governments reduce benefits to families there are longer lineups at voluntary agencies. Rising unemployment increases the demand for counseling and the informal help of family members. Social assistance recipients turn to the voluntary sector for help when food runs low. As the government 'deinstitutionalizes' people from facilities that have historically cared for them, demands on community organizations to offer more services rise dramatically.

Increasing the use of volunteers in providing health and social services poses some dilemmas for social policy and the essence of citizenship in Canada. Mishra (1990a:111) points out that using volunteers to provide essential services undermines the structure of the welfare system. Since charity is voluntary action, the nature and scope of assistance remains unspecified and uncertain. Conversely, those in need do not have any right to assistance from private sources and must be grateful for what they may receive. Our position is that placing greater emphasis on the role of communities in solving social problems must not mean the abandonment of the traditional goals of the welfare state. Reducing poverty, offering economic security, and investing in people through education and health care remain as important now as they did when the Canadian welfare state was envisaged in the 1940s. Looking to local communities, therefore, should not result in letting go of essential public services. The capacity of communities, and marginalized groups in particular, to tackle serious public issues and risks of everyday living is closely linked with the broader context of social policies and other state policies.

The challenge, then, is for governments and community organizations to develop and link social policy and social capital in ways that strive for a number of balances: attending to the long-term and short-term in planning and funding; committing to economic security and social security in national and provincial policies; addressing the needs of the majority and of minority groups; incorporating the experiences of men and of women, and of different groups within each gender; and paying close attention to the rights and responsibilities of citizens, to be sure, but also those of corporations, unions, voluntary agencies, the media, and governments.

10

Creating a New Policy Agenda

The previous chapters have provided an account of the origins, nature, and implications of the changing politics facing social policy and the welfare state in Canada. We have outlined the evolution of programs over the twentieth century, identifying changes in the ideas, policy instruments, interests, and institutions connected with the development of welfare. We have viewed the contemporary politics of social policy as tensions arising from the capacity of local communities to address social problems in the face of the globalization of the economy and the pluralization of the population.

In this last chapter we offer some observations on the study of the welfare state and the practice of social policy. We first review the lessons we have learned about social policy, tracing a number of essential concepts and issues touched on throughout the book. We next place these lessons in the context of the welfare state at the end of the twentieth century. This includes the changing role of women, the aging of the population, the changing relationship between the federal and provincial governments, and the elimination of many provincial and federal budget deficits (but not the debt). Finally, we argue for the development of a policy agenda which recognizes the new politics of social policies and the changing relationships between the market and the community, and between the citizen and the state. We believe this new agenda needs to broaden the scope of social policy analysis, recognize the important role played by governments in developing social policies, and encourage the democratization of the welfare state and social agencies.

Changing Politics and Social Policies: Where Have We Come From, and Where Are We Now?

As Chapters 2 and 3 point out, the history of modern Canadian social policy spans 100 years and is made up of four broad periods: the colonial pre-welfare state phase, the period of establishing the national system of social security, the crisis period, and the current phase of changing politics. Each of these periods is associated with a particular economic context and policy direction, state form, and model of social programming. It began with the colonial period, when people turned to their neighbours and community for help during difficult times, and the local economy had a direct impact on people's ability to meet their needs – that is, people could take care of themselves if work was available. In those communities where the economy was seasonal, or where there was not enough work to meet everyone's needs, communities had a difficult time helping people solve pressing problems. When the problems were too difficult for local resources to solve, community members turned to their governments for help, and the municipal, provincial, and federal governments created basic social policies to meet their most pressing needs. Early policies were based on the principle of 'less eligibility,' and provided income support in a limited, means-tested fashion.

The colonial period reflected the development of local welfare programs provided by voluntary agencies and fledgling government programs which created the foundations of the welfare state. It became clear during this period that people could not protect there own well-being without the support and help of the community. Even when the country was growing and the processes of industrialization and urbanization were creating opportunities for advancement there were many people who were hurt by the changes, could not adapt, and had to turn to their communities and governments for support.

The provision of this basic form of welfare lasted until the Great Depression of the 1930s, which brought home the point that individuals could not protect themselves from the consequences created by the economy. Every major social thinker of the time called for the introduction of programs and services to protect the population from the ravages of economic turmoil. New ideas began to emerge about the role governments should play in helping people meet their basic needs. The ideas of people like Leonard Marsh, Harry Cassidy, Charlotte Whitton,

C.A. Curtis, and J.J. Heagerty came to define the politics of envisioning and then establishing a system of social security for Canadians. These new ideas, as we have shown in Chapter 3, led to the expansionist era of building a social security system leading to an expanded public realm. Government intervention became the norm and between the 1940s and the 1970s many new programs were developed. Based in part on Keynesian economics, the conception of social programs underpinning this period stressed comprehensive provision for a range of risks and needs. Canadians learned that in a complex society such as Canada, the federal and provincial governments must work together if they are to deal with systemic problems such as poverty, unemployment, or social dislocation, or provide universal access to education, health care, or housing.

The expansion of the welfare state came to an end by the mid 1970s as a new period of welfare crisis and restraint began to take hold. The oil crisis and economic problems of the early 1970s created a period of stagflation and economic instability, which led to a questioning of the welfare state. The old economic ideas of *laissez-faire* began to have greater impact on the thinking of policy makers, and a new attitude developed which called for dramatic changes to the existing system. In response, governments cut some programs, froze others, and allowed for limited new initiatives over the 1970s and 1980s. The welfare state came under criticism from community members as well as political activists on the left and the right. Critics claimed the welfare system was overbearing, underachieving, patriarchal, too bureaucratic, and – ultimately most damaging politically – in fiscal crisis. There was a resistance by policy making elites to introduce any further major reforms such as national child care, and various social programs were changed to those with a more residual character.

During this crisis period provincial and federal governments began exploring ways of dismantling aspects of their welfare programs. Family Allowance and Old Age Security, both universal programs, were replaced by geared-to-income programs; the Canada Assistance Plan was replaced by the Canada Health and Social Transfer (CHST), bringing with it deep cuts to federal spending; and the Unemployment Insurance program was replaced, leading to significantly reduced coverage for the unemployed. Some provincial governments, made deep cuts in their social assistance programs and removed many people from their welfare rolls. By the 1990s many programs had been altered and benefits reduced, shifting responsibility from the federal government to the provincial and territorial governments, and through these governments onto the community and voluntary and informal sectors.

Canadians learned that social programs were not protected from the economic winds of change. A number of commentators pronounced the postwar social security system – the Keynesian welfare state – dead or near extinction. To be sure, Brian Mulroney's Conservative federal governments of the 1980s and early 1990s, and Jean Chrétien's Liberal governments of the 1990s, as well as provincial administrations such as those of Ralph Klein and Mike Harris, reduced social spending, often deeply, and retreated from economic stabilization policies and the idea of a comprehensive social safety net. Because of this era of restructuring and retrenchment, Janine Brodie (1995) argued that the foundations of the Keynesian welfare state are disappearing, and Jane Pulkingham and Gordon Ternowetsky argued that the introduction of the Canada Health and Social Transfer in 1996 contributed to 'demolishing what may be left of the Keynesian welfare state in Canada' (1996:9). This idea is echoed by other social policy writers who suggest that the dismantling and privatizing of the welfare state will continue; that under economic globalism the nation state could become obsolete; and that we need to ponder what will come after the welfare state (Teeple 1995; Collier 1997).

Certainly government, as the central agency in society for financing, guaranteeing, and providing services, cash benefits, and social rights, has been criticized by various interests and constrained by deficits and the debt. Important elements of the welfare state are gone: universal income programs for families with children and for seniors, the political commitment to and policies for high and stable levels of employment, and a specific federal role in the financing of employment insurance and in the provision of social assistance across the country. Other elements have been reduced and residualized: the regulation and stabilization of the economy, the coverage of employment insurance, and the provision of social housing. In many respects, the income support levels for those in need are less adequate today than a decade or more ago.

Within the past fifteen years governments have gone beyond fiscal restraint and talk of crisis to the retrenchment of social programs and the restructuring of the government's role in providing social support. The neo-liberal state based on monetarist economic ideas has come to dominate. Many people who support the idea of welfare are glad to see certain aspects of the system disappear. They are pleased with the elimination of sexist employment practices; overtly racist immigration laws; discriminatory regulations in social assistance, such as the 'man in the house' rule for single-mother families; and the closing of residential schools for Aboriginal peoples. As Alan Cairns (1986:82–3) has said, 'it is not necessary to shelter every activity of modern government in Canada under the rubric of the welfare state and thus impervious to criticism. It is far from evident that the major beneficiaries of modern state activity are the poor, the downtrodden, the disadvantaged, and the helpless.'

All has not been lost, however. Much of the welfare system survives even if in an altered state. The core sectors of universal health care and education remain. The personal income tax system continues to be broadly progressive, and several tax credits have been created and enriched over the past fifteen years. Another major development was the entrenchment of the Canadian Charter of Rights and Freedoms into the Constitution in 1982. Canada is the only country in the world with constitutional recognition and protection of people with disabilities. The Charter provides that the rights and freedoms referred to in it are guaranteed equally to males and females, and that the existing Aboriginal and treaty rights of the Aboriginal peoples of Canada are recognized and affirmed. Human rights legislation and other kinds of civic regulation (discussed in Chapter 7) have been introduced and extended in scope at both the federal and provincial levels. Reforms in 1998 to the financing of the Canada Pension Plan serve to sustain this important retirement income support.

In public spending terms, social policy remains the largest share of governmental budgets. Since 1980 social policy expenditures of all governments in Canada have increased not only in absolute terms, but also as a share of total program spending and as a share of the Gross Domestic Product (GDP), the national income produced each year. In 1980–81 social expenditures by the federal, provincial, territorial, and municipal governments were $73.3 billion, representing 64.1 per cent of all program spending by all governments, the equivalent of 23.7 per cent of the GDP. In 1994–95, social expenditures were $215.6 billion; 75.3 per cent of consolidated government program spending and 28.8 per cent of the GDP.[1]

In many ways, social policies have become economic policies. The recent reforms to social programs are designed to reward work effort, facilitate job searches and retraining, and discourage reliance on social assistance and employment insurance. Investment in education and lifelong learning were used as tools for improving economic adaptability and productivity. These changes meant that social policies were realigned not with the needs of people but with the needs of international trade and labour markets. This orientation has altered the nature of social policy from being simply the non-market allocation of benefits and services to people, to include market-based, or at least market-informed, provisions.

This latest period has opened social policy contradictions leading to ongoing struggles and debates. Fiona Williams (1992:204) has written that 'contradictions are nothing new in the state of welfare, but the 1990s marks an intensification of contradictions as well as a shifting of debates.' While many social programs have been marketized to support economic needs, as we show in Chapter 6, the economic security and well-being of many citizens has been decreasing. People are pushed into paid work through workfare measures while the real value of minimum wages has declined over time. Economic growth has been slowing while change in the economy has been accelerating. There has been a fragmentation of social services through contracting out and a financial restriction of community-based services while provincial governments act to centralize authority and control. Canadian pollster Angus Reid (1997:276) has found 'far more willingness to ascribe blame to the poor these days even though it's getting much easier to sink into poverty than it used to be.'

Still another consequence of this latest period is that program cuts often intensify inequalities even though there has been 'a growing awareness and resistance to inequalities of race, gender and disability' (Williams 1992:203). In Chapter 7 we drew attention to one aspect of the changing politics: the shift away from universalism and standardization in program design and organizational processes towards particularism and diversity. While in many ways this has been positive because it offers community recognition to groups who have been excluded by the policy process, in other ways it has been negative because it stigmatizes those who are targeted for social benefits.

Balancing the needs of the community with the needs of the market economy has long been a central challenge of social policy, as Chapters 2, 3, and 4 have shown. Changes in the economy, whether at the local, provincial, or national level – changes which threaten people's security and livelihood – prompt community demands for social protection. Economic globalization and civic pluralization raise new risks and needs for the state and community. There are competing pressures and ideas about the state's role in protecting citizens. A large part of the changing politics is the tension created between global economic interests pressing for the liberalization and reduction of state policies, and social movement claims for further interventions by the state to address inequities and disadvantages.

One of the contradictions of social policy reform in Canada over the last fifteen years has been that universal income programs have been eliminated supposedly to better target benefits to those most in need, while poverty and welfare caseloads have increased and little of the 'savings' from eliminating Old Age Security payments and Family Allowance benefits have actually gone to lower-income families or seniors (Rice and Prince 1993). Behind this contradiction, however, the Canadian welfare state does perform a redistributive role. It has been a disingenuous critique by the Right and an exaggerated claim by some on the Left, that the welfare state has failed to eradicate inequalities or implement a strategy of egalitarianism. In a social policy system built on universal health care and education, and various social insurance programs, all within the context of a market economy, a modest redistribution effect is to be expected. Cash transfers and tax provisions do shift the distribution of market-based income towards greater equality. A study on market incomes and family poverty by the Canadian Council on Social Development reported that 'In the absence of government income supports, many more Canadian families would be left poor by the marketplace ... [also that] government transfers and benefits rescued 557,000 families from market poverty in 1994, and brought the incomes of other poor families a little closer to the poverty line' (Schellenberg and Ross 1997:4). Income support through tax and transfer provisions, we believe, is critical and needs to be sustained if not enhanced. A new approach to improving the incomes of working poor and welfare poor Canadians should also place greater stress on job creation, child care, pay equity, and tax reforms.

Social Policy and Politics in the Post-Deficit Era: Salvation by Surplus?

The crisis period of the welfare state has come to an end. For over a generation the federal deficit has been a principal issue on the Canadian political agenda, and all federal governments since 1975 have been committed to deficit reduction in one form or another, with varying degrees of success.[2] The prevailing discussions conerning deficits is articulated in an ideological set of beliefs that claim excessive growth of expenditures, particularly social spending, as the main cause of rising deficits, despite evidence to the contrary. Critics of social spending claim the deficit has led to impairing the market economy, fueling inflation and high interest rates, eroding people's self-reliance, and burdening future generations with huge debts.

Under this ideology of deficit politics, the recommended policy responses, as we discussed in Chapters 4, 5, and 6, were aimed at retrenching the state: program cutbacks, downsizing of employees, the privatization of activities, deregulation of certain sectors of the economy, and generally lowering expectations of what government can or should do. The ascendancy of this discourse created a powerful deficit politics in which new program ideas were left unfulfilled. The national child-care program was not completed. Old federal policy involvements, such as social housing, were abandoned. Other social transfers were retrenched and burdens shifted to others. The voices of social movements and public interest groups were simply ignored, or, more troubling, deliberately marginalized. Deficits loomed over Ottawa and the country like a harsh arctic cold front.

Political and fiscal seasons, however, are changing from deficit politics to dividend politics. We are entering a post-deficit era in government budgets, initially at the provincial level and more recently at the national level. The federal deficit was eliminated in the 1997–98 budget year, the first time since 1969–70, and the government has estimated budget balances or surpluses into the next century. The Chrétien Liberals have stated that for every billion dollars of a fiscal dividend, half will go to a combination of reducing taxes and reducing the national debt and half will address public priorities by making strategic investments in children and youth, health care and education.

The post-deficit era will not be an easy return to the expenditure politics of the 1960s, and the public will not accept a new round of taxing, borrowing, and spending. The politics and economics of the deficit ideology have seriously altered public attitudes and expectations as well as the platforms of political parties and the policy agendas of governments. The post-deficit era promises to be as contentious as the period of deficit reduction politics. Conflict and debate over what to do with a fiscal dividend is apparent among the federal political parties, in the realm of intergovernmental relations and across interest groups and policy communities. Like deficit politics, fiscal dividend politics is a debate over the appropriate size and role of the federal government in relation to the provinces, the economy, and civil society. Easing of the fiscal constraints on the federal and many provincial governments widens the array of policy instruments available. From an intense concentration on deficit reduction and program spending controls, governments are developing an enhanced ability to respond to issues with expenditures and/or tax cuts. The boundaries of what is financially possible are therefore expanding. New money makes it possible, in principle at least, for new objectives to be addressed and new programs to be established. Issues and concerns previously held to be financially irresponsible and politically naive by the dominant deficit discourse, now seem possible again for genuine consideration by governments. Budgetary surpluses open new 'political spaces' for groups such as the women's movement, and the provinces to make claims for improved services and actions by Ottawa on key problems of the day.

Where Do We Go from Here?

In considering what might be done to find a new balance between the marketplace and community, we discuss three strategies Canadians can use in the study and the practice of social policy in Canada. These strategies include broadening the scope of policy debate to heighten the importance of the community in the policy process; re-establishing the capacity and social role of governments so that new ideas can be put on the policy agenda; and democratizing the welfare state so that it fully includes people from a wide variety of community groups.

The welfare state as an idea is not obsolete but remains relevant precisely because of changing economic and social conditions. Economic globalism will continue to exert a major influence on the making of social policy. A central idea of this book, though, is the need to consider globalization in relation to social pluralization, and to examine the interplay of both trends in relation to the federalized welfare state in Canada. While the economic winners in the new global economy may want to restrict some decisions in some policy areas, the modern state is not rendered powerless. Governments must maintain their ability to direct the course of social policy development. Following Esping-Andersen (1996b) on the Left, and Watson (1998) on the Right, we believe it is an exaggeration to conclude that globalism renders governments powerless to make policy choices and to meet social objectives.

Broadening the Social Policy Debate

The political challenge for the new millennium is to find new ways of thinking about the relationship between market forces and community claims. Though they have contradictory logic, as Karl Polanyi among others has noted, the paradox is that we need both markets and communities to prosper and ensure a vital democracy. An essential barrier in achieving such a new relationship has been the belief, expressed most forcefully by the Right, that markets are the primary institution for attaining well-being. The role of the state and to a lesser extent civil society is being downplayed or ignored as an essential part of this new relationship. The results of excluding the community is that the well-being of many Canadians becomes dependent upon the whims of private investors, the volatility of free markets, the fashions of foreign exchange, and the decisions of bankers and corporate presidents outside of the country.

Polanyi was deeply concerned about the relationship between self-regulating markets and the community's ability to take care of its members. If he were alive today he would understand the rise of globalism and the forces for free trade. He would also understand the growing demands of community groups for recognition of their rights and interests. He would recognize the important role the state must play in balancing the forces of self-regulating markets, and he would expect the state to build social structures that protect the sovereignty of the community against the impositions of market forces. We also believe that governments have the power and authority to create a new relationship between the market and the community as a way of meeting the need for social protection and the desire for cultural recognition.

Opening up a new debate about the changing role of welfare is difficult but absolutely vital because of the pluralization of society. Many more groups want a voice in how the government should address social issues, but are finding it difficult to influence the dominant political parties in Canada. These groups are struggling to have their issues placed on the policy agenda. They seek not only to open the debate about the policy agenda, but also to go further and articulate how and why their issues should be central to the well-being of the community. To be effective, however, community groups must find a way to place their self-interest in a larger context and to relate to other interest groups. A major challenge is that there are few national forums in which community groups come together to talk about their issues or place their concerns into a more encompassing social policy vision.

New forms of federal-provincial and provincial-municipal cooperation must be created to support a more inclusive policy debate. Public structures and processes must provide a way for emerging interest groups to find a legitimate voice on behalf of the communities they represent. Governments must also find ways to help create community-based policy structures to address the changing politics of social policy. The new social policy agenda must be built on the political discourse about the community and the rights and responsibilities of citizenship. It must reject the individualistic notions created by market competition and assert the importance of social connection, social harmony, and social solidarity. It must embrace the notion of cooperation as a central tenant of a functioning society. At the deepest level, the new politics of social policy must champion the idea of interdependence and interconnection between all communities. Moving towards a more cooperative society must be based on the notion that all people have value and that social differences are what make the community rich and resourceful.

The new social policy agenda must encompass the idea that we live in a finite world with limited resources existing in a fragile environment. While the search for new ways of doing things, new forms of energy, and new ways to make life better must continue, it must do so with the recognition that if the community is to provide the support for economic activity it must take into consideration the implications of growth and development for the community and the environment. Governments must find ways of protecting the nation and its citizens from the destructive forces of world trade. While there are important advantages to having increased connections between producing sectors of the world economy, a country cannot allow these relationships to undermine the human rights, income security, health and safety, and working conditions of its citizens. New debates must be developed which argue for trading relationships that protect people, communities, and the environment.

One way to enrich this debate is to invite nongovernmental groups into the discussions. This invitation could include those groups concerned with the environment, human rights, and the rights of particular interests. The opening of such discussions could place people with a wide variety of interests – pro-traders as well as protectionists – into debates that will make the policy trade-offs more visible and understandable to the broad public. When left to market decisions, poverty, pollution, crime, and social dislocations increase. The sum total of decisions made by self-regarding individuals or firms does not create social conditions free from the problems that governments may fail to solve. Rather, they create social arrangements that provide advantages to some and disadvantages to others. Those who are disadvantaged have a more difficult time meeting their needs and are less well off. Those who can take advantage of their position to make private decisions are able to meet their needs more effectively and also to gather more decision-making power (Finlayson 1996; Langille 1997).

The intent of widening the scope of social policy debate is to expand intellectual, political, and everyday discussions of the welfare state and public interventions. Debates should 'encompass the interests of various muted groups, particularly women and oppressed racial and ethnic groups' (Bryson 1992:4–5). What is urgently required, we believe, is to find a new balance between the market economy, civil society, and the welfare state. An important part of that new balance is for government to stop offloading responsibilities onto communities and start supporting local initiatives. In the words of the Social Justice Commission (1994:370), 'Government can never take the place of community: what it can and should do, however, is create political, institutional and financial frameworks which help local people rebuild their communities from the bottom up, making them safer places in which to live and generating a better quality of life which can support wider economic opportunities.'

The changing politics are about the waning of the Right, though not its demise, and a resurgence of the centrist liberal perspective on state intervention and social policy. There is a renewed willingness among policy leaders, though one still conditioned by caution, to undertake the extension of social benefits and services by the public sector. The fiscal capacity of the state, to some extent, is always politically negotiable. The public finance culture will most likely evolve through give and take among the viewpoints and pressures of the federal government, provinces, public and elite opinions, and interest structures. Federal Liberals now refer to new social spending as 'strategic investments' for enhancing economic growth and social well-being. This language is reminiscent of a vital point made long ago by Leonard Marsh (1943:273–4): 'social security payments are not money lost,' but rather, 'are investments in morale and health, in greater family stability, and from both material and psychological viewpoints, in human productive efficiency. They demand personal and community responsibilities; but in the eyes of most of the people who are beneficiaries, give a more evident meaning to the ideas of common effort and national solidarity. It has yet to be proved that any democracy which underwrites the social minimum for its citizens is any the weaker or less wealthy for doing so.'

Rebuilding the Social Role and Capacity of Governments

Back in 1943 Marsh faced a number of questions when thinking about the social role governments should play in providing social and economic security to all citizens. What are the causes of unemployment and what is the proper role of the government in managing the economy? What universal and employment risks do individuals and families face and how should the government share these risks? How should governments protect citizens' well-being? His answers led to the development of a broad series of social policies that protected Canadians from the worst problems created by the process of industrialization and urbanization. These included universal programs for families and the elderly, insurance programs for the unemployed and those injured at work, and social assistance programs for those who were excluded from the labour market.

We face the same questions in trying to *rebuild* the social role of government. What is the proper role of the government in a global economy? Under what conditions should people receive social benefits? How can the government develop new social programs in the face of a globalizing economy? Recent studies offer a number of answers, each focusing on a specific aspect of government that must be rebuilt.

For some studies it is a question of maintaining a just and fair society. Daniel Drache and Andrew Ranachan (1995) call for re-establishing the capacity of governments in order to invest in human capital and get people back to work, to preserve social cohesion and nation building, and to achieve a more equitable society. This is similar to the call by people such as Ken Battle and Michael Mendelson (1997), of the Caledon Institute of Social Policy, who believe governments must take action if they are to eliminate poverty among children; or Sherri Torjman (1998), who believes governments must support community-based initiatives to deal with poverty. Analysts from this perspective make the case that the federal government's fiscal dividend must be spent on social programs because the surplus is a result of the retrenchment of social programs. The cuts had painful consequences for low-income Canadians as well as weakened the presence of Ottawa within federalism. They recommend reinvesting the fiscal dividend in a series of national social initiatives designed to renew the capacity of the government to deal with social problems.

For others such as Judith Maxwell (1994) it is a matter of maintaining the essential role of government in addressing the social deficits in the country. For her a social deficit exists when large numbers of people are on employment insurance or welfare, children and youth are going to school hungry, there are limited opportunities for skill development and retraining, and there is a lack of adequate and affordable child care and elder care. Maxwell argues that rebuilding the social role of the state is essential for no less a reason than restoring the political legitimacy and credibility of our governing institutions; that one step towards rebuilding the role of government is to develop a clearly defined long-term view of cultural, economic, environmental, and social objectives that work towards a new social contract. 'This means rethinking the political values that describe the obligations and rights of all the players – governments, citizens, employers, unions and interest groups' (1994:56).

The literature identifies many initiatives governments could take:

- strengthening the commitment to health care and 'healthy public policy'
- eliminating child poverty
- developing a national child care system
- introducing fairer student loans
- making a new commitment to affordable social housing
- recognizing the rights of Aboriginal peoples, persons with disabilities, and gays and lesbians
- making a renewed commitment to employment and fairer taxes

Taking action on these or any number of other policy issues would strengthen the social role of the government and increase its capacity to deal with social issues.

We believe the federal and provincial governments must rebuild their social role and capacity in order to re-energize the politics of social policy. This requires that governments recommit themselves to developing a more equitable society, a society in which all Canadians have adequate income and a community in which they have a voice in the new social policy debates. Beyond this it requires governments, both federal and provincial, to work together to influence the international social policy environment so that a more global principle of citizenship develops. By taking bold steps the government will rebuild its social role and increase its capacity to govern.

While governments can choose from a long list of social problems that need to be addressed, we have focused on two issues: poverty at the domestic level and international social policy agreements at the global level. Poverty focuses on issues inside the country and challenges governments to develop innovative programs which help individuals and families deal with the risks of the globalizing economy. International agreements focus on broader issues and force Canadians to think about the wider policy domain and the needs of others. In both areas we have set out a policy agenda and called for renewed commitments on the part of the government in addressing social issues.

A Renewed Attack on Poverty

Canada has an ongoing problem with people living in poverty. While the actual number of low-income families has shifted over time, there has been a relatively consistent 15 to 20 per cent of the population whose incomes are near or below the Statistics Canada Low-Income Cut-Off Lines. Historically, economic growth reduced the number of people with low incomes by providing employment opportunities. However, the traditional relationship between economic growth and poverty seems to be weakening (OECD 1997:2). As the global economy comes to have a greater influence on employment, people with a good education are doing better in the labour market while people with limited skills and education are finding it more difficult to find work. A 1994 discussion paper by the Canadian government on reforming social programs (Human Resources Development Canada 1994:9) frankly noted that in the past fifteen years, 'our society increasingly has begun to be polarized between well-educated, highly skilled Canadians in demand by employers – today's economic elite – and less educated people – those without specialized, up-to-date job skills – who have been losing ground.' The differences are widening between well-paying, permanent work in the primary labour forces and poor-paying, part-time jobs in the secondary labour force. The result is an increase in the number of people with jobs that do not provide a living wage.

While increased training and more education will solve some of these problems, there will be a portion of Canadians who will need sustained help to insure they do not live in poverty. The way of providing income support to the poor that best meets our goal of rebuilding the social role of governments is to develop a comprehensive social security program based on a negative income tax. In a recent article, John Myles and Paul Pierson (1997) examined the role of the negative income tax in providing a policy instrument that uses the tax system and is able to provide effective targeting while maintaining broad political support. The negative income tax can be used to provide income through the tax system so that people do not 'apply' for social assistance; rather, when their income falls below a certain level they receive a top up, which helps maintain income security.

The program is relatively simple. The government sets a basic allowance that provides an income floor for eligible individuals and families: as a person's income declines, either because the individual cannot work or there is no work available, the level of the basic allowance rises until it reaches the maximum benefit level; when he or she has income from any other source, the basic allowance is reduced so that as income rises the amount of the allowance falls. The government can set the rate of the reduction so that it encourages people to seek work and thereby increase their income while not 'punishing' them for finding other sources of income by removing all their benefits. At a predetermined point, depending upon the tax-back rate, the benefit disappears and the person starts to pay taxes. Since the tax-back rate is always less than 100 per cent, some portion of the benefits are provided to people with middle incomes who are firmly attached to the world of employment. This means there would be increased political support for the system from the broad middle classes.

The utility of a negative income tax is that it can be theoretically universal while being targeted on needy groups. From this perspective everyone is a taxpayer, and therefore a negative income tax program has a universal orientation. A second advantage is that the system can be tailored to give people a choice about the way they earn or receive income. By providing choice the program can be used to support work incentive programs without forcing people into mandatory workfare programs. People are left to make their own decisions about how much they are able to contribute to their own well-being.

The program is not 'welfare' as we commonly know it, but rather acts as an income stabilizer. While the program seems to have a general appeal to the middle classes, it can be used to target money where it is most needed: for the poor. Similarly, because it does not have to be based on previous earnings and can be based on any number of conditions, it does not have to be focused on wage earners. Stay-at-home parents could have the same rights and be as much a part of the system as those who work outside the house, although their income level would reflect these choices.

The use of negative income tax programs could be designed to encourage any number of different activities. It could be used to support low-income parents who are taking care of other people's children, students who are going to university, or poor people who provide volunteer assistance to social agencies. It could be used for low-income families who are taking care of the elderly or providing community support to someone who is mentally challenged. Traditional complaints against selectivity as being intrusive and stigmatizing for clients, and administratively complex and expensive to deliver, are then largely overcome by using the tax system to income test social benefits.

The expanded use of a negative income tax may be the most positive way governments can address the problems of poverty. The program does not create sharp divisions between the employed and the unemployed or the able-bodied and the disabled. It provides all citizens with a basic guarantee: income that does not fall below a given level.

We believe there is yet another advantage. The greatest feature of the negative income tax system is that it is invisibly attached to the tax system. Even though governments may lose some of their ability to intervene in the social environment, they are much less willing to give up their influence when it comes to the tax system. In a social-policy environment seemingly overshadowed by global interests it is easier for governments to introduce changes in the tax system than it is to introduce new social welfare programs. The tax system is less visible than most welfare programs and does not provide the same political target for restructuring. As such, a negative income tax program can be used to replace social insurance programs without the political protests that come when governments endeavor to introduce new welfare measures.

Myles and Pierson (1997:8) believe negative income tax programs are well adapted to the new politics of social policy. 'They rely on new political coalitions which employ new, low-profile strategies suitable for an environment of austerity.' The negative income tax programs can provide a cost-effective transition from needs-based programs to income-tested programs in a time when there is resistance to any new welfare measures. While they allow for targeting the most needy, the structure of the program provides benefits well into the middle-income ranges and are supported politically by the middle classes.

Developing More Inclusive International Agreements

An important step in rebuilding the government's capacity to deal with social problems is to encourage the development of a new range of international relationships and agreements concerned with the rights of citizens. Part of this strategy would be to have the Canadian government take the lead in calling for a new form of global citizenship. The underlying principle of such a form of citizenship would build on the activities of the United Nations and would seek to ensure everyone's right to live a decent life. This new balance would contribute to the important place of 'community' in the lives of people. The development of this idea encourages governments to negotiate for a more community sensitive form of economic development. This would require negotiating limits on unrestrained exploitation of resources, the development of global trade, and the international flow of capital. The goal in this negotiation would be to highlight the social costs of unregulated economic development and to place social policy issues on the international agenda. Wiseman (1996) argues that the only way to deal adequately with the globalization of economic power is through a system of globalized democratic decision making and regulations.

This is a difficult challenge. The development of new social agreements with other countries will require a broadening of the alternative policy institutions based on community interests. The European experience provides insight into how the process can develop: interest groups in Europe work through their national governments to press for issues that are important to them; at the same time leaders of these interest groups are developing international links with other organizations in the European Union (EU). In this way they create two paths through which they can influence the policy agenda: directly and through the local governments. The Canadian government could encourage the same type of development in Canada. Interest groups could be supported in their quest to influence the international social policy agenda through government activities, while at the same time they could be supported in developing international relationships with interest groups from other countries or within the United Nations.

There are many obstacles to developing networks that support transnational organizations. National governments must find it in their interest to have nongovernmental partners concerning themselves with social issues and working to have these issues place on the policy agenda. They must be prepared to support the agreements and social charters that will eventually emerge from a richer international debate about global citizenship. Governments must be prepared to support grassroots social movements calling for protection from labour exploitation or the degradation of the environment. They will need to foster connections between these grassroots community organizations and encourage them to make links with similar organizations in other countries. They will also have to increase their commitment to international organizations such as the United Nations, Red Cross, and the International Court. The government must support interest groups who are prepared to question the policy directions of the International Monetary Fund, the World Bank, and the World Trade Organization. Groups such as the International Labour Organization, Greenpeace, and Amnesty International need to be encouraged to open the debate about international trade and its implications for global citizens.

The development of a broader international social policy perspective could lead to the creation of international agreements which determine how market activities and social activities can be coordinated. Social policy integration in the EU is based primarily on legal instruments which unify the social policy decisions of different countries. Many of the laws and regulations within the EU have been developed through intergovernmental, rather than political negotiations. Over time they have created a global system (in European terms) of relationships that protect civil, social, and economic rights of citizens across all countries in the Union. At the same time countries have considerable autonomy on purely domestic issues.

The development of such an international approach would encourage Canada and other countries to consider the relationship between economic and social issues in different ways. New social policy agreements would force corporations to take community needs into consideration when they are deciding where and when to locate new production facilities. Corporations would find they had to meet international standards regarding the environment and human rights before they could invest or trade in a country. The agreements could be written in such a way that they punish corporations who violate the agreements by limiting their rights or by imposing taxes.

John Wiseman (1996) has argued that a sequencing of policy initiatives is the key to the development of international agreements. First, countries need to monitor financial flows between countries to ensure present laws are complied with. Next, governments would have to reintroduce some degree of regulation regarding exchange rates to prevent dramatic interest rate changes. Finally, as Wiseman claims, governments would have to levy taxes on globalized financial transactions as a way of building the resources necessary to deal with the social implications of world trade. Pulkingham and Ternowetsky (1996) explore the idea of a financial transaction tax as a means for raising revenue and dampening currency speculation, thus stabilizing exchange rates and interest rates. This financial transaction tax is a possible policy instrument not commonly discussed in social welfare circles, although this may be changing (McQuaig 1998).

Over time the Canadian government could evolve a set of agreements with other countries for controlling transnational corporations. Such actions can include cultural, environmental, and labour clauses in trade agreements; stand-alone multinational social charters to regulate trade and investment relations; and building or reforming public institutions at the international level. These actions represent varying degrees of effort at controlling capital and the power of transnational corporations (Broad 1995; Collier 1997). A prominent Canadian thinker on this is Marjorie Griffin Cohen, who has suggested that international institutions need to be designed to control capital, raise money, and redistribute it worldwide. Cohen (1997a:7) adds that 'there is an urgent need to recognize *economic pluralism* in international trade and investment agreements. A tolerance for pluralism requires the recognition that different goals, conditions, and cultures throughout the world require very different solutions to problems. One system, the western system based on a U.S. kind of economy and social system, will not serve the needs of all people in all circumstances.' In advocating for the continued diversity of social policy worldwide, Cohen is echoing the observations of Maxwell and Esping-Andersen on the relation between globalization and welfare states. They suggest that governments are still relatively autonomous agents, acting within a context of economic, social, and political constraints and opportunities to safeguard people and the conditions of life.

Democratizing the Welfare State, and Beyond

The fundamental characteristic of what constitutes an 'inclusive' welfare state is that it be democratic. In order to have a democratic welfare state the government must be freely elected by citizens who have the right to change it by peaceful means if they are dissatisfied with its performance (Robson 1976:16) . Moreover, the public must be free to criticize the government if it is not meeting citizens' expectations. Democracy from this perspective requires secret ballots, competitive elections among mass political parties, and a popular press separate from the state. These political freedoms and many more are included in the Canadian Charter of Rights and Freedoms.

Since the 1970s crisis period of social policy these fundamental notions of democracy have been challenged by several competing notions about how the welfare state should operate. Those on the far Right have called for the rolling back of the state with a reduction of laws and taxes as the route to more freedom and individual liberty. Some on both the moderate Right and Left, as well as the political centre, have viewed the increasing role for institutions in civil society as a kind of democratization by encouraging active citizenship and limiting the need for state interventions. Others, typically on the Left, have called for the constitutional entrenchment of social rights and welfare entitlements as a way to meet needs, protect individual liberties, and advance group identities; still others, increasingly through the 1990s, have called for global forms of democratic governance. While some observers have welcomed the rise of new social movements and the alternative politics of the women's movement (MacIvor 1996), others have worried that these developments were fractional interests threatening the general public good.

Debates over the nature of democracy are conditioned not just by ideas on the desired separation or connection between the people and political institutions. Another critical dimension is the relation between market economics and democratic politics. Gary Teeple (1995:123) has argued that our political system 'is democratic more in form and rhetoric than in content' because it operates within a capitalist society, although 'it has been possible to impose certain mitigating effects in the shape of reform on the operation of the market.' Philip Resnick strikes a similar and fuller chord:

> there are significant flaws in the operation of democracy as we know it in the West, and as our elites would like to project it to the rest of the world. There is the ongoing problem of the power of capital and the control it has over our media and our political parties. One does not have to subscribe to the wooden language of Marxism-Leninism with its glib dismissal of 'bourgeois' democracy as a sham; but we would be equally naive to ignore the disproportionate power which large corporations and corporate-funded media or pressure groups bring to the political arena, not only during elections but all the time. Can there be real equality of citizen rights and

far-reaching pluralism when we begin with such an uneven playing field? There is also the serious problem of voice, of citizen participation above and beyond the casting of ballots during periodic elections. This is not to disparage representative institutions, which are the privileged form which democracy needs to take in large-scale societies of the nation state variety. (1997:70)

Resnick adds that in many long-standing liberal democracies 'there has been increasing talk about a democratic deficit' (1997:15). The origins of discontents with democracy are related, he suggests, to high rates of unemployment, disenchantment with governing elites, and disillusionment with old-style party politics. To these we would add status anxiety and possibly moral panic associated with the politics of identity, economic and social insecurity associated with the economic liberalization of free trade agreements, and the closed nature of most intergovernmental policy and administrative relations in Canada.

Some fault lies with the welfare state as a complex amalgam of organizations, professions, programs, and rules. We need to be clear about what in social policy is worth lamenting and defending, and what is worth changing or letting go. We need to heed the critiques of the old welfare state – the calls for decentralization of authority, for more racial and cultural sensitivity in programming, for de-bureaucratizing agencies, and for the de-medicalization of health care policy and provision. In a remarkable essay, Leo Panitch writes, 'welfare state reforms had little to do with changing the state itself – that is, with altering the mode of administration in which social policy became embedded.' From Panitch's perspective, government administration is 'fundamentally undemocratic, constructed according to strict doctrines of secrecy and hierarchy that owe much to the nineteenth-century British Colonial Office, or even the Indian army on which it was modeled' (1994:41). Consequently, the welfare state has very limited potential for mobilizing people with shared interests to come together to share common experiences and assert their beliefs and claims. One of the factors contributing to the success of the retrenchment strategies in the 1980s and 1990s, Panitch suggests, was that 'Few employees or "clients" of the welfare state felt that the public agencies really belonged to them – were theirs to influence and control'; and we agree with Panitch's argument that 'social policy can be revived only by its explicit association with social participation, empowerment, and mobilization – or, in a word, with the democratization of the state'

(1994:39). The democratization of the welfare state requires a shift in ideology, social policy making structures and the involvement of a much wider range of interest groups in the identification of social needs.

Recent Canadian social work and policy texts (Mullaly 1997; Wharf 1992) call for democratizing social service agencies to reduce controls over clients and enhance services and supports instead. The struggle for democratizing the workplace 'may take various forms, such as union activity to build and increase service user participation in the decision-making process, more peer supervision, development of a consultative relationship with supervisors rather than that of boss-subordinate, and a struggle to implement more democratic means of sharing decisions, responsibilities, and information' (Mullaly 1997:183).

A more democratized social policy agenda will allow community groups to find ways of encouraging politicians to stop offering corporations an open-door policy in which environmental standards are overlooked, unions are undermined, wages are cut, tax breaks are given, and a blind eye is turned to working conditions. A more open policy debate will encourage community groups to find ways of supporting governments who require corporations to meet fundamental community expectations. Community groups will be able to work with governments to develop regulations that shape the ways corporations enter a community, to ensure that issues such as pollution, health and safety, and working conditions are included in corporate plans. Again history teaches us an important lesson – that community activities can set the stage for government action. Many of the early labour codes and health and safety issues started as local initiatives to be picked up and promoted by provincial governments first, and later expanded through dialogue and support at the national level. In the beginning it was assumed that it was impossible to regulate economic development in an industrializing country; later it was found that the regulations were essential to the growth of the economy.

The democratization of social policy is gradually putting gender, sexual orientation, and race, among other social divisions, alongside traditional concerns regarding poverty and redistribution when considering economic policies and welfare programs and practices. Feminist writers have drawn attention to limitations in the conventional models of social policy and theories of the welfare state, and have generated new concepts and perspectives by emphasizing gender relations and the experiences of women. Feminist research is leading the way in the search for more democratic forms of social policy development by going beyond traditional analyses of entitlement (need, labour market status, and citizenship) to consider other issues central to women, such as motherhood and caregiving. The tasks of socialization and reproduction, and the interrelationships of the family, the market, and the welfare state are now highlighted. These are important themes of inquiry that counterbalance the usual focus on industrial activities and the usual neglect of unpaid, caring work.

The welfare state's own history suggests that 'it will be the old, the poor, the workers, women, Aboriginal peoples, the ill, and the disabled who will have to struggle for, and invent, new self-help and mutual aid methods, and the organizational arrangements to go along with them' (Collier 1997:140).

As part of the process of pluralization, many groups and social movements are looking to the public sector to gain recognition of their identities and needs; perhaps compensation for past wrongs; for provision of services and resources to support their autonomy; and for the realization of citizenship rights. In contemporary identity politics, struggles for citizenship may not mean gaining equal rights and participating in a common culture, but rather attaining a bundle of equivalent individual rights and group rights. Citizenship, then, is about crafting connections and defining differences. An interesting opportunity opens up because of the developments within the global community: it is now possible for community groups to communicate more effective via the Internet, thus creating stronger local social movements, more democratic local institutions, and more cooperative local relationships.

Be we administrators or caregivers, professionals or volunteers, clients or policy makers, students or teachers of policy, there is work to do in finding a new balance of democratic social provisions within our increasingly global economy and pluralistic society.

Notes

Chapter 1: Changing Politics

1 Official bilingualism has grown modestly over the past generation, from 13 per cent of the population in 1971 reporting an ability to speak both English and French, to 17 per cent in 1996.

2 The regulations to the Employment Equity Act specify the following groups as visible minorities: Chinese, South Asians, Blacks, Arabs and West Asians, Filipinos, Southeast Asians, Latin Americans, Japanese, Koreans, and Pacific Islanders.

Chapter 2: Early Developments in Canadian Social Welfare

1 Earlier, Parliament enacted the Annuities Act of 1908, a modest system of government-operated annuities for building pension income for old age, which few Canadians could make real use over the next twenty years (Guest 1985:34–6).

2 Bryden (1974:79) adds that 'The veterans had an additional advantage: a higher pension was paid to a married man regardless of his wife's age and to a widower with one or more dependent children.' An amendment to the War Veterans Allowance Act in 1936 provided for special consideration to veterans over fifty-five years of age who, because of 'pre-aging' combined with disabilities, were incapable of maintaining themselves. A further amendment in 1938 made it possible for veterans with disabilities even younger than fifty-five to be considered for benefits. We briefly discuss this difference in policy generosity between veterans and other citizens in Chapter 6.

3 The following discussion draws from Rice (1985:225–7).

4 Our calculations are from the Appendix, Table 1, in Guest (1985:242–3).

5 The federal government had earlier entered the housing field in 1919 with a $25 million scheme to combat high unemployment at the end of the First World War (Prince 1995).

6 Bennett's package of social and economic policy reforms was dubbed a New Deal after the highly popular New Deal of activist government measures unveiled in 1933 by F. D. Roosevelt, president of the United States.

Chapter 3: Envisaging and Establishing a System of Social Security

1 The children's allowance recommended by Marsh differed with the mother's allowance programs then existing in Canada in several important ways. The mother's allowances were usually targeted to widows with dependent children; seven of the then nine provinces had such programs, which were provincially financed and administered. The programs therefore had varying rules and practices across provinces; and the mother's allowance programs were based on the traditional public relief philosophy. Marsh's children's allowance was based on modern ideas of social insurance and was to be a national program for all families, wholly administered by the federal government and financed through general tax revenue. In hindsight, Marsh (1975) saw the proposal as a precursor to the concept of a guaranteed annual income.

2 We discuss housing policy and veterans' benefits in the war years, but because of space limitations we do not discuss it for the later periods; nor can we examine education, fiscal federalism, Indian affairs, training, or rural rehabilitation and regional development, among others.

3 The Liberals increased the maximum blind allowance effective July 1, 1957, from $40 to $46 monthly. The Conservatives then increased the maximum allowance effective November 1957 from $46 to $55 monthly. As of February 1962, the maximum monthly allowance was raised to $65 by the Conservatives and then to $75 by the Liberals as of December 1963. That was the last time the benefit was boosted by the federal government.

4 The 1951 Blind Persons Act was finally repealed in 1983, having ceased to be necessary.

5 An interesting story could be told of the politics and administration of representation, which we can not explore here. In 1961, under the Vocational Rehabilitation of Disabled Persons Act, the thirty-seven member council was replaced with a twenty-five-member national advisory council on the rehabilitation of disabled persons, to advise the Labour minister, with members appointed by cabinet. In 1967 this advisory council was dissolved, replaced by a twelve-member advisory board on the coordina-

tion of rehabilitation services for disabled persons, for the minister of Manpower and Immigration.

6 When the eligible age for the Old Age Security pension reached age sixty-five in 1970, the Old Age Assistance Act of 1951 was no longer operative, as persons who had been receiving old age assistance could now collect benefits under the OAS legislation.

7 The two deputy ministers of National Welfare in this period were George Davidson (1944–59) and Joseph Willard (1960–72). For more details on these officials see Splane (1987).

Chapter 4: The Crisis of the Welfare State

1 Major works on the welfare crisis are Collier (1997), Esping-Andersen (1996a), Teeple (1995), Pierson (1994), and Mishra (1984 and 1990b). This chapter is by necessity a selected review of the perspectives. Moreover, other perspectives could be added, such as those on ethnicity, race, and sexuality.

2 Armitage (1996) sees the Piven and Cloward (1971) theory on social assistance reflected somewhat in the modern history of Canadian social welfare. Moscovitch and Drover (1987:15), by contrast, say the theory 'appears to explain little in Canada ... [but] does highlight the necessity to look at state expenditures in national historical context.'

3 A political economy approach to studying the welfare state and social policy generally looks at the nature of capitalist relations of power and production; the patterns of inequality in society and the economy; and historical program developments as well as contemporary policies. The approach in Canada has drawn on neo-Marxist thinkers from Britain, Europe, and the United States. Canadian writers tend to adopt a fairly broad view of social welfare that includes the media, culture, the arts, and taxation, along with the more traditional areas of income support, health, education, and housing. Social welfare is regarded as a form of control and care, and as a form of intervention that can both modify, and, more importantly, reinforce structures of disparity and inequality.

4 The term 'Fordism' is derived from Henry Ford, the American automaker who applied the assembly-line approach to mass production in the car industry. Ford thus achieved significant productivity gains, corporate profits, and capital expansion, as well as the promotion of mass consumption of the Model T Ford, other vehicles, and commodities more generally. In part, the concept of Fordism is a synonym for twentieth-century industrial capitalism – mass production and mass consumerism, the scientific

management of the workplace, urbanization, and international markets – coupled with Keynesian policy, collective bargaining in certain sectors of the economy, and social welfare programs. Janine Brodie (1995:15) adds that 'Fordism also rested on a very particular model of the workplace, the home, and the gender order. It presumed a stable working and middle class, a nuclear family supported by a male breadwinner, a family wage, a dependent wife, and children, and women's unpaid domestic labour.'

5 This quote is from the Fraser Institute's web site, www.fraserinstitute.ca. Since its formation in 1974, the Fraser Institute has published over 120 books and thousands of articles, offering critiques on such social welfare fields as affirmative action, education, government deficits and debt, health care, housing policy, labour markets, poverty, public sector unions, rent controls, tax loads, and unemployment insurance. Other conservative policy institutes founded in this period were the Canada West Foundation and the National Foundation for Public Policy Development. More recently, the C.D. Howe Institute launched 'The Social Policy Challenge' series, which has published at least fifteen studies on Canadian social issues and programs. See www.cdhowe.org for details.

6 The reader will notice, from Chapters 2 and 3, that our own view of the development of social policy in Canada differs from that of Courchene in a number of respects. We believe that traditional sources of support were not replaced or suppressed by the emergence of social programs; in fact, most public programs assumed the continued vitality and responsibility of informal supports. Second, comprehensiveness and generosity of benefits are in the eye of the beholder. Third, while some universal programs were established, most notably Family Allowance in 1945, Old Age Security in 1952, and national health insurance (Medicare) over the 1957–72 period, most social programs continued to be selective and targeted. Fourth, the argument that economic growth rendered social policy expansion politically costless in the 1950s and 1960s is simplistic. There were other political costs besides financial ones, namely, jurisdictional fights, constitutional amendments, and the concerns of business and producer interest groups. Finally, Courchene overlooks the forces of pluralization taking place in Canadian society at the time. Aside from economic growth or indeed economic decline as a trigger for demands, numerous claims are rooted in cultural, ethnic, regional, and gender factors. Such claims frequently are not demands for rights to the status quo but rather to a more equitable and inclusive social order.

7 Several thoughtful papers on the culture of poverty are contained in W. Edward Mann (1970).

8 Like other belief systems, feminism has several branches, such as anti-racist, liberal, radical, and socialist perspectives. Each takes a particular approach to social policy and women's experiences of the welfare state. The discussion here is what may be called a mainstream approach, which other branches share to some extent.

9 We turn to those agencies and organizations closest to clients, such as the Canadian Council on Social Development, the National Council of Welfare, and the National Anti-Poverty Organization, to hear about the concerns of those inside the system. Information can also been gathered from federal, provincial, and nongovernmental studies, which have asked clients about their opinions. Some academic work also provides detailed examinations of the experiences of clients and non-clients. See, for example, a special issue of *Canadian Woman Studies* (1992) on the lived experience of poverty by disabled women, visible minority women, single-parent women, Aboriginal women, and others.

Chapter 5: Response to the Crisis

1 There are several other measures for remixing the social economy of care and provision, which, because of space limitations, cannot be discussed here. These include non-intervention, deregulation, privatization, the creation of internal markets within the welfare state, land claims settlements, and self-government agreements for Aboriginal peoples, as well as the creation of tax policies for supporting the care of dependents and for encouraging charitable donations.

2 Margaret Biggs (1996:1) has defined the social union as 'the web of rights and obligations between Canadian citizens and governments that give effect and meaning to our shared sense of social purpose and common citizenship.' She adds that 'The social union has been most closely identified with the policies and programs of the postwar welfare state from equalization to health care and social programs. Federal-provincial fiscal arrangements have helped nurture it.' The official web site for the social union is http://socialunion.gc.ca.

3 For details on these and other countries, see Esping-Andersen (1990 and 1996b), Mishra (1990b), and Pierson (1994).

4 For detailed examinations of the retrenchment records of the Mulroney and Chrétien governments, see Rice and Prince (1993); Rice (1995b); Prince (1997); and Battle (1997). On provincial governments: see Ralph, St-Amand, and Regimbald (1997) on Ontario, and Taft (1997) on Alberta.

5 It can be argued that the Goods and Services Tax (GST) is a form of systemic

retrenchment in that, by raising the visibility of and thus hostility towards the GST, the Mulroney government raised the political cost of any future attempts to raise the tax. The apparent flip-flop of the first Chrétien government on replacing the GST added to the controversial nature of this tax.

Chapter 6: Global Capitalism and the Canadian Welfare State

1 Some challengers, who Marjorie Griffin Cohen (1997b) calls 'purists,' confine their critiques to opposing all new trade agreements and calling for the abolition of existing agreements. Cohen labels as 'revisionists' other challengers who seek to establish strong clauses protecting the environment, labour, and social programs in international trade arrangements. Cohen finds both approaches unsatisfactory, and presents a third approach for establishing international control of corporate rule and behaviour. We discuss this further in Chapter 10, briefly.

2 Numerous social policy writers focus on aggregate social spending levels as a measure for defining and comparing welfare states. For a discussion on the uses and limitations of this approach, see Esping-Andersen (1990), Mishra (1990b), and Prince (1996a).

3 A complete listing of the social security agreements in effect and those under negotiation between Canada and other countries is available from Human Resources Development Canada's web site, http:// HRDCDRHC.GC.CA/hrdc/isp/internat/abroad.

4 Other processes where governments extend the state's realm into the market and community include nationalization or state ownership, economic and civic regulation, taxation, and expenditures and public services. These all represent the penetration of the political system into the economy. By contrast, the processes of taking governments out of the market include the privatization of public assets and services; the full or partial deregulation of economic sectors; tax cuts, especially for corporations; and spending cutbacks and the contracting out of public service provision to for-profit agencies. In the latter case, the result would be a marketization of society, by subjecting more areas of life to the influence of private sector values and market mechanisms.

5 The marketization of social programs can be distinguished from the concept of the 'social market,' which refers either to the welfare state sector or to the state and the nongovernmental provision of health and social services in the voluntary sector. Our concept is also different from 'occupational welfare' and 'corporate welfare' – the development and administration of social benefits and services in the workplace, such as daycare or employee assist-

ance plans. A related concept is 'commercialization,' which is the adoption of business methods to operating public assets such as airports and harbours. Like marketization, it can involve collecting user fees from clients.

Chapter 7: Diversity and Equality in a Pluralist Welfare Community

1 Under the Canada Health Act, 1984, universality is one of the conditions that each provincial and territorial health insurance plan must meet in order to receive full federal cash contributions under the Canada Health and Social Transfer. Universality means that 100 per cent of the insured persons of a jurisdiction are entitled, on uniform terms and conditions, to the insured health services provided for by the plan. A related condition is accessibility, which requires that provincial and territorial plans must provide reasonable access to insured health services unimpeded by financial charges or other means.
2 The Veterans' and Civilians' Disability Pensions (VCDP) program provides pensions to those with disabilities related to military service with the Canadian Armed Forces. The amount of the pension is based on the degree of disability as determined by medical examination. The universalistic feature of the VCDP relates to eligibility in that the applicant's financial circumstances have no bearing on entitlement to a pension or to the amount of the pension.
3 Moreover, the universal education and health care sectors have also experienced cutbacks and challenges. On education, see Barlow and Robertson (1994); and on health care, see Armstrong et al. (1997).
4 Other factors contributing to the distinctive treatment accorded veterans in federal social policy: veterans have had a specific department and minister representing them, in one form or another, since 1918; and through the Royal Canadian Legion and other associations, veterans have a highly institutionalized and effective network of interest-group representation.

Chapter 8: Gender and Social Policy

1 Another classification is by Ramesh Mishra (1984), who distinguishes between 'differentiated welfare states' and 'integrated welfare states.' The first type refers to a relatively delimited group of social policies and institutions appended but largely unrelated to the economic, industrial, and public sectors. In 'integrated welfare states' social policies are linked to the larger society and regarded in close relation to the economy and to the polity. Mishra also refers to this type as the 'corporatist welfare state,' in that the

key interests represented and addressed by the state are those of business and organized labour.

2 A patriarchal social structure is one 'based on male authority, male power and male privilege' (McCormack 1991:3). Whether in a business firm, local community, family, or government, patriarchy refers to rule, exclusively or primarily, by men.

3 Besides gender divisions, other dualisms are apparent in the welfare state, economy, and larger society. These include patterns of stratification between Aboriginal and non-Aboriginal people, people of colour and Caucasians, the poor and the well off, straight people and gays and lesbians, younger and older generations, and the federal and provincial governments.

4 Dual-earner couples who share housework fairly equally tend to be younger with few children, and the woman has a university education (Marshall 1993). Employed women with children over age five, and women with no children, work fewer hours a day on household chores than women with young children, but still do more than their partners. The difference in the number of hours men and women spend on domestic work appears to be narrowing over the last fifteen years or so, though a gap remains. Women continue to do most of the household work (Statistics Canada 1995b).

5 Unless otherwise noted, the following discussion on labour force trends is drawn from *Women in Canada* (Statistics Canada 1995b). While we are discussing overall averages for women as a group, there are differences by different categories of women. For instance, 52 per cent of all women were in the labour force in 1994. This breaks down to 56 per cent of women in a visible minority, 50 per cent of immigrant women, 47 per cent of Aboriginal women, and 41 per cent of women with disabilities.

6 New Federal tax rules stipulate that child support paid under a court order or written agreement made on or after 1 May 1997, when the legislation came into effect, will no longer be deductible to the payer or included in the income of the recipient for tax purposes. The legislation also strengthened enforcement procedures across Canadian jurisdictions for ensuring that family support obligations were honoured.

Chapter 9: Civil Society and Community Capacity

1 Beyond the cluster of concepts related to community capacity that we review here are, of course, other concepts with their own definitional issues and theoretical frameworks. These include renewed interest in the social

policy literature with community development and community organizing (Wharf and Clague 1997), and, in political science and public administration among other literatures, with social cohesion and social economy (Jenson 1998).

2 In the voluntary and nonprofit sector itself, efforts are underway to enhance both the legitimacy and the capacity of local and nationally based organizations. See the report of the panel on Accountability and Governance of the Voluntary Sector (Broadbent 1999). Building the capacity of the voluntary sector is extending beyond traditional ideas of infrastructure supports to include information technology systems and training as well as public policy capacity. In 1998 the Chrétien government established a joint table of federal senior officials and representatives of the voluntary sector on strengthening capacity. Important, related work is being done by the Canadian Centre for Philanthropy, Canadian Policy Research Networks, Public Policy Research Networks, Public Policy Forum, other think-tanks, and research institutes at various universities.

3 We are persuaded by the argument made by Brian Wharf (1992:21–2) 'that senior levels of government have the clear responsibility for resolving what is, after all, the most fundamental social problem – poverty. However, their continuing reluctance to attack the problem in a serious and committed fashion places a particular responsibility on social reform organizations.' With local communities across Canada, large and small, the meeting ground between social problems associated with poverty and the delivery of social programs, municipal governments, and voluntary agencies are increasingly engaged in social planning, research, and advocacy. The challenge, though, as Wharf identifies it, is that the grand issues of social policy, such as poverty, wealth, and redistribution, cannot be addressed adequately on a community-by-community basis; national organizations, coalitions, and sustained campaigns are needed. See also Wharf and Clague (1997) on poverty reduction strategies and movements.

Chapter 10: Creating a New Policy Agenda

1 Our calculations are based on information in Statistics Canada, *Public Sector Finance* (Ottawa: Supply and Services Canada. Cat. No. 68–212). Social policy refers to education, health, housing, income security and social services, employment and immigration, the protection of persons and property, and recreation and culture.

2 The following section draws on Prince (1998a).

Bibliography

Abramovitz, Mimi. 1988. *Regulating the Lives of Women*. Boston: South End Press.

Abu-Laban, Yameen. 1994. The Politics of Race and Ethnicity: Multiculturalism as a Contested Arena. In *Canadian Politics*. 2d ed. Ed. James P. Bickerton and Alain-G. Gagnon. Peterborough: Broadview Press.

Adams, Michael. 1997. *Sex in the Snow: Canadian Social Values at the End of the Millennium*. Toronto: Viking Books.

Almond, Gabriel A., and Sidney Verba. 1963. *The Civic Culture: Political Attitudes and Democracy in Five Nations*. Princeton: Princeton University Press.

Anderson, D.C., J. Lait, and D. Marsland. 1981. *Breaking the Spell of the Welfare State*. London: Social Affairs Unit.

Anderson, Sarah, and John Cavanagh. 1996. Cororate Empires. *Multinational Monitor* 17, no. 12 (December):26–7.

Andrew, Caroline. 1984. Women and the Welfare State. *Canadian Journal of Political Science* 17:667–83.

Armitage, Andrew. 1975. *Social Welfare in Canada: Ideals and Realities*. Toronto: McClelland & Stewart.

– 1988. *Social Welfare in Canada: Ideals, Realities, and Future Paths*. 2d ed. Toronto: McClelland & Stewart.

– 1996. *Social Welfare in Canada: Facing Up to the Future*. 3d ed. Toronto: Oxford University Press.

Armstrong, Hugh. 1977. The Labour Force and State Workers. In *The Canadian State: Political Economy and Political Power*, ed. Leo Panitch. Toronto: University of Toronto Press.

Armstrong, Pat, Hugh Armstrong, Jacqueline Choiniere, Eric Mykhalovskiy, and Jerry P. White. 1997. *Medical Alert: New Work Organizations in Health Care*. Toronto: Garamond Press.

Aronson, Jane. 1991. Dutiful Daughters and Undemanding Mothers: Constraining Images of Giving and Receiving Care in Middle and Later Life. In *Women's Caring: Feminist Perspectives on Social Welfare*, ed. Carol Baines, Patricia M. Evans, and Sheila M. Neysmith. Toronto: McClelland & Stewart.

Aspen Institute Rural Economic Policy Program. 1996. *Measuring Community Capacity*. Version 3. Aspen: Aspen Institute/Rural Economic Policy Program.

Azmier, Jason, and Robert Roach. 1997. *Welfare Reform in Alberta: A Survey of Former Recipients*. Calgary: Canada West Foundation.

Bach, Michael, and Marcia Rioux. 1996. Social Policy, Devolution and Disability: Back to Notions of the Worthy Poor. In *Remaking Canadian Social Policy: Social Security in the Late 1990s*, ed. Jane Pulkingham and Gordon Ternowetsky. Halifax: Fernwood Publishing.

Bach, Sandra, and Susan D. Phillips. 1997. Constructing a New Social Union: Child Care Beyond Infancy? In *How Ottawa Spends 1997–98, Seeing Red: A Liberal Report Card*, ed. Gene Swimmer. Ottawa: Carleton University Press.

Badgley, Robin F., and Samuel Wolfe. 1967. *Doctors' Strike: Medical Care and Conflict in Saskatchewan*. Toronto: Macmillan.

Baines, Carol, Patricia M. Evans, and Sheila M. Neysmith, eds. 1991. *Women's Caring: Feminist Perspectives on Social Welfare*. Toronto: McClelland & Stewart.

Bakker, Isabella, ed. 1996. *Rethinking Restructuring: Gender and Change in Canada*. Toronto: University of Toronto Press.

Banting, Keith. 1987. Visions of the Welfare State. In *The Future of Social Welfare Systems in Canada and the United Kingdom*, ed. Shirley B. Seward. Halifax: Institute for Research on Public Policy.

– 1996. Social Policy. In *Border Crossing: The Internationalization of Canadian Public Policy*, ed. G. Bruce Doern, Leslie A. Pal, and Brian W. Tomlin. Toronto: Oxford University Press.

Banting, Keith, and Kenneth Battle, eds. 1994. *A New Social Vision for Canada: Perspectives on the Federal Discussion Paper on Social Policy Reform*. Kingston: Caledon Institute of Social Policy.

Barlow, Maude, and Heather-jane Robertson. 1994. *Class Warfare: The Assault on Canada's Schools*. Toronto: Key Porter Books.

Battle, Kenneth. 1990. [written under Gratten Gray, pseud.]. Social Policy by Stealth. *Policy Options* 11.

– 1993. The Politics of Stealth: Child Benefits Under the Tories. In *How Ottawa Spends 1993–1994: A More Democratic Canada ...?*, ed. Susan D. Phillips. Ottawa: Carleton University Press.

– 1996. Back to the Future: Reforming Social Policy in Canada. Paper Presented at a Conference in Honour of Allan J. MacEachen, St. Francis Xavier University, Antigonish, Nova Scotia. June 6.

– 1997. *Transformation: Canadian Social Policy, 1985–2001.* Ottawa: Caledon Institute of Social Policy.

Battle, Kenneth, and Michael Mendelson. 1997. *Child Benefit Reform in Canada: An Evaluative Framework and Future Directions.* Ottawa: Caledon Institute of Social Policy.

Battle, Kenneth, and Sherri Torjman. 1995. *How Finance Reformed Social Policy.* Ottawa: Caledon Institute of Social Policy.

Battle, Kenneth, Sherri Torjman, and Michael Mendelson. 1998. Reinvest the Fiscal Dividend. *Policy Options Politique* 19, no. 1:19–22.

Baum, Gregory. 1996. The Practice of Citizenship in Today's Society. Annual General Meeting of the Social Planning Council of Metro Toronto, 1996.

Begin, Monique. 1997. The Canadian Government and the Commission's Report, Women and the Canadian State. In *Women and the Canadian State,* ed. Caroline Andrew and Sanda Rodgers. Montreal and Kingston: McGill-Queen's University Press.

Berman, Marshall. 1988. *All That Is Solid Melts into Air: The Experience of Modernity.* New York: Penguin Books.

Bernard, Mitchell. 1994. Post-Fordism, Transnational Production, and the Changing Global Political Economy. In *Political Economy and the Changing Global Order,* ed. Richard Stubbs and Geoffrey R.D. Underhill. Toronto: McClelland & Stewart.

Beveridge, William. 1942. *Social Insurance and Allied Services.* Cmd. 6404. London: His Majesty's Stationery Office.

Biggs, Margaret. 1996. *Building Blocks for Canada's New Social Union.* Working Paper No. R 02. Ottawa: Canadian Policy Research Networks.

Black, Edwin R. 1975. *Divided Loyalties: Canadian Concepts of Federalism.* Montreal and London: McGill-Queen's University Press.

Bliss, Michael. 1975. Preface. In *Report on Social Security for Canada,* ed. Leonard Marsh. Toronto: University of Toronto Press.

Boyd, Susan B, ed. 1997. *Challenging the Public/Private Divide: Feminism, Law, and Public Policy.* Toronto: University of Toronto Press.

Broad, David. 1995. Globalization versus Labour. *Canadian Review of Social Policy,* no. 36: 75–85.

Broadbent, Edward. 1999. Building on Strength: Improving Governance and Accountability in Canada's Volunteer Sector. Ottawa: Panel on Accountability and Governance in the Voluntary Sector.www.pagvs.com.

Brodie, Janine. 1995. *Politics on the Margins: Restructuring and the Canadian Women's Movement.* Halifax: Fernwood Publishing.

– ed. 1996. Canadian Women, Changing State Forms, and Public Policy. In *Women and Canadian Public Policy.* Toronto: Harcourt Brace, 1–28.

Brooks, Stephen. 1993. *Public Policy in Canada: An Introduction*. 2d ed. Toronto: Oxford University Press.

Brown, David M. 1994. Economic Change and New Social Policies. In *The Case for Change: Reinventing the Welfare State*, ed. William G. Watson, John Richards, and David M. Brown. Toronto: C.D. Howe Institute.

Browne, Paul Leduc. 1996. *Love in a Cold World? The Voluntary Sector in an Age of Cuts*. Ottawa: Canadian Centre for Policy Alternatives.

Bryden, Kenneth. 1974. *Old Age Pensions and Policy-Making in Canada*. Montreal: McGill-Queen's University Press.

Bryson, Lois. 1992. *Welfare and the State: Who Benefits?* London: Macmillan.

Burt, Sandra. 1994. The Women's Movement: Working to Transform Public Life. In *Canadian Politics*. 2d ed. Ed. James P. Bickerton and Alain-G. Gagnon. Peterborough: Broadview Press.

Byrne, Lesley Hyland. 1997. Feminists in Power: Women Cabinet Ministers in the New Democratic Party (NDP) Government of Ontario, 1990–1995. *Policy Studies Journal* 25(4), 601–612.

Cairns, Alan. 1986. The Embedded State: State-Society Relations in Canada. In *State and Society: Canada in Comparative Perspective*, ed. Keith Banting. Toronto: University of Toronto Press.

– 1991. *Disruptions: Constitutional Struggles, from the Charter to Meech Lake*. Toronto: McClelland & Stewart.

Cairns, Alan, and Cynthia Williams. 1985. Constitutionalism, Citizenship and Society in Canada: An Overview. In *Constitutionalism, Citizenship and Society in Canada*, ed. Alan Cairns and Cynthia Williams. Toronto: University of Toronto Press.

Callahan, Marilyn, Andrew Armitage, Michael J. Prince, and Brian Wharf. 1990. Workfare in British Columbia: Social Development Alternatives. *Canadian Review of Social Policy*, no. 26:15–26.

Calvert, John. 1984. *Government Limited: The Corporate Takeover of the Public Sector in Canada*. Ottawa: Canadian Centre for Policy Alternatives.

Cameron, Duncan, and Andrew Sharpe, eds. 1988. *Policies for Full Employment*. Ottawa and Montreal: Canadian Council on Social Development.

Campbell, Robert M. 1987. *Grand Illusions: The Politics of the Keynesian Experience in Canada, 1945–1975*. Peterborough: Broadview Press.

Campbell, Robert M., and Leslie A. Pal. 1989. *The Real Worlds of Canadian Politics: Cases in Process and Policy*. Peterborough: Broadview Press.

Canada. 1985. *1985 Royal Commission on the Economic Union and Development Prospects for Canada*. Ottawa: Minister of Supply and Services Canada.

- 1994. *Improving Social Security in Canada: A Discussion Paper.* Ottawa: Human Resources Development Canada.
- 1997a. *Inclusive Social Policy Development: Ideas for Practitioners.* Ottawa: Canadian Council on Social Development.
- 1997b. Message to the 36th Parliament. September 10. Ottawa: Canadian Council on Social Development.

Canadian Woman Studies/*les cahiers de la femme.* 1992. Women in Poverty. *Canadian Woman Studies/les cahiers de la femme* (special issue) 12, no. 4.

Cassidy, Harry M. 1947. The Canadian Social Services. *Annals of the American Academy of Political and Social Science* 253:190–201.

Cassin, A. Marguerite. 1993. Equitable and Fair: Widening the Circle. In *Fairness in Taxation: Exploring the Principles,* ed. Allan M. Maslove. Toronto: University of Toronto Press.

Catano, Janis Wood, and Linda Christiansen-Ruffman. 1989. *Women as Volunteers in Canada,* ed. Voluntary Action Directorate, Multiculturalism and Citizenship. Ottawa: Supply and Services Canada.

Charlton, Mark W. 1992. *The Making of Canadian Food Policy.* Montreal and Kingston: McGill-Queen's University Press.

Chrétien, Jean. 1998. A Global Quest for Volunteer Effort. Speech to the Biennial World Volunteer Conference of the International Association for Volunteer Effort, August 23–27, Edmonton.

Clement, Wallace. 1975. *The Canadian Corporate Elite: An Analysis of Economic Power.* Toronto: McClelland & Stewart.

Clutterbuck, Peter. 1997. A National Municipal Social Infrastructure Strategy. *Canadian Review of Social Policy* 40 (winter):69–75.

Cohen, Marjorie Griffin. 1992. The Canadian Women's Movement and Its Effort to Influence the Canadian Economy. In *Changing Times: The Women's Movement in Canada and the United States,* ed. Constance Backhouse and David H. Flaherty. Montreal and Kingston: McGill-Queen's University Press.
- 1997a. Presentation to the House of Commons Sub-Committee on International Trade, Trade Disputes and Investment: Hearings on the Multilateral Agreement on Investment Panel on Corporate, Consumer and Social Implications. http://www.policyalternatives.ca/maipresentation.html.
- 1997b. What to Do About Globalization. Toronto/Vancouver: Canadian Centre for Policy Alternatives. http://www.policyalternatives.ca/apec.html.

Coleman, James S. 1990. *Foundations of Social Theory.* Cambridge, Mass.: Harvard University Press.

Coleman, William D. 1991. Financial Services and Government Intervention.

In *Canada at Risk? Canadian Public Policy in the 1990s*, ed. G. Bruce Doern and Bryne B. Purchase. Toronto: C.D. Howe Institute.

Coleman, William D., and Tony Porter. 1996. Banking and Securities Policy. In *Border Crossings: The Internationalization of Canadian Public Policy*, ed. G. Bruce Doern, Leslie A. Pal, and Brian W. Tomlin. Toronto: Oxford University Press.

Collier, Kenneth. 1995. Social Policy versus Regional Trading Blocs in the Global System: NAFTA, the EEC and 'Asia.' *Canadian Review of Social Policy* 35 (spring) 50–9.

– 1997. *After the Welfare State*. Vancouver: New Star Books.

Commission on Social Justice. 1994. *Social Justice: Strategies for National Renewal*. The Report of the Commission on Social Justice. London: Vintage.

Cooper, Andrew F., and Leslie A. Pal. 1996. Human Rights and Security Policy. In *Border Crossings: The Internationalization of Canadian Public Policy*, ed. G. Bruce Doern, Leslie A. Pal, and Brian W. Tomlin. Toronto: Oxford University Press.

Courchene, Thomas J. 1980. Towards a Protected Society: The Politicization of Economic Life. *Canadian Journal of Economics* 13:556–77.

– 1987. *Social Policy in the 1990s: Agenda for Reform*. Policy Study No. 3. Toronto: C.D. Howe Institute.

– 1994. *Social Canada in the Millennium: Reform Imperatives and Restructuring Principles*. The Social Policy Challenge. No. 4. Montreal: C.D. Howe Institute.

Cusson, Sandra. 1990. Women in School Administration. *Canadian Social Trends* 18:24–5.

Davies, Linda, and Eric Shragge, eds. 1990. *Bureaucracy and Community*. Montreal: Black Rose Books.

Dear, Michael J., and Jennifer R. Wolch. 1987. *Landscapes of Despair: From Deinstitutionalization to Homelessness*. Princeton N.J.: Princeton University Press.

Deaton, Rick. 1973. The Fiscal Crisis of the State in Canada. In *The Political Economy of the State*, ed. Dimitrios I. Roussopoulos. Montreal: Black Rose Books.

DeVoretz, Donald J. 1995. *Diminishing Returns: The Economics of Canada's Recent Immigration Policy*. Ottawa: C.D. Howe Institute and the Laurier Institute.

Djao, Angela Wei. 1979. The Welfare State and Its Ideology. In *Economy, Class and Social Reality*, ed. John Allan Fry. Toronto: Butterworths.

– 1983. *Inequality and Social Policy: The Sociology of Welfare*. Toronto: John Wiley.

Doern, G. Bruce, Allan M. Maslove, and Michael J. Prince. 1988. *Public Budget-*

ing in Canada: Politics, Economics and Management. Ottawa: Carleton University Press.

Doern, G. Bruce, Leslie A. Pal, and Brian W. Tomlin, eds. 1996. *Border Crossings: The Internationalization of Canadian Public Policy*. Toronto: Oxford University Press.

Doern, G. Bruce, and Richard W. Phidd. 1983. *Canadian Public Policy: Ideas, Structure, Process*. Toronto: Methuen.

– 1992. *Canadian Public Policy: Ideas, Structure, Process*. 2d ed. Toronto: Nelson.

Doern, G. Bruce, and Bryne B. Purchase, eds. 1991. *Canada At Risk: Canadian Public Policy in the 1990s*. Toronto: C.D. Howe Institute.

Economic Council of Canada. 1990. *Good Jobs, Bad Jobs – Employment in the Service Economy*. Ottawa.

Drache, Daniel, and Duncan Cameron. 1985. Introduction. In *The Other Macdonald Report*, ed. Daniel Drache and Duncan Cameron. Toronto: James Lorimer.

Drache, Daniel, and Andrew Ranachan. 1995. *Warm Heart, Cold Country: Fiscal and Social Policy Reform in Canada*. Ottawa/Toronto: Caledon Institute on Social Policy and the Robarts Centre for Canadian Studies.

Drucker, Peter F. 1993. *The Post-Capitalist Society*. New York: Harper Business.

Esping-Andersen, Gosta. 1990. *The Three Worlds of Welfare Capitalism*. Princeton, NJ: Princeton University Press.

– 1996a. After the Golden Age? State Dilemmas in a Global Economy. In *Welfare States in Transition: National Adaptations in Global Economies*, ed. Gosta Esping-Andersen. London: Sage.

– ed. 1996b. *Welfare States in Transition: National Adaptation in Global Economics*. London: Sage.

Etzioni, Amitai. 1993. *The Spirit of Community: Rights, Responsibilities and the Communitarian Agenda*. London: Fontana Press.

– 1995. The Attack on Community: The Grooved Debate. *Society* (July/August):12–17.

Evans, Patricia M. 1991. The Sexual Division of Poverty: The Consequences of Gendered Caring. In *Women's Caring: Feminist Perspectives on Social Welfare*, ed. Carol Baines, Patricia M. Evans, and Sheila M. Neysmith. Toronto: McClelland & Stewart.

Evans, Patricia M., and Gerda R. Wekerle. 1997. *Women and the Canadian Welfare State: Challenges and Change*. Toronto: University of Toronto Press.

Evans, Patricia M., Lesley A. Jacobs, Alain Noel, and Elisabeth R. Reynolds. 1995. *Workfare: Does It Work? Is It Fair?* Montreal: Institute for Research on Public Policy.

Fagan, Tony, and Phil Lee. 1997. 'New' Social Movements and Social Policy: A

Case Study of the Disability Movement. In *Social Policy: A Conceptual and Theoretical Introduction*, ed. Michael Lavalette and Alan Pratt. London: Sage.

Fast, Janet E., and Judith A. Frederick. 1996. Working Arrangements and the Time Stress. *Canadian Social Trends* 43 (winter):14–19.

Fay, Jeanne. 1997. Back to the Future: Nova Scotia's Retrograde Social Assistance Reforms. *Canadian Review of Social Policy* (spring) 39:92–3.

Finlayson, Ann. 1996. *Naming Rumpelstiltskin: Who Will Profit (and Who Will Lose) in the Workplace of the 21st Century*. Toronto: Key Porter Books.

Findlay, Peter C. 1983. The Case for Universality. *Canadian Social Work Review* 1:17–24.

Firestone, Shulamith. 1979. *The Dialectic of Sex*. London: The Women's Press.

Fisher, Robert, and Joe Kling. 1994. Community Organization and New Social Movement Theory. *Journal of Progressive Human Services* 5, 2:5–21.

Freeman, Linda. 1985. The Effect of the World Crisis on Canada's Involvement in Africa. *Studies in Political Economy*, 17:107–39.

George, Victor, and Paul Wilding. 1976. *Ideology and Social Welfare*. London; Boston: Routledge & Kegan Paul.

– 1985. *Ideology and Social Welfare*. London and Boston: Routledge & Kegan Paul.

Gidengil, Elisabeth, and Richard Vengrof. 1997. Representational Gain of Canadian Women or Token Growth? The Case of Quebec's Municipal Politics. *Canadian Journal of Political Science* 20, no. 3:513–37.

Gillespie, W. Irwin. 1978. *In Search of Robin Hood: The Effects of Federal Budgetary Policies During the 1970s on the Distribution of Income in Canada*. Montreal: C.D. Howe Institute.

– 1991. *Tax, Borrow and Spend: Financing Federal Spending in Canada, 1867–1990*. Ottawa: Carleton University Press.

Goffman, Irving J. 1968. Canadian Social Welfare Policy. In *Contemporary Canada*, ed. R.H. Leach. Toronto: University of Toronto Press.

Gonick, Cy. 1987. *The Great Economic Debate: Failed Economics and a Future for Canada*. Toronto: James Lorimer.

Gordon, Linda. 1990. The New Feminist Scholarship on the Welfare State. In *Women, the State, and Welfare*, ed. Linda Gordon. Madison: University of Wisconsin.

Gough, Ian. 1979. *The Political Economy of the Welfare State*. London: Macmillan.

Graham, Katherine A., Susan D. Phillips, and Allan Maslove. 1998. *Urban Governance in Canada: Representation, Resources, and Restructuring*. Toronto and Fort Worth: Harcourt Brace.

Guest, Dennis. 1985. *The Emergence of Social Security in Canada*. 2d ed. Vancouver: University of British Columbia Press.

– 1997. *The Emergence of Social Security in Canada*. 3d ed. Vancouver: University of British Columbia Press.

Gwyn, Richard. 1996. *Nationalism Without Walls: The Unbearable Lightness of Being Canadian*. 2d ed. Toronto: McClelland & Stewart.

Harrison, Trevor. 1996. Class, Citizenship, and Global Migration: The Case of the Canadian Immigration Business Program, 1978–1992. *Canadian Public Policy* 21, no. 1:7–23.

Hewitt, Martin. 1994. Social Policy and the Question of Postmodernism. In *Social Policy Review 6*, ed. Robert Page and John Baldock. Canterbury: University of Kent.

Hirsch, Werner Z. 1991. *Privatizing Government Services: An Economic Analysis of Contracting Out by Local Governments*. Los Angeles: Institute of Industrial Relations, University of California.

Hodgetts, J.E. 1973. *The Canadian Public Service: The Physiology of Government 1867–1970*. Toronto: University of Toronto Press.

Hogg, Peter W. 1985. *Constitutional Law of Canada*. 2d ed. Toronto: Carswell.

Howlett, Michael, and M. Ramesh. 1995. *Studying Public Policy: Policy Cycles and Policy Subsystems*. Toronto: Oxford University Press.

Human Resources Development Canada. 1994. *Improving Social Security in Canada*. Ottawa: Supply and Services Canada.

Jacobs, Jane. 1961. *The Death and Life of Great American Cities*. New York: Vintage Books.

Jenson, Jane. 1998. Mapping Social Cohesion: The State of Canadian Research. Ottawa: *Canadian Policy Research Networks*. CPRN Study No. F/03.

Johnson, Albert W. 1987. Social Policy in Canada: The Past As It Conditions the Present. In *The Future of Social Welfare Systems in Canada and the United Kingdom*, ed. Shirley B. Seward. Halifax: Institute for Research on Public Policy.

Kent, Judy. 1989. *Volunteers in Health Organizations*, Voluntary Action Directorate, Multiculturalism and Citizenship. Ottawa: Supply and Services Canada.

Kent, Tom. 1999. *Social Policy 2000: An Agenda*. Ottawa: Caledon Institute of Social Policy.

Kerans, Patrick. 1994. Universality, Full Employment and Well-Being: The Future of the Canadian Welfare State. *Canadian Review of Social Policy*, no. 34:119–35.

Keynes, John M. 1936. *The General Theory of Employment, Interest and Money*. London: Macmillan.

Kitchen, Brigitte. 1995. Scaled Social Benefits: Are They a Step Up from Universality? In *Warm Heart, Cold Country: Fiscal and Social Policy Reform in Canada*, ed. Daniel Drache and Andrew Ranachan. Ottawa/Toronto: Caledon Institute of Social Policy and the Robarts Centre for Canadian Studies.

– 1996. Round Up – Ontario. *Canadian Review of Social Policy* 38:165–6.

– 1997. The New Child Benefit: Much Ado About Nothing. *Canadian Review of Social Policy* 39 (spring):65–74.

Kuusisto, Nils, and Rick Williams. 1981. Social Expenses and Regional Underdevelopment. In *Inequality: Essays on the Political Economy of Social Welfare*, ed. Allan Moscovitch and Glenn Drover. Toronto: University of Toronto Press.

Langille, David, ed. 1997. *Exposing the Facts of Corporate Rule*. Toronto: Jesuit Centre for Social Faith.

Lash, Scott, and John Urry. 1987. *The End of Organized Capitalism*. Cambridge: Polity.

Laxer, James. 1984. *Rethinking the Economy: The Laxer Report on Canadian Economic Problems and Policies*. Toronto: New Canada Publications.

Lazar, Harvey. 1991. Investing in People: A Policy Agenda for the 1990s. In *Canada At Risk: Canadian Public Policy in the 1990s*, ed. G. Bruce Doern and Bryne B. Purchase. Policy Study No. 13. Toronto: C.D. Howe Institute.

Lee, Bill. 1992. *Pragmatics of Community Organization*. 2d ed. Mississauga: Commonact Press.

Lee, Phil, and Colin Raban. 1988. *Welfare Theory and Social Policy: Reform or Evolution?* London: Sage.

Lewis, David. 1972. *Louder Voices: The Corporate Welfare Bums*. Toronto: James Lewis & Samuel Publishers.

Lightman, Ernie S. 1995. Equity in Lean Times. In *Warm Hearts, Cold Country: Fiscal and Social Policy Reform in Canada*, ed. Daniel Drache and Andrew Ranachan. Ottawa/Toronto: Caledon Institute on Social Policy and the Robarts Centre on Canadian Studies.

Lightman, Ernie S., and Allan Irving. 1991. Restructuring Canada's Welfare State. *Journal of Social Policy*. Vol. 20, no. 1:65–86.

Lindblom, Charles. 1977. *Politics and Markets: The World's Political-Economic Systems*. New York: Basic Books.

Lipsky, Michael. 1980. *Street-Level Bureaucracy: Dilemmas of the Individual in Public Services*. New York: Russell Sage.

Lochhead, Clarence. 1997. *From the Kitchen Table to the Boardroom Table: The Canadian Family and the Work Place*. Ottawa: Vanier Institute of the Family.

Low, William. 1996. Wide of the Mark: Using 'Targeting' and Work Incentives to Direct Social Assistance to Single Parents. In *Remaking Canadian Social*

Policy: Social Security in the Late 1990s, ed. Jane Pulkingham and Gordon Ternowetsky. Halifax: Fernwood Publishing.

MacIvor, Heather. 1996. *Women and Politics in Canada*. Peterborough: Broadview Press.

Mann, W. E, ed. 1970. *Poverty and Social Policy in Canada*. Vancouver: Copp Clark Publishing.

Manzer, Ronald. 1985. *Public Policies and Political Development in Canada*. Toronto: University of Toronto Press.

– 1994. *Public Schools and Political Ideas: Canadian Educational Policy in Historical Perspective*. Toronto: University of Toronto Press.

Marsh, David. 1991. British Industrial Relations Policy Transformed: The Thatcher Legacy. *Journal of Public Policy* 11, no. 3 (July–September).

Marsh, Leonard. 1943. *Report on Social Security for Canada*. Toronto: Reprint, Toronto: University of Toronto Press, 1975.

Marshall, Katherine. 1993. Dual Earners: Who's Responsible for Housework? *Canadian Social Trends* 31 (winter):11–14.

Marshall, Thomas H. 1963. Citizenship and Social Class. In *Sociology at the Crossroads*. London: Heinemann.

Marsland, David. 1996. *Welfare or Welfare State? Contradictions and Dilemmas in Social Policy*. London: Macmillan.

Martin, Paul. 1994. The Budget Speech. Ottawa: Department of Finance (February 22).

Maslove, Allan M., Michael J. Prince, and G. Bruce Doern. 1986. *Federal and Provincial Budgeting: Goalsetting, Coordination, Restraint and Reform*. Toronto: University of Toronto Press.

Maxwell, Judith. 1993. Globalization and Family Security. In *Family Security in Insecure Times: National Forum on Family Security*, ed. Canadian Council on Social Development. Ottawa: Canadian Council on Social Development.

– 1994. Rethinking the Social Role of Government. *Policy Options Politique* 16, no. 3:54–8.

– 1995. The role of the state in a knowledge-based economy. In *Redefining Social Security*, ed. P. Grady, R. Howse, and J. Maxwell. Kingston: School of Policy Studies, Queen's University.

McBride, Stephen. 1992. *Not Working: State, Unemployment and Neo-conservatism in Canada*. Toronto: University of Toronto Press.

McCormack, Thelma. 1984. Culture and the State. *Canadian Public Policy* 10, no. 3:267–77.

– 1991. *Politics and the Hidden Injuries of Gender: Feminism and the Making of the Welfare State*. Ottawa: Canadian Research Institute for the Advancement of Women.

McGilly, Frank. 1990. *An Introduction to Canada's Public Social Services: Understanding Income and Health Programs*. Toronto: McClelland & Stewart.

– 1998. *Canada's Public Social Services*. 2d ed. Toronto: Oxford University Press.

McKnight, John. 1992. *The Future of Low-Income Neighborhoods and the People Who Reside There: A Capacity-Oriented Strategy for Neighborhood Development*. Chicago: Center for Urban Affairs and Policy Research, Northwestern University.

McLeod, R. C., and D. Schneiderman. 1994. *Police Powers in Canada: The Evolution and Practice of Authority*. Toronto: University of Toronto Press.

McQuaig, Linda. 1993. *The Wealthy Banker's Wife: The Assault on Equality in Canada*. Toronto: Penguin Books.

– 1995. *Shooting the Hippo: Death by Deficit and Other Canadian Myths*. Toronto: Penguin Books.

– 1998. *The Cult of Impotence: Selling the Myth of Powerlessness in the Global Economy*. Toronto: Viking Books.

Miller, Dorothy C. 1990. *Women and Social Welfare: A Feminist Analysis*. New York: Praeger.

Mishra, Ramesh. 1984. *The Welfare State in Crisis : Social Thought and Social Change*. Brighton, Sussex: Wheatsheaf Books.

– 1990a. The Collapse of the Welfare Consensus? The Welfare State in the 1980s. In *Housing the Homeless and the Poor: New Partnerships among the Private, Public, and Third Sectors*, ed. George Fallis and Alex Murray. Toronto: University of Toronto Press.

– 1990b. *The Welfare State in Capitalist Society: Policies of Retrenchment and Maintenance in Europe, North America and Australia*. New York: Harvester Wheatsheaf.

Morissette, Rene, John Myles, and Garnett Picot. 1995. Earnings Polarization in Canada, 1969–1991. In *Labour Market Polarization and Social Policy Reform*, ed. Keith G. Banting and Charles M. Beach. Kingston: School of Policy Studies, Queen's University.

Moscovitch, Allan. 1990. 'Slowing the Steamroller': The Federal Conservatives, The Social Sector and Child Benefits Reform. In *How Ottawa Spends 1990–91: Tracking the Second Agenda*, ed. Katherine A. Graham. Ottawa: Carleton University Press.

Moscovitch, Allan, and Jim Albert, eds. 1987. *The Benevolent State: The Growth of Welfare in Canada*. Toronto: Garamond Press.

Moscovitch, Allan, and Glenn Drover, eds. 1981. *Inequality: Essays on the Political Economy of Social Welfare*. Toronto: University of Toronto Press.

– 1987. Social Expenditures and the Welfare State: The Canadian Experience in Historical Perspective. In *The Benevolent State: The Growth of Welfare in Canada*, ed. Allan Moscovitch and Jim Albert. Toronto: Garamond Press.

Mullaly, Robert. 1997. *Structural Social Work: Ideology, Theory, and Practice*. 2d ed. Toronto: Oxford University Press.

Murphy, H.B.W., B. Pennee, and D. Luchins. 1972. Foster Homes: The New Back Ward. *Canada's Mental Health* 20 (Supplement 71):1–17.

Murray, Charles. 1984. *Losing Ground: American Social Policy 1950–1980*. New York: Basic Books.

– 1990. *The Emerging British Underclass*. London: Institute of Economic Affairs.

– 1994. *Underclass: The Crisis Deepens*. London: Institute of Economic Affairs.

Myles, John, and Paul Pierson. 1997. *Friedman's Revenge: The Reform of 'Liberal' Welfare States In Canada and the United States*. Toronto: Caledon Institute of Social Policy.

National Council of Welfare. 1976. *The Hidden Welfare System*. Ottawa: Supply and Services Canada.

– 1978. *Bearing the Burden, Sharing the Benefits*. Ottawa: Supply and Services Canada.

– 1983. *Family Allowances for All?* Ottawa: Supply and Services Canada.

– 1987. *Welfare in Canada: The Tangled Safety Net*. Ottawa: Supply and Services Canada.

– 1995. *Legal Aid and the Poor*. Ottawa: Supply and Services Canada.

– 1996–97. *Welfare Incomes 1995*. Ottawa: Supply and Services Canada.

– 1997. *Poverty Profile 1995*. Ottawa: Supply and Services Canada.

National Forum on Family Security. 1993. Keynote paper. In *Family Security in Insecure Times*, ed. Canadian Council on Social Development. Ottawa: Canadian Council on Social Development.

Neary, Peter, and J.L. Granatstein, eds. 1998. *The Veterans Charter and Post-World War II Canada*. Montreal and Kingston: McGill-Queen's University Press.

Neysmith, Sheila M. 1991. From Community Care to a Social Model of Care. In *Women's Caring: Feminist Perspectives on Social Welfare*, ed. Carol Baines, Patricia M. Evans, and Sheila M. Neysmith. Toronto: McClelland & Steward.

Ng, Roxana, Gillian Walker, and Jacob Muller, eds. 1990. *Community Organization and the Canadian State*. Toronto: Garamond Press.

O'Connor, James. 1973. *The Fiscal Crisis of the State*. New York: St Martin's Press.

Offe, Claus. 1984. *Contradictions of the Welfare State*, ed. John Keane. London: Hutchinson.

– 1985. *Disorganized Capitalism*. Cambridge, Mass.: MIT Press.

O'Higgins, Michael. 1985. Inequality, Redistribution and Recession, 1976–1982. *Journal of Social Policy* 14, no. 3, 279–307.

Ontario Fair Tax Commission. 1993. *Fair Taxation in a Changing World: Highlights.* Toronto: Queen's Printer for Ontario.

Organization for Canadian Economic Development. 1997. *Beyond 2000: The New Social Policy Agenda.* A Paper Prepared for a Conference on the Challenges of Change in Social Policy: North American Perspectives.

Orloff, Ann Shola. 1993. Gender and the Social Rights of Citizenship: The Comparative Analysis of Gender Relations and Welfare States. *American Sociological Review* 58, no. 3:303–25.

Osberg, Lars. 1981. *Economic Inequality in Canada.* Toronto: Butterworths.

Owram, Doug. 1986. *The Government Generation: Canadian Intellectuals and the State 1900–1945.* Toronto: University of Toronto Press.

Pal, Leslie A. 1988. *State, Class, and Bureaucracy: Canadian Unemployment Insurance and Public Policy.* Montreal and Kingston: McGill-Queen's University Press.

– 1997. *Beyond Policy Analysis: Public Issue Management in Turbulent Times.* Scarborough: Nelson.

Panitch, Leo, ed. 1977. *The Canadian State: Political Economy and Political Power.* Toronto: University of Toronto Press.

– 1994. Changing Gears: Democratizing the Welfare State. In *Continuities and Discontinuities: The Political Economy of Social Welfare and Labour Market Policy in Canada,* ed. Andrew F. Johnson, Stephen McBride, and Patrick J. Smith. Toronto: University of Toronto Press.

Pante, Michelle. 1996. Social Partnerships, Sustainable Social Policy and Community Capital. In *Sustainable Social Policy and Community Capital,* ed. Caledon Institute of Social Policy. Ottawa: Caledon Institute of Social Policy and the Canada Mortgage and Housing Corporation.

Pascall, Gillian. 1986. *Social Policy: A Feminist Analysis.* New York: Tavistock.

Pateman, Carole. 1988. The Patriarchal Welfare State. In *Democracy and the Welfare State,* ed. Amy Gutmann. Princeton: Princeton University Press.

Penna, Sue, and Martin O'Brien. 1996. Postmodernism and Social Policy: A Small Step Forward? *Journal of Social Policy* 25, no. 1:39–61.

Phillips, Susan D. 1989. Rock-a-Bye, Brian: The National Strategy on Child Care. In *How Ottawa Spends 1989–90: The Buck Stops Where?* Ed. Katherine A. Graham. Ottawa: Carleton University Press.

Philp, Margaret. 1997. Child-Care Plan Makes Quebec Distinct. *The Globe and Mail.* 17 June, A1, A6.

Piat, Myra. 1992. Deinstitutionalization of the Mentally Ill. *Canadian Social Work Review* 9, no. 2 (summer):201–13.

Pierson, Paul. 1994. *Dismantling the Welfare State? Reagan, Thatcher, and the Politics of Retrenchment*. New York: Press Syndicate of the University of Cambridge.

Piven, Frances Fox, and Richard A. Cloward. 1971. *Regulating the Poor: The Functions of Public Welfare*. New York: Vintage Books.

Polanyi, Karl. 1957. *The Great Transformation: The Political and Economic Origins of Our Times*. Boston: Beacon Press.

Porter, John. 1965. *The Vertical Mosaic: An Analysis of Social Class and Power in Canada*. Toronto: University of Toronto Press.

Pratt, Alan. 1997. Neo-liberalism and Social Policy. In *Social Policy: A Conceptual and Theoretical Introduction*, ed. Michael Lavalette and Alan Pratt. London: Sage.

– 1997b. Universalism or Selectivism? The Provision of Services in the Modern Welfare State. In *Social Policy: A Conceptual and Theoretical Introduction*, ed. Michael Lavalette and Alan Pratt. London: Sage.

Pratt, Cranford, ed. 1994. *Canadian International Development Assistance Policies: An Appraisal*. Montreal and Kingston: McGill-Queen's University Press.

Prince, Michael J. 1989. *Social Policy Commissions: A Review of Findings and Implications for Housing*. Ottawa: Canada Mortgage and Housing Corporation.

– 1991. Universality in Canadian Social Programs: Theory and Practice. Paper prepared for the Consultative Committee on Social Policy, Department of National Health and Welfare, Government of Canada.

– 1992. Touching Us All: International Context, National Policies, and the Integration of Canadians with Disabilities. In *How Ottawa Spends 1992–93, The Politics of Competitiveness*, ed. Frances Abele. Ottawa: Carleton University Press.

– 1995. The Canadian Housing Policy Context. *Housing Policy Debate* 6, no. 3:721–58.

– 1996a. At the Edge of Canada's Welfare State: Social Policy-Making in British Columbia. In *Politics, Policy, and Government in British Columbia*, ed. R.K. Carty. Vancouver: University Of British Columbia Press.

– 1996b. From Expanding Coverage to Heading for Cover: Shifts in the Politics and Policies of Canadian Pension Reform. In *Aging Workforce, Income Security, and Retirement: Policy and Practical Implications*, ed. Anju Joshi and Ellie Berger. Proceedings of the 12th Annual McMaster Summer Institute on Gerontology. Hamilton: Office of Gerontological Studies.

– 1997. Lowering the Boom on the Boomers: Replacing Old Age Security with the New Seniors Benefit and Reforming the Canada Pension Plan. In *How Ottawa Spends 1997–98: Seeing Red: A Liberal Report Card*, ed. Gene Swimmer. Ottawa: Carleton University Press.

– 1998. New Mandate, New Money, New Politics: Federal Budgeting in the Post-Deficit Era. In *How Ottawa Spends 1998–99: Balancing Act: The Post-Deficit Mandate*, ed. Leslie A. Pal. Toronto: Oxford University Press.

– 1999. Civic Regulation: Regulating Citizenship, Morality, Social Order and the Welfare State. In *Changing the Rules: Canadian Regulatory Regimes and Institutions*, ed. G. Bruce Doern, Margaret Hill, Michael J. Prince, and Richard Schultz. Toronto: University of Toronto Press.

Prince, Michael J., and Neena L. Chappell. 1997. Voluntarism By Canadian Seniors: Silver Threads or Golden Opportunities for Social Care. Unpublished Paper, National Welfare Grants Program.

Prince, Michael J., and James J. Rice. 1981. Department of National Health and Welfare: The Attack on Social Policy. In *How Ottawa Spends Your Tax Dollars*, ed. G. Bruce Doern. Toronto: James Lorimer and Company.

– 1989. The Canadian Job Strategy: Supply Side Social Policy. In *How Ottawa Spends Your Tax Dollars*, ed. K. Graham. Toronto: Lorimer.

Pulkingham, Jane, and Gordon Ternowetsky, eds. 1996. *Remaking Canadian Social Policy: Social Security in the Late 1990s*. Halifax: Fernwood Publishing.

Putnam, Robert, D. 1993. The Prosperous Community: Social Capital and Public Life. *The American Prospect* 13 (spring 1993):35–42.

– 1996. The Strange Disappearance of Civic America. *The American Prospect*, no. 24 (winter) http://epn.org/prospect/24/24putn.html.

Ralph, Diana. 1994. Fighting for Canada's Social Programs. *Canadian Review of Social Policy*, No. 34:75–85.

Ralph, Diana, Neree St-Amand, and Andre Regimbald, eds. 1997. *Open for Business/Closed to People, Mike Harris's Ontario*. Halifax: Fernwood Publishing.

Reid, Angus. 1997. *Shakedown: How the New Economy Is Changing Our Lives*. Toronto: A Seal Book.

Resnick, Philip. 1997. *Twenty-First Century Democracy*. Montreal and Kingston: McGill-Queen's University Press.

Rice, James J. 1979. Social Policy, Economic Management, and Redistirbution. In *Public Policy in Canada*, ed. G. Bruce Doern and Peter Aucoin. Toronto: Macmillan.

– 1985. Politics of Income Security: Historical Developments and Limitations to Future Change. In *Royal Commission on Economic Union and Development Prospects for Canada*, ed. G. Bruce Doern. Toronto: University of Toronto Press.

– 1986. The MacDonald Commission: Social Policy Recommendations. *Canadian Review of Social Policy* 14 and 15:96–106.

– 1987. Restitching the Safety Net: Altering the National Social Security System. In *How Ottawa Spends 1987–88: Restraining the State*, ed. Michael J. Prince. Toronto: Methuen.

– 1990. Volunteering to Build a Stronger Community. *Perception* 14, no. 4:9–14.

– 1995a. A National Treasure at Risk: Changing the Social Security System Threatens the Voluntary Sector. In *Critical Commentaries on the Social Secruity Review*. Ottawa: The Caledon Institute of Social Policy.

– 1995b. Redesigning Welfare: The Abandonment of a National Commitment. In *How Ottawa Spends: Mid-life Crises*, ed. Susan D. Phillips. Ottawa: Carleton University Press.

Rice, James J., and Michael J. Prince. 1993. Lowering the Safety Net and Weakening the Bonds of Nationhood: Social Policy of the Mulroney Years. In *How Ottawa Spends: A More Democratic Canada ...?*, ed. Susan D. Phillips. Ottawa: Carleton University Press.

Riches, Graham. 1997. The Renewal of Social Citizenship: Right to Food Central to an Alternative Agenda. http://www.policyalternatives.ca/articles/article111.html.

Rifkin, Jeremy. 1995. *The End of Work*. New York: Tarcher Putnam.

Robson, William A. 1976. *Welfare State and Welfare Society: Illusion and Reality*. London: Allen & Unwin.

Rosenblum, Sidney, and Peter Findlay, eds. 1991. *Debating Canada's Future: Views from the Left*. Toronto: James Lorimer.

Ross, David P. 1986. Local Economic Initiative: An Overview. In *Employment and Social Development in a Changing Economy*, ed. Canadian Council on Social Development, Ottawa.

Ross, David P., and Peter Usher. 1986. *From the Roots Up: Economic Development As If Community Mattered*. Toronto: James Lorimer.

Rothman, Jack. 1974. *Planning and Organizing for Social Change: Action Principles from Social Science Research*. New York : Columbia University Press.

Ryan, William. 1971. *Blaming the Victim*. New York: Vintage Books.

Sainsbury, Diane. 1996. *Gender, Equality, and Welfare States*. Cambridge: Cambridge University Press.

Saul, John Ralston. 1995. *The Unconscious Civilization*. Concord, Ontario: House of Anansi Press.

Schellenberg, Grant. 1996. Diversity in Retirement and the Financial Security of Older Workers. In *Remaking Canadian Social Policy: Social Security in the Late 1990s*, ed. Jane Pulkingham and Gordon Ternowetsky. Halifax: Fernwood Publishing, 151–67.

Schellenberg, Grant, and David P. Ross. 1997. *Left Poor by the Market: A Look at*

Family Poverty and Earnings. Social Research Series Paper No. 2. Ottawa: Centre for International Statistics at the Canadian Council on Social Development.

Scott, Alan. 1990. *Ideology and the New Social Movements.* London: Unwin Hyman.

Segalman, R., and D. Marsland. 1989. *Cradle to Grave: Comparative Perspectives on the State of Welfare.* London: Macmillan.

Seligman, Adam B. 1992. *The Idea of Civil Society.* New York: The Free Press.

Selznick, Philip. 1995. Thinking about Community: Ten Theses. *Society* (August):33–7.

Shragge, Eric, ed. 1997. *Workfare: Ideology for a New Under-Class.* Toronto: Garamond Press.

Silver, Jim. 1997. Round-up, Manitoba. *Canadian Review of Social Policy* (Spring) 39:86–7.

Simeon, Richard. 1991. Globalization and the Nation-State. In *Canada At Risk: Canadian Public Policy in the 1990s.* Policy Study No. 13, ed. G. Bruce Doern and Bryne B. Purchase. Toronto: C.D. Howe Institute.

Smith, George. 1990. Policing the Gay Community. In *Community Organization and the Canadian State,* ed. Roxana Ng, Gillian Walker, and Jacob Muller. Toronto: Garamond Press.

Social Justice Commission. 1994. The Report of the Commission On Social Justice. *Social Justice: Strategies for National Renewal.* Toronto: Vintage.

Solomon, Andrew. 1994. Defiantly Deaf. *The New York Times Magazine.* 28 August, Section 6, 39–68.

Spivey, W. Allen. 1985. Problems and Paradoxes in Economic and Social Policies of the Modern Welfare States. *Annals of the American Academy of Political and Social Science* 479:14–30.

Splane, Richard B. 1965. *Social Welfare in Ontario 1791–1893: A Study of Public Welfare Administration.* Toronto: University of Toronto Press.

– 1987. Social Policy-Making in the Government of Canada, Further Reflections: 1975–1986. In *Canadian Social Policy.* Rev. ed. Ed. Shankar Yelaja. Waterloo: Wilfrid Laurier University Press.

Statistics Canada. 1994. *Public Sector Finance.* Cat. no. 68–212. Ottawa: Supply and Services Canada.

– 1995a. *Education in Canada.* 81–229. Ottawa: Statistics Canada.

– 1995b. *Women in Canada; A Statistical Report.* 3d ed. Ottawa: Statistics Canada.

– 1997. *1996 Census: Marital Status, Common-law Unions and Families; Mother Tongue, Home Language and Knowledge of Languages; Immigration and Citizenship.* Ottawa: Supply and Services Canada.

– 1998. *1996 Census: Aboriginal data; Ethnic origin, Visible Minorities*. Ottawa: Supply and Services Canada.

Studlar, Donley, and Gary Moncrief. 1997. The Recruitment of Women Cabinet Ministers in the Canadian Provinces. *Governance* 10, no. 1:67–81.

Swimmer, Gene, and Mark Thompson, eds. 1995. *Public Sector Collective Bargaining in Canada: Beginning of the End or the End of the Beginning?* Kingston: Industrial Relations Centre Press. Queen's University.

Taft, Kevin. 1997. *Shredding the Public Interest: Ralph Klein and 25 Years of One-Party Government*. Edmonton: University of Alberta Press.

Taylor, Malcolm G. 1978. *Health Insurance and Canadian Public Policy: The Seven Decisions that Created the Canadian Health Insurance System*. Montreal and Kingston: McGill-Queen's University Press.

Taylor-Gooby, Peter. 1994. Postmodernism and Social Policy: A Great Leap Backwards? *Journal of Social Policy* 23, no. 3:385–404.

Teeple, Gary. 1995. *Globalization and the Decline of Social Reform*. Toronto: Garamond Press.

Ternowetsky, Gordon W. 1987. Controlling the Deficit and a Private Sector-Led Recovery: Contemporary Themes of the Welfare State. In *The Canadian Welfare State: Evolution and Transition*, ed. Jacqueline S. Ismael. Edmonton: University of Alberta Press.

Tester, Frank James, Chris McNiven, and Robert Case, eds. 1996. *Critical Choices, Turbulent Times*. Vancouver: School of Social Work, University of British Columbia.

Thompson, Kelly. 1989. *Volunteerism in the International Sector*. Voluntary Action Directorate, Multiculturalism and Citizenship. Ottawa: Supply and Services Canada.

Titmuss, Richard M. 1968. *Commitment to Welfare*. London: Allen & Unwin.

– 1974. *Social Policy: An Introduction*, ed. Brian Abel-Smith and Kay Titmuss. London: Allen & Unwin.

Torjman, Sherri. 1996. Sustainable Social Policy. In *Sustainable Social Policy and Community Capital*, ed. Caledon Institute of Social Policy. Ottawa: Caledon Institute of Social Policy and the Canada Mortgage and Housing Corporation.

– 1997a. *Cash Poor, Community Rich*. Toronto: Caledon Institute of Social Policy.

– 1997b. *Civil Society: Reclaiming Our Humanity*. Toronto: Caledon Institute of Social Policy.

– 1998. *Community-Based Poverty Reduction*. Ottawa: Caledon Institute of Social Policy.

Trainor, John, Bonnie Pape, and Edward Pomeroy. 1997. Critical Challenges for Canadian Mental Health Policy. *Canadian Review of Social Policy* 39: 55–64.

Trebilcock, Michael J., Leonard Waverman, and J. Robert Prichard. 1978. Markets for Regulation: Implications for Performance Standards and Institutional Design. In *Government Regulations*. Toronto: Ontario Economic Council.

Tudiver, Neil. 1987. Forestalling the Welfare State: The Establishment of Programmes of Corporate Welfare. In *The Benevolent State: The Growth of Welfare in Canada*, ed. Allan Moscovitch and Jim Albert. Toronto: Garamond Press.

Tyhurst, James S. 1963. *More for the Mind: A Study of Psychatric Services in Canada*. Toronto: Canadian Mental Health Association.

Ursel, Jane. 1997. Considering the Impact of the Battered Women's Movement on the State: The Example of Manitoba. In *Women and the Canadian State*, ed. Caroline Andrew and Sanda Rodgers. Montreal and Kingston: McGill-Queen's University Press.

Vanier Institute of the Family. 1979. *Exploring Work and Income Opportunities in the 1980s: Our Future in the Informal Economy*. Ottawa: Vanier Institute of the Family.

Vickers, Jill. 1994. Why Should Women Care about Federalism? In *Canada, The State of the Federation 1994*, ed. Douglas M. Brown and Janet Hiebert. Kingston: Institute of Intergovernmental Relations, Queen's University.

Voluntary Action Directorate. 1989. *National Survey of Volunteer Activity*. Edited by the Social Trends Analysis Directorate. Ottawa: Supply and Services Canada.

Walker, Michael. 1985. The Welfare State. In *Free Enterprise and the State: What's Right? What's Left? What's Next?*, ed. Jan Federowicz. Toronto: CBC Enterprises.

Wallace, Elisabeth. 1950. Origin of the Welfare State in Canada, 1867–1900. *Canadian Journal of Economics and Political Science* 16, no. 3:383–93.

Walzer, Michael. 1983. *Spheres of Justice*. New York: Basic Books.

Watson, William. 1998. *Globalization and the Meaning of Canadian Life*. Toronto: University of Toronto Press.

Wharf, Brian, ed. 1979. *Community Work in Canada*. Toronto: McClelland & Stewart.

– ed. 1990. *Social Work and Social Change in Canada*. Toronto: McClelland & Stewart.

– 1992. *Communities and Social Policy in Canada*. Toronto: McClelland & Stewart.

Wharf, Brian, and Michael Clague, eds. 1997. *Community Organizing: Canadian Experiences*. Toronto: Oxford University Press.

White, Joe, and Aaron Wildavsky. 1989. *The Deficit and the Public Interest: The Search for Responsible Budgeting in the 1980s*. Berkeley and Los Angeles: University of California Press and the Russell Sage Foundation.

Wildavsky, Aaron. 1988. *The New Politics of the Budgetary Process*. 4th ed. Boston: Little, Brown.

Wilensky, Harold, and Charles Lebeaux. 1958. *Industrial Society and Social Welfare*. New York: Russel Sage.

Williams, Fiona. 1989. *Social Policy: A Critical Introduction*. Cambridge: Polity Press.

– 1992. Somewhere Over the Rainbow: Universality and Diversity in Social Policy. In *Social Policy Review 4*, ed. Nick Manning and Robert Page. Canterbury: University of Kent, 200–19.

Wilson, Elizabeth. 1977. *Women and the Welfare State*. London: Tavistock Publications.

Wiseman, John. 1996. National Social Policy in an Age of Global Power: Lessons from Canada and Australia. In *Remaking Canadian Social Policy: Social Security in the Late 1990s*, ed. Jane Pulkingham and Gordon Ternowetsky. Halifax: Fernwood Publishing.

Wolf, Daniel. 1994. Brotherhood in Biker Bars. In *Doing Everyday Life: Ethnography as Human Lived Experience*, ed. Mary Lorenz Dietz, Robert Prus, and William Shaffir. Mississauga: Copp Clark Longman.

Wolfe, David. 1985. The Politics of the Deficit. In *The Politics of Economic Policy*, ed. G. Bruce Doern. Toronto: University of Toronto Press.

Woodcock, George. 1985. *Strange Bedfellows: The State and the Arts in Canada*. Vancouver: Douglas & McIntyre.

Woodsworth, J.S. 1972. *My Neighbor*. Originally published in 1911. Toronto: University of Toronto Press.

Yeatman, Anna. 1990. *Bureaucrats, Technocrats, Femocrats: Essays on the Contemporary Australian State*. Sydney: Allen & Unwin.

Young, Iris Marion. 1990. *Justice and the Politics of Difference*. Princeton: Princeton University Press.

Author Index

Subject Index

International economies, 131; economic institutions, 133; trading
agreements, 6–7, 33, 131–3; trading blocs, 133, 135–6
International Monetary Fund (IMF),
136, 144, 250
International social policy agreements, 148, 246, 249–51
Internationalization: of human
rights, 132; of public policy, 148
Internet, 19–20, 31; privacy concerns,
12; VolNet, 212
Inuit, 32, 77; Women's Association of
Canada, 96
Investments, 57, 171, 243–4; corporate, 20–1; in education and
learning, 237; social, 224

Keynesian welfare consensus, 98–9,
128–9
Keynesian welfare state: as dead or
near extinction, 235
Kinship networks, 12, 209

Labour: codes, 254; non-unionized,
20; organized, 11; relations, 151;
union movement, 116
Labour market, 22, 32, 246; effects of
globalization on, 146–8; participa-
tion of women and volunteering,
227; trends, 146–8; 264n5
Land claims, 10–11
Language groups in Canada, 27–8
Left-wing critiques, 15, 84–90
Legal aid, 105, 203–4
Lesbians, 105; community, 10, 32,
157–8
Less eligibility principle, 36
Liberal(s), 243, 258; federal govern-
ment, 45, 63, 69, 72, 76, 80, 84, 109,

118, 126, 135, 166, 176–7, 235, 239;
perspective, on state intervention,
243
Liberalism: individualism, 86;
market, 19
Liberty, 90–4; 252; community,
215–16
Library boards, 39, 52, 121
Locality development, 208, 221
Lone parent families, 26. *See also*
Families
Lottery revenues: as regressive
taxes, 204
Low-income families, 50, 246, 248

Male breadwinner model of social
policy, 20, 184–5, 198
Market, 13, 241; economy, 243;
failures, 123; forces, 8; liberalism,
19; liberalization, 5; risks, 125; self-
regulating/labour, 8–9, 11
Marketization of discourse and
programs, 23–4; contrasted to
other processes, 262n5; of services,
22; of social programs, 148–53
Marsh Report/Report on Social
Security for Canada, 15, 60–3,
65–8, 71, 73, 75, 77–8, 98, 143,
171, 177
Marxist, 84, 184–5
Maternity/parental benefits, 68, 202
Means testing, 41, 44–5, 94, 110,
168–9, 233; assistance, 60, 65, 73,
80; assistance for women, 187–8
Media: press, 38, 97, 104, 145, 252
Medicare, 78, 80, 103–4, 107, 125–8,
140–1, 159, 166, 168–9, 174
Men, dominant roles, 16; social
policy, 98–9; work, 118
Men's experiences with social